LIGHTS, CAMERA, WAR

LIGHTS,
CAMERA,
WAR

Is Media Technology Driving
International Politics?

Johanna Neuman

ST. MARTIN'S PRESS
NEW YORK

Production Editor: Miranda Ford
Copyedited by Karen Pilibosian Thompson
Design by Ellen R. Sasahara

Library of Congress Cataloging-in-Publication Data

Neuman, Johanna.
    Lights, camera, war : is media technology driving interna-
tional politics? / Johanna Neuman.—1st ed.
        p.   cm.
    ISBN 0-312-14004-5
    1. Broadcast journalism. 2. Television broadcasting of
news. 3. Journalism—Political aspects. 4. War in mass media.
I. Title.
PN4784.B75N48   1995
070.1'9—dc20   95-40352
                                                   CIP

First Edition: January 1996

            10 9 8 7 6 5 4 3 2 1

Books are available in quantity for promotional or premium use. Write to Director of Special Sales, St. Martin's Press, 175 Fifth Avenue, New York, NY 10010, for information on discounts and terms, or call toll-free (800) 221-7945. In New York, call (212) 674-5151 (ext. 645).

To my father, Seymour,
Who taught me the love of history
and the beauty of words
And to my mother, Evelyn,
Who taught me their meaning

Contents

Preface

SECRETARY OF STATE James A. Baker III climbed up on a makeshift podium draped in camouflage in an air hangar in Taif, Saudi Arabia, to deliver the latest U.S. ultimatum to Iraqi president Saddam Hussein. It was January 11, 1991, four days before war would begin, two days after a failed mission in Geneva to avert war in all-day talks with Iraqi foreign minister Tariq Aziz. Parked behind Baker, nose-to-nose, were an F-111 fighter-bomber and an EF-111A Raven electronics-jamming warplane. In front of him were several hundred U.S. airmen and -women from the Forty-eighth Air Force Tactical Fighter Wing, most wearing camouflage gear and an edge of impatience. After months of training in the desert, they were eager to see action. Baker reminded them that the UN deadline for Iraq to leave Kuwait or risk war by an unprecedented coalition of thirty-four Western and Arab nations was only days away. "As the clock ticks down to midnight January fifteenth," he said, "I can tell you this: You will not have to wait much longer." The troops whooped their approval. Baker also spoke of Saddam's propensity to miscalculate, to "wait until he is on the very brink before he moves." With the crowd hushed, Baker added, "Just so there is no misunderstanding, let me be absolutely clear. We pass the brink at midnight January fifteenth."

With other journalists, I watched this dramatic scene, convinced it marked a turning point in the history of international relations—not so much because Baker had laid down another warning to Baghdad, nor even because he had done so in front of 400 bellowing troops. This appeal to a vast audience was unusual for Baker, who more often filled his calendar with private visits to sometimes obscure foreign ministers. The scene had a distinctly Deaveresque feel to it, as if Baker were still chief of staff in Ronald Reagan's first White House and strategist Mike Deaver were still painting flattering backdrops for important political speeches. But that was not the epiphany either. No, the remarkable thing about this emotional encounter in the hangar in Saudi Arabia was that Saddam could see it within the hour. Covered by Cable News Network, Ted Turner's twenty-four-hour-a-day, all-news television network, the speech could be heard and seen in Baghdad before Baker went to sleep. "I sent a message from Taif," Baker explained later. "We didn't send that message through Joe Wilson [top U.S. diplomat in Baghdad]. We sent it through CNN."

For decades, diplomats had conveyed their messages in private, using diplomatic pouches to hide great secrets of state. Henry Stimson, Herbert Hoover's secretary of state, had in 1928 closed down the agency at the State Department assigned to break telegraphic codes of other countries, explaining that "gentlemen do not read each other's mail." Since then, of course, there had been much code breaking, and no shortage of intercepted messages, so in some sense diplomacy had long since made Stimson a quaint if sweet anachronism. But even when they were attempting to peek inside the envelopes of other sovereign nations, diplomats were careful to shield their own secrets from the press and the public. It was one thing to telegraph intentions to competing countries, quite another to broadcast them to the world. Leaks there had always been, often targeted, sometimes random. Clever policy makers had, since the days of kings and their court scribes, sought to influence history's view of their work by appealing to their writers for a sympathetic accounting. But never had the news media been used quite so conspicuously, almost without their consent, to convey policy. Or so it seemed.

Real-time information had arrived in that hangar in Saudi Arabia, and it was, seemingly, changing the rules of international governance. Governments watched history with their publics, losing the luxury of time to deliberate in private before the imperative to "do something" stood on their doorsteps. Instant information, accessible to anyone with a television and a cable, had removed a sheath of mystery from the mantle of leadership, costing politicians some measure of respect. And the disenfranchised were suddenly media celebrities, basking in what Andy Warhol forever labeled as their fifteen minutes of fame, soaking up the international spotlight while it was warm. That was the context for Baker's remarks in the desert, a mirror of the larger debate within foreign-policy circles about what they called the CNN curve. There was angst about a television network setting the agenda for international policy, worry about a public unduly swayed by the emotions of the moment. Among print journalists there was a resentment toward this omnipotent creature, one that could convey news faster than anything gone before. Mostly, in that hangar in the days before that war, there was a feeling that power had shifted to technology, that CNN was driving diplomacy, that governments and newspapers were no longer the guardians of public information.

To Baker, whose first job in national public life was to count votes for Gerald R. Ford at the 1976 Republican convention and who had spearheaded the presidential campaigns of Ronald Reagan and George Bush, all of this hand-wringing about the power of television seemed like false hysteria. Baker was a politico, not a member of the Council on Foreign Relations. From his perspective, speeding a message through CNN instead of conveying it through an ambassador was an advantage to be exploited, one more tactical weapon in an international arsenal. He seemed puzzled that any diplomat would view CNN as anything but a tool. "You have more tools at your disposal now to accomplish your goals," was how he put it.

Baker's successes as secretary of state owed not a little to his political instincts, his intuition about how far he could push Israeli prime minister Yitzhak Shamir before the Israeli conservative would feel the heat from his own right wing, or how much spine he had to show Syrian president Hafez al-Assad before he could force him toward the peace table. He was a tactician for the most part, measuring his achievements by whether he had met his goals. Contemplating the impact of media technology on international relations in the late twentieth century, he likened it to a high-stakes campaign where the pace is hurried, the window for decisions is narrowed, and the cost of mistakes is enormous. "It makes it more like a permanent campaign," he observed. "Your reaction time is in minutes and hours, not days."

Professional diplomats were not as sanguine. Many still nursed the image of the striped-pants courier delivering diplomatic messages in secret pouches. They chuckled knowingly over British diplomat Henry Wotton's famous description of the ambassador in the seventeenth century as "an honest man sent to lie abroad for the good of his country." They bristled when, during the 1992 presidential campaign, independent candidate Ross Perot argued that new communication technology had made ambassadors obsolete. Mostly they derided the new technology and its use by political leaders without proper training in the rhythms of diplomacy. Their contempt reached its heights over President Bush's use of the telephone. When, in the run-up to the Persian Gulf War, Bush used the phones to keep in touch with other world leaders, the media dubbed it "Rolodex diplomacy." Some diplomats were appalled. "I've always trembled when a president picks up the phone to talk to his counterparts," said David Newsom, former U.S. ambassador and director of the Georgetown University's Institute of Diplomacy. "The idea of solving difficult international issues through personal rapport is a very risky one." This was old school diplomacy, which held that nations act for strategic reasons and that leaders do not go to war because a friend called. The real fear was that Bush might promise too much in return for too little, giving away the game before the poker players at the State Department could protect the U.S. hand.

Among the foreign-policy community, there were other questions too, about whether the increased pace of international relations was forcing governments to make mistakes, whether the politicization of foreign policy would hurt the deliberative, cautious, steady craft of diplomacy that had served the world of nations so well for so long. Baker dismissed these latter musings as the sour grapes of those whom technology had cut out of the loop, but other serious people worried about them. Lawrence Eagleburger, a career foreign-service officer who followed Baker as secretary of state, viewed the haste as a danger. Pressed to give an example of where the government had erred in the rush to take action, he cited U.S. policy toward Haiti in 1991 after President Jean-Bertrand Aristide was ousted in a bloody coup. A lifelong smoker who alternates cigarettes with an inhaler, Eagleburger exhaled deeply as he opined that the error was one of degree, that the White House should not have embraced Aristide quite so tightly, should not have equated his return with the restoration of democracy, a policy that three years later required 16,000 American troops to escort Aristide home at the end of the barrel of a gun. Eagleburger's example is a bit nuanced, because a hug is still a hug. Still, his worry over U.S. policy in Haiti speaks to the instinct among diplomats that haste can breed mistakes.

Even as politicians and diplomats debated the impact of the new tools of technology on international affairs, some in the business of information marveled at their consequences for journalism. Enthusiasts like Mark Brender of ABC-TV News saw in the commercial satellite the fruits of the information revolution. Freed of government control in a post–cold war era, the satellite gives news organizations access to photographs from space that until now were available only to governments. When Iraqi troops mass near the Kuwaiti border and sensory images are available for a price, the news media can report on Iraq's movements to the public at the same time that U.S. government officials are analyzing the images. This is a major check on government control of information, much as television was in the Vietnam War. "You can get on a train from Washington to Philadelphia and you'll see what's left of the industrial revolution," Brender said as he welcomed a group from NASA to discuss the uses for satellite imaging with ABC. "You see burnt factories with chimneys in the grass. We're in the information revolution now. All these satellites are the harvesters of information. They go around the earth just pulling up information." For technology's true believers, the satellite gives journalism the promise of more power and influence than ever before.

Like other journalists, political leaders, and professional diplomats weighing technology's legacy for international affairs, I came to this book convinced that recent media inventions had dramatically recast the way nations deal with other nations. In introducing this project to my colleagues at the Freedom Forum Media Studies Center at Columbia University, where I first researched the book, I said, "Modern communication media—everything from the fax machine to satellite television, from CNN to computer E-mail—have revolutionized the way nations interact. In the process, these modern technologies have also given the news media a larger role in foreign policy than ever before."

But intervening months of thought—both in the dusty stacks of Butler Library and in the quiet contemplation of a journalist facing no deadlines—gave me new perspective. The changes in international relations brought by the satellite and the computer, by digital technology and global networks, by CNN and real-time television, are profound. These changes are marvelous and sobering and frightening and dramatic, but what my readings through history demonstrated is that they are not new. The changes information technology has visited on the worlds of diplomacy and journalism in the late twentieth century are little different from the price exacted by technology in earlier eras.

What is new, what has changed, is the speed with which new technology is assaulting the political world. From the invention of the printing press to the advent of the telegraph lie three centuries in which diplomats and journalists grew accustomed to their news roles. Only a decade separates the dawning of satellite television and the promise of digital information, ten years in which to absorb the requirements of real-time television and prepare for the changes unleashed by the Internet.

The changes may be coming faster now, but every excursion into history confirms a consistent pattern of social change. Whenever a new communication technology arrived on the scene, diplomats scoffed at the new invention, journalists boasted that their influence had exploded, the public noticed that its world was shrinking, as if the boundaries of home were stretching to meet the horizon.

So striking was this pattern that it began to seem as if the tribulations of the past were an echo to the passions of our own day. There was a consistent theme threading the history, an insistence that each new technology promised to strip power from the elites and vest it in the public, giving democracy a new hope. Many predict today that cyberspace will empower the disenfranchised, putting information directly in the hands of people, unfiltered by governments. This view can also be heard in the musings of writer Thomas Carlyle, who in 1836 looked back in wonder at the invention of the printing press in the 1450s. "He who first shortened the labor of copyists by the device of moveable types," Carlyle wrote, "was disbanding hired armies and cashiering most kings and senates, and creating a whole new democratic world." This is an intoxicating promise of technology, to abet democracy.

True, each new media technology dislodges the middleman, bringing the audience closer to the stage, offering the potential for wider dissemination of information. This too is part of the pattern, one that is repeated, absorbed, and soon unnoticed. But the 550-year history of media technology suggests that democracy's triumph is not inevitable. For better or worse, intermediaries usually find new uses for their talents, inserting themselves between the public and the media. Technology opens the door to wider involvement by the public, but it does not hustle the audience inside. That still requires leadership, and a message.

For that is the other lesson in the history, that media technology is rarely as powerful in the hands of journalists as it is in the hands of political figures who can summon the talent to exploit the new invention. In this contest for public opinion, what Teddy Roosevelt called the bully pulpit of high office, the platform from which to summon a great cause and marshal political will, is mightier than the power of the pen or the presses.

It is often said that ours is an era of media power where instant communication has given life to Marshall McLuhan's prophesy of a global village. Borders have been erased by computers, goes the refrain, and pictures are driving international affairs. It is my contention, by contrast, that pictures drive diplomacy—as words did in an earlier era—only when there is a vacuum of political leadership.

If there is a better example of the failure of policy at the top and its deadly impact on the ground than the crisis in Bosnia-Herzegovina in the 1990s, I cannot imagine it. It was as if the West decided to parody Teddy Roosevelt by speaking loudly and carrying a soft stick. A headline in the *Washington Post* in the spring of 1993 announced, DIPLOMACY FAILS TO HALT SERB ATTACK. The headline writer presumed that diplomacy had been tried. But diplomacy, a discipline where words still matter, is not an exercise in frequent-flyer points. Without a policy to guide diplomatic efforts, or a consistency of language, everything from TV pictures to the false promises of Serb military leaders will carry too much weight. To blame the media and its technology for this inflated influence is to misunderstand the imperatives of power.

This, then, is a book about technology and leadership, about the news media and journalism, about diplomacy and war. It is a book that documents the sweep of changes technology has visited on international affairs, but also puts them in historic context. At its heart is a contention that in the end, in war and peace, on television and in print, leadership tells. Influenced perhaps unduly by having covered Ronald Reagan's White House and James Baker's State Department, I believe that individuals can have a strategic impact on events, and that to do so, they must evidence several qualities of leadership—among them an ability to communicate, an appreciation for the domestic politics of their counterparts, a fidelity to words and understanding of the importance of symbols, and, finally, a clarity about the bounds of national interest and the consequences of crossing them.

Throughout my reflections on history, I kept in touch with a wide range of public officials, respected academics, and thoughtful journalists. I listened, in more than 100 interviews, for evidence of a revolution. The more carefully I listened, the more I began to hear something else: an undercurrent of doubt that the computer or the satellite or the fax machine or whatever other marvel of technology was then under discussion had changed more than the outer garments of international affairs. Many proclaimed a revolution, but when pressed for examples, few gave answers that could not be interpreted to make the opposite case. Quite a few were angry about the changes technology had visited on international relations, sure that things had been better "in the old days." To those who continue to believe that the sky has fallen, I only hope that the pages of this book at least provide reason to reexamine the ground beneath their feet.

In speeches to foreign-service students and midcareer Pentagon officials, I am often asked how a leader can possibly maintain a sense of proportion in the face of a media blitz. This is the plaint of today's public officials, that the media drumbeat—delivered instantly, with a battery of microphones stuck in the face—requires immediate action and robs them of time for careful deliberation. My answer is to quote a marine official who, at the end of the Persian Gulf War, was asked why marines were better than the army at coping with the onslaught of reporters, producers, cameramen, and photographers. "We didn't view the news media as a group of people we were supposed to schmooze," replied Chief Warrant Officer Eric Carlson. "We regarded them as an environmental feature of the battlefield, kind of like the rain. If it rains, you operate wet." His answer is one I would offer besieged policy makers. The noise may be louder, the herd bigger, but the basics of international governance are unchanged.

Nations interact with other nations for self-interest and high moral purpose, for economic gain and market cooperation. From the cynical schemes of Italian political philosopher Niccolò Machiavelli to Henry Kissinger, America's foremost practitioner of *real politik*, diplomacy over the last three centuries has measured its steps in geopolitics, viewing the world and its nation-states as a giant chessboard in a game of deadly pursuit. With the end of the cold war and the rise of what Neil Postman calls technopoly, relations between nations, even sovereignty, are losing ground to the imperatives of the global market and the demands of worldwide, real-time communication. In this exciting milieu, it is tempting to assume that technology has modernized the old-fashioned. In the end, though, these new forces may represent less a revolution than a shifting of loyalties, from geopolitics to ecopolitics or even cyberpolitics. Then as now, international relations require a community of individuals, joined in temporary and changing alliances, coalescing around different causes that define national identity.

What is new, thanks to real-time satellite television and the advent of interactive computers, is that policy makers now watch events unfold at the same time as their constituents. Of necessity, this time crunch prizes those who are quick on their feet and nimble with their thoughts. But in truth nearly every technology had that effect. The new speed of delivery that so fascinated me as I watched Baker in an airport hangar in Saudi Arabia as he sent a message to Saddam Hussein in his bunker in Baghdad, the marvel that technology could bypass passport control, has consequences. A kind of virtual reality has come to diplomacy, as it has to everything else in the world of the 1990s. Diplomats may be especially aggrieved, feeling that they are being forced to hurry inquiries and speed decisions and perhaps make mistakes. Journalists may feel falsely empowered, believing that they are swaying public opinion and forcing leaders to "do something" about the latest crisis. But in the hands of gifted leaders, the new tools of communication technology are, like the rain, but the newest elements of leadership. Undeniably, it has been raining a lot lately.

1

The CNN Curve
Through History

I T WAS LATE Sunday night in Washington, early Monday morning in Moscow, when Strobe Talbott, ambassador-at-large to Russia and the former Soviet republics, picked up the telephone to talk to an official at the Russian Foreign Ministry. Both were watching CNN—Talbott on the cable network, the Russian official on a feed via local television—as the drama of Russia's past clashed with the promise of its future. What they saw was a Russian White House suddenly in crisis, with soldiers ringing its perimeter and parliamentarians inside making a desperate last stand against Yeltsin–style reform of the old Soviet system. In the distance, helicopters appeared on screen, carrying President Boris Yeltsin from his weekend dacha outside Moscow to his office in the Kremlin.

"Wait a minute, here come the helicopters," said the Russian official. "Let's watch how this plays out."

So for several minutes, as the dramatic events of Black Monday were unfolding, a U.S. diplomat and his Russian counterpart said not a word to each other on a secure telephone line as they concentrated on watching a live television broadcast of a crisis they were trying to resolve diplomatically. They stopped talking the logistics of diplomacy and began watching the unfolding of real-time history. They stopped talking to each other and listened instead to a newscaster. The freeze-frame picture of their halted conversation made clear what the foreign-policy community has been buzzing about since the end of the cold war: Communication technology is now a player in international diplomacy.

The next day, TV pictures from Somalia flooded the airwaves, searing the national memory with images of horror: the corpse of an American body dragged through the streets of Mogadishu, the pained words of U.S. airman Michael Durant as he anxiously eyed his captors. The imagination reeled. Wasn't this the same Somalia of starving babies and bloated stomachs that the United States had come to feed only a few months before? "The people who are dragging American bodies don't look very hungry to the people of Texas," said Republican senator Phil Gramm as he called for withdrawal of U.S. forces.

The one-two punch of Moscow and Mogadishu unleashed a flurry of blame-laying in Washington. As questions arose about whether Yeltsin was a democrat worthy of U.S. embrace, and the public opinion registered disapproval for keeping U.S. troops in Somalia, the Clinton administration's foreign policy came in for criticism. In the first instance, Clinton was questioned for backing Yeltsin at the expense, seemingly, of democracy. In the second, he was criticized for letting a humanitarian mission evolve into a manhunt for one warlord, an example of "mission creep" that engendered a firefight that left eighteen dead and seventy-eight wounded, some with gruesome and painful injuries, the worst single fight in U.S. military history since Vietnam. On the defensive, some administration figures blamed television. "Television's ability to bring graphic images of pain and outrage into our living rooms has heightened the pressure both for immediate engagement in areas of international crisis and immediate disengagement when events do not go according to plan,"

UN ambassador Madeleine Albright complained to the Senate Foreign Relations Committee.

Others were even ready to proclaim a New World Media Order, ceding diplomacy to the cameras in a kind of permanent post–cold war confusion. "CNN was become a universal intervener," said George Stephanopoulos, adviser to President Clinton. "It's an immediate actor. We're often forced to respond to them as much as to actual activity." This was the worry of policy makers, that CNN and other international television networks had overtaken the agenda of international affairs, usurping the government's traditional role of identifying problems, outlining options, and pursuing solutions. Television pictures in "real time" meant that the public and the leadership watched events together. Boutros Boutros-Ghali, as UN secretary-general and the nominal keeper of the international agenda, found it unsettling that television was setting the agenda. "The member states never take action on a problem unless the media take up the case," he said in a speech to CNN's *World Report* contributors in May. "When the media gets involved, public opinion is aroused." So "intense" is this public emotion, said Boutros-Ghali, that "United Nations work is undermined" and "constructive statesmanship . . . is almost impossible."

It is an article of faith in foreign-policy circles these days that the advent of instantaneous and global technology has given the news media more of a voice in international communication and robbed diplomacy of its rightful place at the helm. Foreign-policy types call it the CNN curve, and the term is not a compliment. It suggests that when CNN floods the airwaves with news of a foreign crisis, policy makers have no choice but to redirect their attention to the crisis at hand. It is also suggests that crisis coverage evokes an emotional outcry from the public to "do something" about the latest incident, forcing political leaders to change course or risk unpopularity. This curve of public emotion may ebb as news recedes from the screen, but in the meantime, the enormous power of images broadcast in real time—students rebelling in Beijing, bombs falling in Baghdad, marines landing on the beaches of Mogadishu, a Russian White House set to fire by diehard Marxists, paratroopers landing in Haiti—has, in this view, eviscerated political will.

This book argues, instead, that while technology has enabled faster feedback from the public in matters of war and peace, while it has speeded the deliberative process and shortened reaction time, while it has written a new job description for diplomats and given the public a sense of being there, it has not, in the end, changed the fundamentals of political leadership and international governance. Once past the wonder and marvel at the specter of two diplomats watching television together while telephones dangle in their hands, there comes the question, So what? Their mutual viewing influenced not at all the outcome of events, except to speed the flow of information. To view this increased pace of knowledge as a revolution in diplomacy and journalism is to misread history.

But that is not to diminish the magic of watching history in real time, which one viewer—glued to a television set in Los Angeles while the Russian White House burned in Moscow—compared to a feeling that "CNN had handed out guns." There is undeniably something new afoot when the Clinton White House, monitoring events at a crisis moment in Moscow, discards the cables of its own embassy staff in favor of watching CNN. Or when Secretary of State James Baker, standing in an air force hangar in Taif, Saudi Arabia, makes a speech to hundreds of airmen and -women about the brink of war that is directed to an audience of one, Saddam Hussein, sitting in his bunker in Baghdad watching television. And there is no denying that the profusion of new communication channels—from cellular telephones to computer E-mail, from the fax machine to Internet—has created headaches for officials trying to keep apace of the information flow. When microphones are thrust in the face of policy makers whose job is to consider implications, when sound bites take precedence over substance, policy can suffer.

These developments do not, however, constitute a revolution in policy or politics, only in the speed of communication and the breadth of the audience. Nor are they new, having their precedent in earlier clashes of diplomats with media technology. What has been missing so far in the discussion about CNN's impact or technology's primacy is any sense of history. Reviewing the history of media technology over the last 550 years, this book argues that television pictures in the age of television are as powerful as newspapers in the time of print, or broadcasts in the time of radio, or film in the time of newsreels, or computers in an age of cyberspace, in short, a treatise on relative history meant to calm the techno-hysteria of many in the diplomatic, political, and journalistic communities.

It is said, for instance, that real-time satellite television—with its ability to relay events as they are happening—empowers the powerless, busting up the elite circle of policy makers accustomed to setting policy without interference from the less enlightened. In just one example, Israel in 1992 expelled 415 Palestinians suspected of being terrorists, hoping to quiet the domestic outrage at the recent killing of five Israeli policemen, and to send a message to the Islamic Resistance Movement, better known by its Arabic acronym, Hamas, that violence would not go unpunished. Instead, the move landed Israel in the middle of a public-relations nightmare, as English-speaking Palestinians, cooking tea in makeshift tents, told their story on international television. So gripping was their tale, so dramatic their surroundings, that when Israel agreed, under pressure from the United Nations, to release some of the men, they refused to leave. They calculated that their cause was better served by staying, by pleading their case on an international stage, than it could ever be at home. Policy makers bemoaned the advent of satellite television, which gave these men an unprecedented global platform.

But Palestinians were not the first to gain a new audience because of a new media technology. Martin Luther, a German monk who challenged the Catholic Church's authority, was blessed with intellect—and good timing. No matter how widespread the interest in Luther's ideas, without the printing press, invented by Johann Gutenberg seventy years earlier, it is doubtful that Lutheranism would have achieved, so quickly, a worldwide following. Lutheranism, said one historian, "was from the first the child of the printed book."

The printing press gave Luther a larger audience for his ideas in the sixteenth century, much as satellite television did for Palestinians in the twentieth century. But the ruling elite in each case had available the same tools of technology to plead its case, to counter the dissent from within. One of the lessons of history is that no matter how much technology levels the playing field and empowers those who were until then powerless, ruling elites retain much influence. There may be more players on the field, and the viewing audience may be larger, but the game is unchanged. "The exercise of power is determined by thousands of interactions between the world of the powerful and that of the powerless," wrote Václav Havel, a Czech dissident playwright and later, after the fall of the Communist regime, president of the Czech Republic. "All the more so because these worlds are never divided by a sharp line: everyone has a small part of himself in both."

It is likewise said that real-time satellite television, and the coming race for cyberspace, robs diplomats of time for due deliberation, and strips ambassadors of power. Former Secretary of State Lawrence Eagleburger blames technology—the telephone and the computer in particular—for allowing world capitals to keep a shorter leash on their envoys than they did in earlier times, when diplomats freelanced policy, and military officers negotiated treaties with other countries, as Matthew C. Perry did in opening diplomatic and trade relations between the United States and Japan in 1854. "In the good old days," said Eagleburger, "you had a lot more flexibility."

But in some sense the good old days never were. To hear them tell it, diplomats have been losing power since the advent of the telegraph, which they blamed for encouraging war. French historian Charles Mazade argued in 1875 that the just-passed Franco-Prussian War could have been avoided if leaders had sat eye-to-eye instead of sending their ultimatums by telegram. The London *Spectator* agreed, lamenting the telegraph's impact in 1889 on diplomacy and journalism. "The world is for purposes of intelligence reduced to a village," the newspaper editorialized. "All men are compelled to think of all things, at the same time, on imperfect information, and with too little interval for reflection." The editors even complained about what the television age would later label sound bites, and charged that the new invention was encouraging emotions instead of rationality in international affairs. "The constant diffusion of statements in snippets, the constant excitements of feeling unjustified by fact, the constant formation of hasty or erroneous opinions, must in the end, one would think, deteriorate the intelligence of all to whom the telegraph appeals." Snippets or sound bites, the impact was the same.

The most telling criticism is that real-time satellite television has forced diplomacy to respond to emotional appeals instead of rational thought. From places like Bosnia, Somalia, Rwanda, and Burundi, television images of war, starvation, and deprivation evoke raw emotions that put new demands on policy makers. When a busload of Bosnian children being escorted out of Sarajevo under United Nations protection was attacked by Serb artillery, the graphic pictures of children caught in the crossfire of ethnic hatred outraged John Fox, an Eastern European specialist at the State Department's planning and policy office. "The images just kept mounting," he said. "The images came, they never stopped, and that's what got to people. Every now and then, even though you had to steal yourself just to get through the day . . . there would be one that you just couldn't ignore." Like three other top State Department officials, Fox resigned.

But emotionalism has always been a factor in international politics. Consider the War of Jenkins' Ear, fought in 1739, when Britain battled Spain over its mistreatment of British smugglers and pirates. Robert Jenkins, an English mariner, picked a barroom brawl with a Spanish customs guard and in the process suffered a bad cut on his ear, which doctors, in the practice of the day, amputated. Amid a commercial rivalry between England and Spain, Jenkins' ear was waved about on the floor of the House of Commons, used to pressure the reluctant in the government to seek revenge for alleged mistreatment of British smugglers. Here was symbolism and emotionalism combined.

In spite of these historic echoes, or perhaps because of them, some maintain that the current explosion of media technology is exponentially more of a burden than past inventions. The U.S. intervention in Somalia is widely cited as an instance where television pictures swayed international events. The oft-heard chorus: Pictures got us in, and pictures got us out. Those who hold this view argue that the vivid and wrenching images of starving Somali children forced

President Bush to act, and that the equally horrible pictures of an American soldier's corpse being dragged through the streets of Mogadishu compelled President Clinton to announce a departure date for U.S. troops. The truth is more textured. If TV pictures *alone* compelled Bush to intervene in Somalia, then they should have had a similar impact in the Sudan, where the starvation was equally devastating, the pictures equally horrific, and, at first, equally in evidence on CNN. If Clinton had wanted to use political capital to explain to the American public why the United States was in Somalia, if he had used the bully pulpit of high office to make a case that the United States had an obligation to stay, he could have countered the weight of those pictures from Mogadishu. By choosing not to expend his political capital for a cause not of his own choosing, the legacy of an earlier administration, Clinton allowed the pictures to dominate. It is not inevitable, or even desirable, that leaders cede this power to television. It is also not the fault of television.

Television was not responsible for the predicament facing policy makers who were forced to shape a response to Somalia, but it did speed events. There is simply no denying that television quickens the pace of international affairs, and one thing more. A medium that combines the visual and the verbal, television taps the emotions. Thousands of words written about mass starvation do not touch the same emotion, in the television age, as the moving picture of a child beset by flies, crying from hunger. Like the photograph and film, satellite television, for all its technological prowess, touches the heart. That is why Americans provided food in Somalia in 1992. But like the other visual media, television provides a fleeting image. Context still matters.

No better example exists than the pictures of famine from Ethiopia in 1984. NBC's London bureau chief Joseph Angotti had seen a BBC Report on the famine, and urged his employers in New York to look at it. Angotti wanted to ship the footage by air, but NBC News president Lawrence Grossman overruled him on grounds that it was too expensive. "To Angotti's credit, he insisted," Grossman recalled years later. "Everybody writes about this but what nobody remembers is that it wasn't just the pictures that convinced us to use the story, it was also the poetry of the script." The pictures were gripping, but they still needed words. The combination did affect policy—public pressure found the Reagan administration increasing federal food aid from $23 million to $98 million—but not for long. Once coverage faded, so did public interest.

George Kennan, the esteemed diplomat who fathered the containment policy of the cold war, was critical of U.S. intervention in Somalia because he believed emotions evoked by television pictures were driving American diplomacy. "If American policy from here on out, particularly policy involving the uses of our armed forces abroad, is to be controlled by popular emotional impulses, and particularly ones provoked by the commercial television industry, then there is no place—not only for myself, but for what have traditionally been regarded as the responsible deliberative" voices in government, he wrote in an article just before U.S. Marines landed on the beaches of Mogadishu. It is a fitting coda to Kennan's lament that when the marines landed, they encountered only one hostile group: a pack of journalists whose bright camera lights mitigated the strategic effect of the soldiers' night-vision goggles. To Kennan, these cameras looked like the enemy.

The old warrior of diplomacy, who had been so prescient in predicting Moscow's aggressions during a time of superpower rivalry, was trying to warn a new generation of the dangers of television and its impact on diplomacy. But Kennan's real quarrel is not with television pictures that hit viewers in the gut but with leaders who too easily yielded to their pull. This grand man of foreign policy may have forgotten, in his rant against the emotionalism of the 1990s, that he was equally incensed by Franklin Delano Roosevelt's decision in the 1930s to grant concessions to the Soviet Union during negotiations over diplomatic recognition. Politicians tend to make decisions for political reasons, with public opinion and emotion much on their radar. Chiding FDR in his memoirs for "showmanship and prestidigitation," Kennan attributes the move to "neurotic self-consciousness and introversion, the tendency to make statements and take actions with regard *not to their effect on the international scene . . . but rather to their effect on . . . American opinion* (italics added)."

Each generation is mesmerized by the innovations of its times, sure that no other generation has experienced the emotional upheaval that comes of technological change. We are in the throes of such an infatuation now. In the most extreme example, a diplomat at the United Nations recently quipped that CNN had become "the sixth vote on the Security Council." Already, there are predictions, similarly, that the World Wide Web will erase national borders, making governments impotent and sovereignty a memory. What history shows, instead, is that despite the vanity of each age, journalists have always had power to sway public opinion, and more, that politicians always credit the news media for souring public opinion when they fail to win favor. What changes as one invention gives way to the next is the way in which the message hits home.

When the telegraph was new—and the telegraph is the closest mirror to changes unleashed by satellite television— it ushered in a revolution in the way international relations were conducted. From an age when messages were delivered at the speed of transportation—a horse, a sailing ship, a train—diplomats braced themselves for what they considered instantaneous communication. The shift was almost beyond imagining. "We can speak to and receive an answer in a few seconds of time from Hong Kong, where ten P.M. here [New York] is ten A.M. there," Samuel F. B. Morse marveled at a reception. "China and New York are in interlocutory communication. We know the fact, but can imagination realize the fact?"

Morse's sense of awe at the impact of his own invention, his amazement that opposite ends of the world could be so quickly connected, is but one similarity to our own fascination with the possibilities of real-time, satellite communication. It is also a humbling reminder that communication technology has always laid out its gifts with wide eyes. No matter the magic, each new communication technology unleashes a similar dilemma on the political players and audience of its day. Technology has always been a burden, calling on leaders in every era to change their habits, to adjust to a new speed or a new imperative, to hurry their decisions and address a larger audience. But technology has also been a gift to those who learned to exploit its blessings to shape public debate instead of being driven by the whims of public opinion. In this history there are echoes.

2

The Telegraph Annihilates
Time and Space

S AMUEL F. B. MORSE sat alone in the visitors' gallery on
a February day in 1843 as Congress debated the merits
of his invention. Poverty-stricken, feared by friends to be
wasting his artistic genius on a "miserable delusion," Morse,
a professor of painting and design at the University of the
City of New York, listened as his machine was ridiculed. A
bill providing $30,000 to "test the expediency of the tele-
graph projected by Professor Morse," passed on a 89-83 vote,
but not before many in the House of Representatives took
the opportunity to mock the telegraph. In a debate not unlike
those that characterize the House floor to this day, Representative George Smith Houston, a Democrat from Alabama,
argued that if the telegraph was everything it was cracked up
to be, it must be akin to the Messiah. In which case, Houston
proposed, Morse should share the $30,000 with the Millerites,
a religious sect predicting the second coming of Christ
sometime in 1844. Others were even more sarcastic, suggesting that the funds be shared with hypnotists, as if science
should compete with witchcraft. Amid "great laughter" from
the floor, a reporter approached Morse in the gallery. Morse
was holding his head in his hands. "You are anxious," he
surmised. "I have reason to be," replied Morse. "I have spent

seven years in perfecting this invention. If it succeeds, I am a made man. If it fails, I am ruined."

Within a year, the $30,000 congressional appropriation (actually, Morse returned $3,500 unused) proved its merit to political detractors. With Democrats meeting in Baltimore for their convention, word came by telegraph that James Polk, the first "dark horse" candidate, had overtaken the front-runner, former president Martin Van Buren. When the convention nominated Senator Silas Wright of New York as vice president, he declined—by telegram. An incredulous convention sent a committee to verify what the telegraph had communicated. Once that was confirmed, "the fame of the telegraph at once took wing." The telegraph's place, at least among American politicians and journalists, was secure. "Even the most inveterate opposers have changed to admirers," Morse wrote in his diary. "And one of them, the Honorable Cave Johnson, who ridiculed my system last session by associating it with the tricks of animal magnetism [hypnotism], came to me and said: 'Sir, I give in. It is an astonishing invention.' "

The telegraph was the first invention of communication technology in history to travel faster than the fastest form of transportation then available. Carried over electronic wires, a message on the telegraph traveled at the speed of light, or 186,000 miles per second, while all the railroad train could muster was 2 miles a minute, and pigeon carriers were clocked at over 35 miles per hour. The telegraph's impact was as revolutionary in the industrial age as any current claims for the computer in the information age. Even now, it is hard to comprehend the magnitude of the transition. Suddenly, from a world where communication depended on the speed of a horse or a carrier pigeon or a balloon or a sailing ship or a train, messages could be received and answered almost instantly. This transition, from a leisurely pace to instantaneous touch, is perhaps the closest mirror to the changes in information technology experienced in the late twentieth century. Looking at the telegraph as a later generation would view the computer, one early witness said, quite simply, "Time and space are now annihilated."

Time and space, annihilated. No other phrase appears so frequently in the literature on the history of technology. It is as if conquering time and space is a human instinct as basic as hunger or thought. "Man may instantly converse with his fellow man in any part of the world," proclaimed one of the telegraph's devotees. "Is it not a feat sublime? Intellect hath conquered time," cooed the masthead of the *Telegrapher*, the official publication of the National Telegraphic Union. Said one Rochester newspaper: "The actual realization of the astonishing fact that instantaneous personal conversation can be held between persons hundreds of miles apart can only be fully attained by witnessing the wonderful fact itself." Even a congressional committee, investigating the telegraph in 1838, concluded that it meant "almost instantaneous communication of intelligence between the most distant points of the country, and simultaneously. Space will be, to all practical purposes of information, completely annihilated." It is fashionable in the late years of the twentieth century to talk about "the information superhighway," with its Internet and promise for global interaction. But long before satellites circled the globe, the telegraph was proclaimed "The Great Highway of Thought," its wires "slender bridges."

Here was an earthquake in diplomacy, in journalism, in war. To nineteenth-century sensibilities, there could be nothing more instantaneous, nothing more immediate, nothing with more of the promise of a global village. "The chilling influences of time and distance are all gone," said Dr. George Loring, former congressman and chairman of the Massachusetts Republican Party, at a reception in Morse's honor in

1871. "All mystery and doubt with regard to passing events and their influences are ended. The events occur, are received, weighed, set down in a moment, and in a moment we pass on to the next."

From the beginning, the telegraph worried some intellectuals, who fretted that the faster dissemination of information by cable would somehow dilute the quality of public discourse, to say nothing of their own influence. Henry David Thoreau, in *Walden*, set the tone. "We are in great haste to construct a magnetic telegraph from Maine to Texas," he wrote, "but Maine and Texas, it may be, have nothing important to communicate." It is, he added, "as if the main object were to talk fast and not to talk sensibly. We are eager to tunnel under the Atlantic and bring the Old World some weeks nearer to the New; but perchance the first news that will leak through into the broad, flapping American ear will be that the Princess Adelaide has the whooping cough."

Technology inspired fears among elitists, whether they ruled politics or literature, that they could no longer control public opinion. Even before Morse perfected the electric telegraph, France banned the visual telegraph, or Chappe system, based on flag signals. "Just imagine what could have happened if the passing success of the Lyons silk workers' insurrection had been known in all corners of the nation at once!" argued a horrified member of King Louis-Philippe's court. Given that official view, it was not surprising that, in 1837, a French law was enacted imposing jail sentences and stiff fines (up to 10,000 francs) on "anyone transmitting unauthorized signals from one place to another by means of the [Chappe] telegraph machine."

Russian czar Nicholas I was likewise terrified by the telegraph's potential to spread information. Fearing that the broad use of the telegraph would prove "subversive," Nicholas turned down a contract with Morse, even though the details had already been worked out with Russian counselor of state Baron Alexander de Meyendorff. It was a strategic blunder that cost Russia dearly. On the eve of World War I, Russian telegraph lines were still so rudimentary that Russian military officials were forced to use radio to transmit marching orders. As a result, during one of the first battles of the war, Germans learned from uncoded Russian radio broadcasts the exact location of two key Russian units. The information proved decisive in the German victory at the Battle of Tannenberg. Nicholas feared the democratizing potential of information so much that, like his Communist successors years later who tried to outlaw the telephone, he was willing to risk victory to keep technology at bay. Many of his troops paid with their lives.

Even as Nicholas saw in the new technology a recipe for war, others saw the prospect of world peace. "Ambassadors can utter each day the voice of the government to which they belong, and communicate the reply from that to which they are sent," said Loring. "The boundaries of states and empires may remain the same, their tongues may differ, their social and civil conditions vary, but united as they are into an international community, intimate with each others' wants and necessities and interests, how can they long remain antagonistic?"

Such optimism about the fruits of technology attests to a naive but endearing view that the knowledge relayed by the telegraph would make nations so conversant with the national interests of their one-time enemies that war would come no more. Queen Victoria may have had this in mind when, during the first of five attempts to lay an underwater trans-Atlantic cable, she telegraphed President Buchanan, "Glory to God in the Highest, peace on earth, good will to men." Sam Morse's brother Sidney was more effusive. "Your invention, measuring it by the power which it will give to man to accomplish his plans, is not only the greatest invention of this age, but the greatest invention of any age," Sidney wrote his brother in 1838, five years before Congress began its debate. "The surface of the earth will be networked with wire, and every wire will be a nerve. The earth will become a huge animal with 10 million hands, and in every hand a pen to record whatever the directing soul may dictate! No limit can be assigned to the value of the invention."

Sidney Morse was likely trying to buck up his brother for the bumpy road to fame still before him. What is remarkable is that these claims to greatness were heard again in 1994, more than 150 years after Sidney wrote in praise of his brother Sam's invention. "Time in this age has been collapsed; there is no time any longer," said Marvin Kalb, director of the Joan Shorenstein Barone Center on the Press, Politics and Public Policy at Harvard University. "Another concept that has been collapsed is distance. Both are gone."

No matter how fulsome Sidney's praise of Sam Morse's invention, the promise of a technology that could end war remained elusive. In fact, with prescience and precision, the generals seized the telegraph to aid in the command of war. Unlike poets and monarchs, the generals viewed technology as a tactical breakthrough, less a threat to the spirit than an advantage to the army. For generals, the telegraph, like a satellite linkup, may have been a mixed blessing, speeding communication and facilitating enemy intelligence, abetting sabotage and manipulation, but always a weapon of choice. It was, in short, as potent and as critical as a new gun.

To journalism and international relations, the telegraph likewise arrived with a clamor. For diplomats, the telegraph, like CNN, cut the time allowed for decision-making and robbed them of power in the field, but allowed for direct and immediate communication around the globe. For journalists, the telegraph, like satellite TV, offered a boost of influence over public opinion, though it ushered in a period of shoddy reporting. For none did it change the essentials of political power—that quality still resided first with leaders who demonstrated both popular appeal and strong convictions—but for all, it increased the number of players on the scene, and, more importantly, radicalized the ways of doing business.

When the first telegraphic machine was readied on May 24, 1844, Morse asked Annie Ellsworth, daughter of U.S. commissioner of patents, to compose a message. She chose a passage from the Bible, Numbers 23:23: "What hath God wrought!" The message—dots and dashes printed on a paper tape—was sent along a wire wrapped in rope yarn and tar from the Supreme Court room in Washington to the B&O Mount Clare station on Pratt Street in Baltimore. The *second* message Morse sent to Baltimore was more to the point. "Have you any news?" he cabled. For what God had wrought was a godsend for the newspapers.

Since the 1830s, when the penny press challenged the establishment newspapers by printing local crime and human-interest stories, newspapers had begun the shift to a mass medium. But even their large circulations and big advertising budgets could hardly compensate for the costs of transporting the news by chartered boats, rail cars, stagecoaches, harbor patrols, and carrier pigeons. The telegraph was the answer to their bottom-line prayers because it allowed reporters to cable news instead of transporting it.

Newspapers leaped at the new technology. In the first week of 1848, the *New York Herald* printed 79,000 words of telegraphic content, at a cost of $12,381, boasted publisher James G. Bennett. In 1861, Western Union opened a line between New York and San Francisco, with two results. One was a neighborhood called Telegraph Hill. The other was the death of the Pony Express, begun the year before in hopes of winning government contracts to deliver the mail, put out of business by the speed and competitive cost of the telegraph. By 1880, Western Union was thriving, delivering 92 percent of the messages sent within the country, over 3 million of them from reporters.

There was a magic to the times, an intoxication about the "telegraphic" newspaper. "We marvel that it has become possible to convey, print, and circulate upon the streets facts concerning a pending battle hundreds of miles away," said one of the Civil War military telegraph operators. The era brought other changes too, chief among them a bravado, a cult of personality, a sense of rooting for the underdog, the beginning of the reporter as rakish seducer of information. That the telegraph's arrival coincided with other technological wonders—the steam engine and the railroads, among others—accounted in part for the shift. Then too, an increasingly urbanized and industrialized population had different needs of its newspapers. News of the cities, not the farms, crowded the pages, crime news often, grimy and dramatic and sensational. In a city of strangers, the newspaper became the community bulletin board, and injustices were addressed on its pages. It is probably too much of a stretch to say the telegraph fathered the trench coat, but it seems arguable that the heady atmosphere of speeded information and inexpensive newspapers paved the way for the raucous, unpretentious, seat-of-the-pants atmosphere of Ben Hecht and Charles MacArthur's newsroom in the 1934 play *The Front Page*.

None of this, however, made the reporting terribly accurate. Journalism from Civil War battles is, with few exceptions, a disappointing chapter in the profession's history, though perhaps the sensationalism owed something to the nature of the battle, with brother fighting brother. Reporters in the South went to battle largely as partisans, describing the North as "the cursed, cowardly nation of swindlers and thieves" that fought "drunken with wine, blood and fury." In the North, correspondents went to fill a tremendous appetite for news from readers scouring every report for news of the welfare of son, brother, husband. Circulation skyrocketed as newspapers discovered they could sell five times their normal run with details of a battle. Reporters often bribed telegraph operators to give preference to their copy over a competitor's. The new trend was best summed up by a publisher hungry for copy. "Telegraph fully all news you can get," *Chicago Times* editor Wilbur F. Storey ordered one of his reporters, "and when there is no news, send rumors."

Exaggeration became the hallmark of Civil War journalism, complete fabrication not at all uncommon. One correspondent begged a wounded officer not to die before he had finished interviewing him, promising him his last words would appear in "the widely circulated and highly influential journal I represent."

How much of this sad journalistic record is attributable to the technology can be answered by the tale of two bylines. The first, which gained popularity in the early years of the war, said, "By Telegraph," a clue to readers that the message was fresh, if not always reliable. The second, imposed briefly in 1863 by General Joseph Hooker of the North's Army of the Potomac, was a byline that gave the correspondent's name. This latter method was meant to fix blame for the legion of inaccuracies in the newspapers. Many believe it worked, as reporters traveling with Hooker's troops tended to be more circumspect in their writings. When individual accountability superseded technological wonders, journalism improved, at least for a while.

The wild excesses of technologically emboldened newspapers were a bane to the generals. William Tecumseh Sherman loathed correspondents and banished them from his camps, resulting in a near absence of coverage of his victorious, torched march from Atlanta to the coast. General George G. Meade, unhappy with the dispatches filed by the *Philadelphia Inquirer*'s Edward Crapsey, ordered him placed backwards on an old horse with a sign around his neck that said LIBELER OF THE PRESS and escorted out of camp to the tune of the "Rogue's March." This banishment aroused sympathy from Crapsey's colleagues, who conspired to boycott any mention of Meade's name in any dispatch ever again. Meade was an ambitious politician who harbored presidential ambitions, and the silent treatment was widely thought to have ended his political career. But he may have had good cause for suspecting Crapsey of disloyalty. Confederate general Robert E. Lee reportedly read the Northern papers for hints on the whereabouts of Union troops, and was particularly enamored of one reporter for the *Philadelphia Inquirer*, saying that the fellow "knew what he reported and reported what he knew."

William Howard Russell, the veteran war correspondent from the *Times of London*, the model of journalistic probity, did not fare well in the Civil War either. Widely recognized as the world's first war correspondent. Russell nearly single-handedly brought down the British government over its handling of the traumatic Crimea War in 1854–1855. So devastating were his disclosures on the horrors of the military hospital at Sevastopol and the disastrous charge of the Light Brigade that the British establishment accused Russell of betraying secrets to the enemy. So accurate were they that Prime Minister Lord Aberdeen suffered a parliamentary vote of no confidence, and the military hierarchy commanding the battle was called to account. So suspenseful were his files that men and women gathered in parlors for a reading of his latest dispatches, which often ran for full pages in the newspaper. No longer.

The telegraph imposed a new format on journalism, requiring correspondents to file their most important information first, leaving to the end their more descriptive sentiments. The telegraph, along with a new mass market for newspapers, begat the inverted pyramid, a form of journalism in which the bottom line is served first, the punch line delivered before the setup. With the telegraph, a line could be cut, a transmission could end in midsentence, so the imperative was to squeeze in the news at the top. This was a vast departure for people like Russell, who found that truth was no defense.

During the first engagement between Union and Confederate forces at Bull Run, members of Congress and their wives came down from Washington with picnic lunches to watch fighting. Russell came too, and reported that the untested federal troops had bolted and fled the scene at the first cracks of Southern fire. His report angered Yankee sympathizers, who advised him to seek protection from angry mobs in the British embassy. Russell himself left the front during the course of the Civil War, discouraged less by bloodshed than by the new pace and seeming bias of the press.

Like the changes that satellite television would later bring to journalism, the telegraph ushered in a period of quick stories, fast-paced copy, racy headlines. Press critic W. J. Stillman lamented that "America has in fact transformed journalism from what it once was—the periodical expression of the thought of the time, the opportune record of the questions and answers of contemporary life—into an agency for collecting, condensing and assimilating the trivialities of the entire human existence." Somehow the new mass audience liked speed of information, the sense of being there as events were unfolding. Russell, with his overview of how a battle was won or lost, his emphasis on the narrative of war instead of the score, had become old school.

In any event, journalism was almost too enamored of the new speed of information to notice his departure. A business that thrives on speed had found a means of near instant com-munication. One of the penny papers, so named because they cost one cent, even scooped the White House. President James K. Polk was waging war with Mexico in 1847 over territories called California and New Mexico. News of the fall of Vera Cruz, a critical city, came not from the War Department but from the *Baltimore Sun*, which telegraphed the White House with the development—after sharing the news with its readers. Far from being distressed at this lapse of intelligence in his own government, Polk declared in his diary, "This was joyful news." Within two hours, Polk got a copy of the newspaper to read a more detailed report of the surrender before sharing the news with his cabinet. If Polk later learned of these war developments through official chan-nels, he did not deem fit to record the fact in his diary. Later he grew angry at the newly empowered media, realizing that it could deliver information to him as well as rob him of it. He had dispatched Nicholas P. Trist, Thomas Jefferson's son-in-law, to negotiate a peace treaty with Mexican authorities, only to find the details had been leaked to the *New York Herald*. "It was a profound Cabinet secret," Polk despaired in his diary. "I have not been more vexed or excited since I have been president. The success of Mr. Trist's mission I knew in the beginning must depend mainly on keeping it a secret."

Secrets obsessed the generals too, and for all of its negative impact, the telegraph served their purposes well. "The value of the magnetic telegraph in war cannot be exaggerated, as was illustrated by the perfect concert of action between the armies in Virginia and in Georgia, in all 1864," Sherman wrote in his memoirs. "Hardly a day intervened when General Grant did not know the exact state of facts with me, more than 1500 miles off, as the wires ran." By the end of the war in 1865, the Union Army had built 15,000 miles of military telegraph lines and handled over 6 million messages, up to

3,000 a day, at a cost of $2.6 million. "No orders had to be given to establish the telegraph," Ulysses S. Grant wrote in his memoirs. "In a few minutes longer time than it took a mule to walk the length of its coil, telegraphic communication would be effected between all the headquarters of the army."

The Confederacy also made use of the telegraph, though it had far fewer lines. Stringing only 1,000 miles of wire, the South depended when it could on commercial lines. Still, it made a difference. Brigadier General J. N. Palmer wrote in a letter to Major General B. F. Butler that the military telegraph, during an attack at New Bern, "had not only informed me of all that was going on in front, but the whole line of posts to Morehead was put upon its guard. During the day, when the enemy were immediately around the town, the Signal Corps kept us advised of the smallest movement of the enemy at any point of the line." Its worth, he told a colleague, "cannot be estimated in money."

As with every new technology, the telegraph was also vulnerable to manipulation by the enemy. Grant reports that several telegrams sent to him by General McClellan were confiscated by a Rebel spy operator, who escaped with "many" of the dispatches. The most successful wiretapping of the war was achieved by Charles Gaston, one of Lee's telegraphic operators, who managed to tap the North's Fort Monroe Line. For six weeks the Confederate operator was on Grant's wire, but this advantage was all but eliminated by a lack of code breakers. Only one message proved of use to the Confederacy, as it was not written in code, but rather instructed Grant on the shipment of 2,486 cattle. Struggling to supply his troops with food, Lee sent troops to intercept the shipment, assuring a forty-day food supply. Then, too, technology abetted cowardice, with deadly consequences. A Confederate telegraph operator captured at his station in

Jacksonville in 1864 was "under the influence of a revolver at his ear, compelled to telegraph in his own style a train order which in due time brought a complete train [of Rebel soldiers] into the Union lines, where it was of course captured." But for the most part, the telegraph was so great a blessing to both sides that units were sent ahead of the army to string wires, often at great risk, guardian angels of information.

For Lincoln too, the telegraph was a risk worth taking, the newly emboldened newspapers a burden to be borne. Public opinion had always mattered in war, but in the Civil War it grew from an undercurrent to a wave, no longer content to stay beneath the surface. The White House courted public opinion because many Northerners, convinced the South was bluffing, assumed the war would be over in short order. That it took four years and took 617,548 lives was a shock, one that nearly cost Abraham Lincoln reelection in 1864. Lincoln had many problems in war, not least the recalcitrance of his generals to lead the fight. But he was not immune to the inaccuracies and slights of a partisan press. After a grim day touring the battlefield at Antietam, a depressed Lincoln retired to his tent. Aides tried to cheer him with lighthearted banter. A passing reporter heard laughter from the tent, and telegraphed his newspaper, which promptly published: "President Lincoln tours the Antietam Battlefield, and laughs in sight of burial parties." Lincoln was pained by the criticism, and considered putting out a statement to clarify what had happened. The statement was prepared but never delivered. "There has already been too much said about this falsehood," Lincoln told his aides. "Let the thing alone. If I have not established character enough to give the lie to this charge, I can only say that I am mistaken in my own estimate of myself. In politics, every man must skin his own skunk. These fellows are welcome to the hide of this one."

Lincoln may have sought to rise above the pains of slander, but his secretary of war, Edwin Stanton, did not. Concerned about public morale, he began to alter casualty figures, so Union losses would look lighter than the battlefield reality suggested. He tried censorship—arresting editors, threatening court-martial, banning correspondents from the front—but found it widely disobeyed. So Stanton began, early in 1864, to report the war himself. Issuing his own files, in a war diary addressed to military officials in New York and distributed through the Associated Press, Stanton put the Northern "spin" on war developments. Not coincidentally, the Associated Press itself was an effort by New York papers to share costs and beat the government's mail service by as much as twenty-four hours during the War with Mexico in 1846. War had always made for big themes, told in breathless prose. The correspondents' play to the emotions clearly sold newspapers, and worried political leaders.

Like other media advances, the telegraph widened the circle of citizens with views on key policy decisions. "The opinion of the world has become a powerful international force," wrote one of the telegraph operators who kept the lines humming during the Civil War. Like real-time television in a later century, the telegraph speeded the delivery of messages in its time. When General Sherman was about to enter surrender negotiations with General Joseph Johnston, he received a telegram saying that Abraham Lincoln had been assassinated. Johnston had come to the meeting sure he could get better terms than Lee had because, while on the run, he was not surrounded. As soon as Sherman handed him the telegram, he knew he would get very little. Sweat broke out on Johnston's forehead "in large drops" as he realized that in this moment of reconstruction, "Mr. Lincoln was the best friend they had," his assassination "the greatest possible calamity to the South." He understood that Northerners would blame the

South for Lincoln's death, further eroding chances of a just peace. Sherman did offer one concession not given to Lee: Johnston's men were allowed to retreat with their guns. The telegram had not changed public opinion, but the assassination itself certainly hardened Northern hearts. The telegram speeded that message, and Johnston could read it between the lines.

In the end, the telegraph speeded communication beyond the expectations of science, and that is legacy enough. More, it redistributed power within journalism. Those who could tell a fast-paced story, embellished for dramatic appeal, would excel. Some might call it sensationalism, others, pandering to the worst instincts of a fickle public. Whatever this new trend might be called, it reached its apogee during the Spanish-American War.

3

A Splendid Little War

THE SPANISH-AMERICAN WAR of 1898 was a shaper of fame and reputation, cementing the image of an adventure-seeking Theodore Roosevelt leading his Rough Riders into battle. There were other images too, of a handsome war correspondent, Richard Harding Davis, charming readers with his good looks and daring pen, of an ambitious publisher, William Randolph Hearst, sensationalizing news for the sake of financial profits and political power. This three-month war fought for Cuba's independence, which dissolved the Spanish empire and put San Juan Hill on the map, had everything: a good cause, a quick rout, even the hint of a world power in the making. "It has been a splendid little war," John Hay, U.S. ambassador to England, wrote to Colonel Roosevelt afterwards, "begun with the highest motives, carried on with magnificent intelligence and spirit, favored by that fortune which loves the brave."

Many argue that this was also a press war, fomented by the highly inaccurate and jingoistic reports of the "yellow" press, fueled by three years' worth of sensationalist accounts in Hearst's *Journal* but with ample support from Joseph Pulitzer's *World* and the war-eager *Sun*. There is evidence aplenty of the sensationalism, and some sense that the war fever in those newspapers did move the body politic, at least on Capitol Hill.

But there is also reason to question whether it was the press that drove this war to the starting gate. For one thing, the newspapers were not a monolith, the *New York Tribune* and the *New York Times* sounding a more reasoned note, and most newspapers outside New York supporting White House mediation efforts. For another, President McKinley's efforts to resolve the conflict diplomatically showed some promise. In response to his entreaties, Spain made concessions that, had they come earlier, might have mitigated the outcome. In short, examined through the prism of technology's historic impact on diplomacy, the Spanish-American War becomes a case study for the core themes of this book: that journalism's influence on policy is often overrated, that political leaders have more sway than journalists in shaping public opinion, and that, finally, diplomats are responsible for diplomacy, no matter how exasperating the press exaggerations.

Exaggerations there surely were. In the run-up to the Spanish-American War, as the Cuban insurrection gained ground, the New York newspapers printed "accounts of battles that never occurred, while remaining ignorant of real battles. They narrated a succession of Spanish atrocities entirely unauthenticated. They dealt in the feeblest of rumor." W. A. Swanberg, in his celebrated biography, *Citizen Hearst*, has culled the libraries for some delightful examples. FEEDING PRISONERS TO SHARKS, read one *Journal* headline, over a perennial theme of Spanish atrocities toward Cuban subjects. Another account reported that Spanish authorities had roasted twenty-five Catholic priests—alive.

While sensationalizing Spanish atrocities and misrepresenting Spanish military intentions (one newspaper reported that Spain had gotten a "money loan" from the Rothschilds to buy warships, an interesting development that proved untrue), the newspapers also suppressed news that might have reflected poorly on the rebels, burying deep in the newspaper's pages stories about *insurrectos* who extorted protection money from American plantation owners in Cuba.

As if these sorry examples of journalism, many fed to headline-seeking publishers by a pro-Cuba junta of expatriates in New York, were not enough, the key players were only too happy to hype their own influence. Hearst set the tone with a telegram. One of his illustrators, artist Frederic Remington, was disappointed in a lack of action in Havana. "Everything is quiet," he cabled Hearst. "There is no trouble here. There will be no war. I wish to return." To which Hearst replied, in a cable that may be apocryphal but is clearly illustrative: "Please remain. You furnish the pictures and I'll furnish the war." Hearst's cockiness swelled on the eve of the battle, when a headline in his newspaper proclaimed: HOW DO YOU LIKE THE JOURNAL'S WAR?

For a long time, his version was gospel. One author, writing in 1967 "an indictment of the war-mongering press," lamented "the great power of newspapers when they work together in fostering international hatred and distrust." This was the conventional wisdom, that the sensationalist, fevered newspapers had forced the hand of rational leaders, that but for the newspapers whipping up public emotion there would have been no war.

There is no question they tried. Hearst and his cohorts gave the interventionists an emotional ballast, showing a gut feel for the power of the symbol. Hearst stoked the embers of war fever in 1897 by making a national heroine of Evangelina Cisneros, who was imprisoned for her role in the insurrection in Cuba. Not so, blared the Hearst newspaper, which reported that Miss Cisneros, the "Cuban Joan of Arc," was actually jailed for protecting her virtue from the lurid intentions of Spanish authorities.

Organizing a petition drive among well-known American women (including Mrs. McKinley, the president's mother), Hearst then had one of his correspondents "rescue" Miss Cisneros from her Cuban jail cell (by paying off guards), and deliver her to a triumphant parade at Madison Square. "Now is the time to consolidate public sentiment," he told an aide. "It must be a whale of a demonstration—something that will make the president and Congress sit up and think."

Hearst demonstrated an uncanny instinct for pushing public leaders to action. When he learned about the sinking of the *Maine*, a U.S. ship blown up in Havana Harbor, he knew it meant war. The Spanish, who told U.S. envoys they were stunned by the incident, claimed the explosion was an internal one. To this day, the evidence is unclear. McKinley sought to sober the nation by ordering flags flown at half-mast to honor the 266 American sailors and officers killed at sea. He convened an official inquiry, and maintained, for five weeks, an official silence as he awaited the results. Five weeks in an era of telegraphic speed of communication is a long time. Hearst needed no such pause. He is said to have called the newspaper the night of the explosion to check late developments.

"What is the important news?" Hearst asked.

"The battleship *Maine* has been blown up in Havana Harbor," replied his editor.

"Good heavens, what have you done with the story?"

"We have put it on the first page, of course."

"Have you put anything else on the front page?"

"Only the other big news," said the editor.

"There is not any other big news," Hearst said. "Please spread the story all over the page. This means war."

Hearst's sagacity in understanding the levers of power made him an adept manipulator of public opinion, and a shrewd businessman. His was a Democratic newspaper battling a Republican president. And nothing sold newspapers like war. Amid a fierce contest for circulation, the *Journal* went from 150,000 readers in 1896 to 800,000 by the time war started two years later. But Hearst's political and financial instincts alone did not propel the nation to war. There were facts on the ground, and national interests. War is rarely committed without them.

Few powers voluntarily leave their empires, but Spain might have retreated with greater class. The Revolt in 1898 was not, after all, the first time Cubans had shown a willingness to die for their freedom. In the period between 1823 and 1855, there were eight Cuban revolts against Spanish rule. After this came a prolonged conflict called the Ten Years War, from 1868 to 1878, followed by yet another rebellion in 1883. By the time tensions flared anew in 1895, Spain had sent 80,000 soldiers and spent $100 million. Spain was also reeling from the assassination of Prime Minister Antonio Canavos del Castillo, "a brilliant intellectual, shrewd, Spain's most important nineteenth-century politician," and wracked by debts from administering its colonies in both the Philippines and Cuba.

Worried about loss of men and morale in Cuba, a new Spanish government led by liberal Práxedes Mateo Sagasta was in a mood, and a position, to compromise. In this window for diplomacy, Sagasta and McKinley maneuvered. But Sagasta's room for negotiation was not unlimited. No Spanish regime could long survive the humiliation of losing Cuba, the jewel of its empire.

Even Spain's efforts to lure European interests to her side—Spanish envoys argued that America would not stop at taking Cuba—ran into geopolitics on the Continent. In Russia, the czar refused Spain's appeals, arguing that if Europe warned the United States against the war in Cuba, Washington might be tempted to lecture Russia on its designs in Japan.

Recovering from its own Civil War, Washington was warming to a sense of manifest destiny, a nineteenth-century doctrine of pride that the United States was meant to play a leadership role in the hemisphere. The navy's second in command, Teddy Roosevelt, was convinced that a large naval encounter—and capture of the Philippines—was the rite of passage for a nation becoming a world power. In fact, the navy had been increasing its shipbuilding for just such a moment.

More importantly, to many American ears, *Cuba Libre* sounded a lot like "The Redcoats are coming." No American president could long survive politically if his heart did not beat to the drums of independence sounded by the Cuban rebels, so like that of the founding fathers. Backing the rebels in Cuba was a safe bet, and politicians eagerly set their sails "to catch the popular breeze." By mid-1897, Senator Henry Cabot Lodge of Massachusetts warned McKinley that if he did nothing to help Cubans fighting for their freedom, the Republican Party "shall go down in the greatest defeat ever known." Politics being fickle, Democrats who had pressed for the war started to distance themselves soon after its victorious conclusion, turning away from what they saw suddenly as a legacy of imperialism.

The unique history with which each country came to the conflict made for some classic misunderstandings. Spain was convinced that the heart of the problem was not in Cuba but in New York, where a pro-independence *junta* of exiled Cuban leaders fed stories of Spanish military atrocities and negotiating bad faith to the newspapers, who were more than happy to spread lies, raise money, even send materiel to the rebels. This, to Madrid, was evidence that the United States was not remaining neutral. Spanish public opinion was also misinformed by the partisan nature of Spanish newspapers, which left many proud Spaniards with the impression that the Americans were "greedy Yankees lacking military virtues" and not up to the "superior fighting spirit" of their own troops. Finally, Spain made the classic mistake of believing that the United States would lose interest, that "the passage of time would make the situation better." They called it a "hand to mouth policy." It was the last meal of the Spanish empire.

National interests aside, there was also a story to be covered. The fact is that Spain's military attempt to put down the insurrection in Cuba resulted in the starvation of tens of thousands of civilians, some who died in full view of diplomats and journalists in Havana. The causes of the mass starvation were several. Brooding over the failure to win independence from Spain during the last insurrection—in the Ten Years War from 1868 to 1878—rebel leader Maximo Gomez hit on a strategy for this new revolt: plunder the Cuban economy so that Spain would abandon the island. This he did by "destroying crops, disrupting transportation, and engaging in incessant hit-and-run assaults" that pinned down Spanish soldiers and rotted the Cuban economy.

Ironically, his best ally in this endeavor was Spain's "vigorous and ruthless" military leader, General Valeriano Weyler, later dubbed "the Butcher" by the New York yellow newspapers. Weyler designed a "civilian re-concentration program" aimed at destroying the insurgents' popular base in the countryside by forcing their supporters into camps and thus robbing the rebels of food, supplies, and information. Ordering the peasants from their homes, Weyler herded them into centers under the control of Spanish military authorities.

But Spanish officials had neither food nor water nor housing nor sanitary equipment to care for them. Within months, the centers had become death camps.

While Gomez was attempting to destroy Cuba's economy from within, Weyler was killing both farms and population from without. By the time a U.S. envoy came in 1897 to take the measure of the land, he found the countryside empty. "Every house had been burned, banana trees cut down, cane fields swept with fire, and everything in the shape of food destroyed," he reported to the White House. "I did not see a house, a man, woman or child; a horse, mule, or cow, not even a dog." Though the motives were surely different, each campaign had a similar impact on people. As people had always been journalism's most compelling subject, the plight of the Cubans gave the newspapers plenty of fodder, even if they had not exaggerated, to tug at readers' emotions. There was a story to be covered. Hearst and Pulitzer no doubt hyped it, they likely distorted it, and they surely exploited it. It is even possible that they created an atmosphere that favored war. But even in the face of such a sensationalist blitz, political leaders had options short of war.

For all the exaggerated headlines in Hearst's New York *Journal*, McKinley had nearly thirteen months, from his inauguration in March of 1897 to the beginning of hostilities in April of 1898, to explore diplomatic alternatives. For all the pressure to go to war from within his administration, McKinley held back, withstanding private barbs from such as Assistant Secretary of the Navy Theodore Roosevelt that he had "no more backbone than a chocolate eclair."

Though most U.S. press histories begin with Franklin Roosevelt, McKinley was actually fairly prescient about the need to reach the public through the press. He was the first president to assign one staffer—first John Addison Porter, later George Cortelyou—to brief White House correspondents daily, at noon and 4 P.M., and to offer them schedules and advance copies of presidential speeches so that they could accompany McKinley out of town and judge public reaction to his policies. He gave them a place to work—a long table was set up on the second floor, and the regulars had assigned seats. He was the first president to attend regularly the correspondents' Gridiron Club dinners, and it was McKinley who first invited reporters to attend the New Year's receptions at the White House. He literally opened the gates of the White House—removing sentry gates that Grover Cleveland had erected—and, while still observing the rule that presidents could not be quoted except in speeches or proclamations, made known that "reporters are at liberty to call upon him or his cabinet for information on public affairs."

Though these openings may seem cosmetic, the small perquisites of leadership, meant to curry favor with reporters, in fact the real import of the changes was to centralize power at the White House, to make it the headquarters for news. An atmosphere that contained both camaraderie and information was a natural draw for reporters. By bringing both to the White House, McKinley acquired a new measure of and influence on public opinion. Bringing reporters inside the White House did not guarantee good press coverage, but it tended to mitigate against bad press coverage. By bringing reporters away from "Newspaper Row" on the North Portico, where they once waited to question visitors, and moving them into their own office space at the White House, McKinley was shifting the focus of attention from the visitors, who might talk loosely about affairs of state, to his own executive staff. McKinley could not muzzle Hearst's *Journal* or Pulitzer's *World*, but he could see his policies defended in most other newspapers.

McKinley's attempts to negotiate the Cuban crisis rather than rush to war were popular throughout the country, according to George Cortelyou's newspaper scrapbooks. Called *Current Comment*, the scrapbooks were a forerunner of the modern *White House News Summary*, providing a window on editorial comment *outside* New York, where Hearst was busy making good on his slogan, "While others talk, the *Journal* acts." Away from the elitist opinion makers of Washington and New York, Americans showed little appetite for war. Before June of 1897, Cortelyou's scrapbook included only two references to Cuba, and his mailbag contained only three letters on the topic. Throughout 1897, McKinley was seemingly under little pressure from the public over Cuba, at least based on the topics aired in newspaper editorials in Cortelyou's scrapbooks. Cuba had not been an issue in the 1896 campaign that elected McKinley over the silver-sloganeering William Jennings Bryan, and McKinley believed from his scrapbooks that the public would support war if necessary but still preferred a peaceful solution.

Stung by congressional charges that he showed McKinley only the positive mail and press clippings, Cortelyou took to the pages of his diary to complain about "the sensational newspapers' public daily accounts . . . of influences that are never felt." He dismissed the charges as "ridiculous," insisting that "the president sees everything, whether in the shape of mail, telegrams or newspapers, that can indicate the drift of public sentiment." He recorded that he briefed McKinley daily on the favorable and unfavorable letters. "The fact is that on a most conservative estimate, ninety percent of the entire correspondence that has come to the office since the beginning of the concluding negotiations on the Spanish-Cuban questions has been an endorsement of the president's course—an emphatic appeal for peace and for the exercise of sound reason in the handling of the whole matter."

To explore the diplomatic track, McKinley in the spring of 1897 sent a personal envoy to Spain. After several big names in business and academia turned him down, McKinley tapped Stewart Woodford, a Civil War general and former lieutenant governor of New York. On his arrival in Madrid, Woodford gave Spain a November 1 deadline to "satisfy the United States that early and certain peace can be promptly secured." In response to this ultimatum, Spain moved a considerable distance. Within two months, Spain removed Weyler from Cuba, released the captured American crew of the schooner *Competitor*, settled all tobacco-export cases, and freed remaining American prisoners. Spain's primary offer was local autonomy, in which Cuba would have control over local affairs while Spain retained foreign-policy rights—as long as the rebels laid down their arms. The yellow press decried autonomy as "sham reforms." But local autonomy went into effect on January 1, 1898, giving Cubans a new measure of home rule, with Spain still in charge of military policy. Eleven days later, riots by Spaniards opposed to the policy broke out in Havana, demonstrating the limits of Spain's diplomatic flexibility. Shouting "Death to autonomy," rioters—led by Spanish officers—sacked four newspapers that had supported the government's plan. This is the moment when McKinley knew the bounds of negotiation had been stretched beyond recall, this moment thirty-five days before the *Maine* exploded.

When war came, the United States was ready, and willing, to serve. This was in no small measure because McKinley played statesman to Hearst's hysteric. But when it came time to declare war and rally the nation, McKinley was less successful, almost as if he was suited to the one task, of corridor diplomacy, and not the other, of public diplomacy. McKinley was not a man to evoke the human drama of war. Here, passion mattered more than reason, pride more than logic. McKinley excelled at bureaucratic leadership, not charismatic leadership. Which may be why history remembers this as

Teddy Roosevelt's war or Richard Harding Davis's war or William Randolph Hearst's war but not as William McKinley's war. No less than journalists, historians like a larger-than-life character.

By war's end, Hearst was running headlines four inches high, often in red ink, anything to get the reader's attention, his kingdom for circulation. Newspapers were feeling newly emboldened, and they reveled in "the new journalism," a partisan, personal approach to the news that made metaphors of facts and made heroes of correspondents. Like Hearst, many publishers were spending money like bullets. "From a correspondent's point of view, it was an ideal campaign," said Phillip Knightley in *The First Casualty*, his study of war correspondents. "Two hundred turned up to cover it, including twenty-five from Hearst's group alone. Expenses were no object. Cable charges for a single story ran to $8,000. The Associated Press chartered a flotilla of boats, which, throughout the naval engagements, cruised at will through the battle lines, ignoring fire from both sides and scurrying back and forth to the nearest cable station."

This was the ultimate in personal journalism, in many ways a byline war. Famous authors like Stephen Crane, author of *The Red Badge of Courage*, which was so popular during the Civil War, were pressed into service. Lyrical description of Colonel Roosevelt and his Rough Riders—members of the landed gentry trained as polo players—ranks as one of the classic legend builders in American politics. Not that TR and his Rough Riders did not charge San Juan Hill, only that few in history who act bravely are so fortunate as to have a poetic and *sympatico* eyewitness to celebrate them for it. "Roosevelt, mounted high on horseback and charging the rifle pits at a gallop and quite alone, made you feel that you would like to cheer," Davis wrote. "No one who saw Roosevelt take that ride expected he would finish it alive. As the only mounted man, he was the most conspicuous object in range of the rifle pits, then only two hundred yards ahead. It looked like foolhardiness, but as a matter of fact, he set the pace with his horse and inspired the men to follow."

Like the Vietnam War more than sixty years later, the Spanish-American War was virtually uncensored, with press boats vying for position in naval battles, rushing back and forth to and from shore to use the telegraph. Like Vietnam, it haunted the national conscience of its times. And like Vietnam, it was for a long time seen as a "victory" for the press.

Richard Harding Davis, whose personal fortunes benefited as much by the Spanish-American War as any other's, later lamented that the war had ended the era of the war correspondent it sought to extol. "The fall of the war correspondent came about through the ease and quickness with which today news leaps from one end of the earth to the other," Davis wrote. In the Crimea War and in the Civil War, he noted, "the telegraph and cable were inadequate and expensive, and the war correspondent depended largely on the mails. As a consequence, before what he wrote appeared in print, the events he described had passed into history, and what information he gave could in no way benefit the enemy." But the speed of modern communication had ended all that.

For access to information was too precious to be left to journalists, at least if military strategists could help it. Presaging the advent of combat censorship, Davis lost his bravado when reporters had to start covering words instead of bullets. "The day his cable from Cuba to New York was relayed to Madrid," Davis wrote on the eve of his bitter experiences trying to cover World War I, "the war correspondent received his death sentence."

It may have been inevitable, this war between a waning colonial power and an ascending global power, but in some sense it was also a contest between the barons of journalism, newly empowered by the speed afforded by the telegraph and the railroad, and the titans of politics, who had not entirely learned how to use the same technology to advantage. McKinley still had "the traditional presidential fear of lese-majesty," a sense that to reach out for public support was somehow to debase the office. But mass media called for public diplomacy, and those who understood the imperatives of what Teddy Roosevelt would soon call the "bully pulpit" had the best lock on leadership.

The Spanish-American War was not the first battle to test the balance of power between the pen and power, nor was the telegraph the first invention to change the boundaries of journalism and diplomacy. That honor belonged to an earlier technology, the printing press, hailed by its enthusiasts as a boon for journalism and a beacon of democracy. "The printing presses transformed the field of communications and fathered an international revolt," wrote Maurice Gravier. "It was a revolution." It would not be the last.

4

Gutenberg's Revolution

JOHANN FUST ARRIVED at the Sorbonne University in Paris in 1456 with a dozen copies of a new Bible in his valise. The merchant from Germany was eager to begin testing the market for the new product, which he priced at 60 crowns, compared to the going rate of 500 crowns for the Bibles then available. Though Fust's Bibles resembled the older models, they represented a stunning departure. Until then, Bibles had been lovingly and painstakingly copied by calligraphers, first by priests and monks, later by professional secular scribes, but always with a reverence for art and religion that made production a labor of love. It also meant that each book took years, sometimes decades, to complete. What Fust hoped would make him rich and famous was a Bible produced by a machine, the moveable-type press invented by a goldsmith named Johann Gutenberg. In the history of civilization, it is hard to imagine more of a watershed invention.

Gutenberg was not the first to envision the utility of printing letters in uniform style. In the centuries of the first millennium, the Chinese developed wood blocks for printing. But the Chinese were burdened by a language requiring some 80,000 symbols, a complexity that meant it took 23 years to edit and print the 130 volumes of Confucian classics.

Gutenberg's genius, aided by an alphabet more suited to the rigors of machine writing, was to apply his skills as a goldsmith to cast letters in metal so that they could be struck repeatedly with nearly identical result at a speed that none had seen before. The marvel was the speed and beauty of its work, having "the singular gift of God in it, seeing one man can print as much, in one day, as the best hand can write in a whole year." This burst of speed in the amount of time it took to deliver a message—a 365 percent increase in productivity—changed not only religion, but governance and communication as well.

For all the speed his invention brought to the art of printing, Gutenberg was not a man who cut corners. So meticulous was he, so particular about duplicating the craftsmanship of the scribes, that his metal alphabet had 290 characters, including eight versions of a lowercase *a* and several letters set together to avoid unsightly spaces between them. Some of his creations, including the pinholes used for keeping paper on track, are still employed in the computer age. His ink—oil paint with a high lead content—may be environmentally incorrect but it remains glossy to this day.

Unfortunately for him, Gutenberg's attention to detail was expensive, and he kept borrowing from backers, including Fust, a wealthy financier who invested a substantial 1,600 guilders in Gutenberg's project. Five years later, Fust still had not seen a return on his investment, so he sued Gutenberg. Fust won his suit and Gutenberg had to pay 2,026 guilders, plus turn over all his materials and equipment, including the first pages and the type for his Bible. With this inheritance, Fust opened a new firm with his future son-in-law, Peter Schoeffer, a calligrapher who had served as Gutenberg's foreman and testified against his boss at the 1455 trial. Fust & Schoeffer thus published the first forty-two-line Gutenberg Bible, though Gutenberg, ever an enthusiast, convinced another backer to stake him to a new printing press. Years later, Johann Schoeffer claimed that the printing press was the sole creation of his father, Peter Schoeffer, and his grandfather, Johann Fust, but the well-publicized, well-documented lawsuit settled the question in Gutenberg's favor among most historians, and even his contemporaries. When he died in 1468, Gutenberg was buried in the Church of St. Francis in Mainz, under a tablet inscribed to "the inventor of the art of printing and deserver of the highest honors from every nation and tongue."

And honors there were, for the printing press was the first media technology, the first machine to give birth to a new method of communication, the pamphlet, and to inaugurate a new power player in international affairs, the printer. This etymology, from invention to influence, took centuries to complete. Still, what is striking about Gutenberg's printing press is that from the beginning, it evidenced all the traits that would emerge as the pattern for the other media technologies to come. Diplomats, in this case the rulers and priests who made up the world's intelligentsia, resisted the new medium as an intrusion on their power. Writers, emboldened by the ease of communication, boasted of newfound influence on public discourse. And readers, whose numbers grew as literacy and economic prosperity beckoned, marveled that their world had gotten smaller, as if the abstractions of time and space—those enduring temptations of media history, the standard by which all media progress is measured—had been conquered.

As with all new technologies, the Gutenberg Bible met with considerable resistance from the ruling elite. A guild of booksellers, on examining the new book, called police to arrest Fust as an impostor. Even at the Sorbonne, center of scholarly books since its foundation in 1250, Fust's lodgings were searched, and rumors spread that the red ink illustrating some of the letters was his own blood. "It was ferociously adjudged that he was in league with the devil," wrote one early historian. Of course, the printing press was not alone in stirring fear. When paper was first introduced, it too was distrusted as unreliable, and important documents were printed on vellum up to the nineteenth century.

Still, objection to Gutenberg's printed materials was particularly fierce. Much of the resistance came from a fear that the printing press would intrude on the creative process, a concern summarized by a character in Victor Hugo's *The Hunchback of Notre Dame*, who encounters his first printed book on the steps of the cathedral. Gazing from the book to the spires, he predicts, "This will kill that." The notion that print would kill art, that type would trample spirituality, amounted to an elitist fear that the spread of information to more people in less time would somehow hurt quality.

This concern is a perennial in the history of media technology, masking a second concern, one harder for the guardians of information to swallow, that the wider dissemination of knowledge would lessen their own power. Clinging to old habits and real fears—in part validated by the coming religious and political revolutions—kings and churches, noblemen and clergymen, continued for the next century to favor calligraphic manuscripts over what they dismissed as the "clumsy and unattractive" printed book.

By 1534, when the price of printed books started to decline, worried scribes prevailed on François I to ban printing. The monks were right to worry. Not only was their livelihood from an old technology (pen and ink) threatened by a new one (print) but, more importantly, so was their monopoly on ideas. The rise of Luther and his reformation is directly attributable to the diffusion of knowledge from the pens of a few to the presses of many. "In the spread of religious ideas it seems difficult to exaggerate the significance of the [printing] press, without which a revolution of this magnitude could scarcely have been consummated," wrote historian A. G. Dickens. "Lutheranism was from the first the child of the printed book, and through this vehicle Luther was able to make exact, standardized and ineradicable impressions on the mind of Europe."

The ban on printing was never enforced, but its very proclamation meant the tide had turned. From its debasement as the devil's work, Gutenberg's printing press now assumed mantle to all the out-sized predictions that befall most technologies, credited for everything from spreading democracy to ending war. The printing press was viewed as an equalizer of the classes. "What otherwise at one time only the rich and the king owned, is now found everywhere, even in the cottage—a book," marveled poet Sebastian Brant.

Indeed, in the first forty years after the printing press was invented, 20 million books were published. In the next 100 years, the total reached 200 million. This explosion of available information to a far vaster audience did not doom the monarchs of the day, but it increased the chances that a literate public would raise questions about their rule. Suddenly, kings and poets were not the only ones reading, and individuals began to form their own ideas about world events. This was an inherently dangerous turn of events to the policy elite. "So many books—so much confusion!" complained Spanish playwright Lope de Vega. "All the most famous men of Europe rushed into print, but once they were published, their ignorance was obvious to all."

The undeniable legacy of the printing press was this spread of literacy, a fact that changed not only the nature of society but the requirements for leadership, which in turn gave rise to a public voice. A population that could read could also influence opinion. A literate citizenry could share ideas as they were promulgated. "Before the invention of this DIVINE

ART, mankind were absorbed in the gravest ignorance," wrote one eighteenth-century author. "The clergy, who before this era held the key of all learning in Europe, were ... proud, presumptuous, arrogant and artful; their devices were soon detected through the invention of typography."

It is important here to distinguish between the ideas and their method of conveyance, between the message and the messenger, but there is no doubt the printing press made possible the delivery of these new and revolutionary themes to a larger audience, in faster time, than ever before. Luther's Reformation, his Protestant challenge to the Catholic Church, would no doubt have been possible without the printing press, but support for his heretical views might have taken much longer to solidify, a delay that could have proven fatal to the ultimate success of his movement. As it was, Luther, a German monk who himself described printing as "God's highest and extremest act of grace, whereby the business of the Gospel is driven forward," published 30 writings between 1517 and 1520 that sold over 300,000 copies. He had the audacity, amid this outpouring, to protest to Pope Leo X that "it is a mystery to me how my theses ... were spread to so many places. They were meant exclusively for our academic circle here. ... They were written in such a language that the common people could hardly understand them."

But if Martin Luther "had no wish nor plan to publicize" his works, his disciples were only too eager to disseminate the word. That those ideas did spread, in a kind of angry, anti-papal wave, owed less to the printing press than to the message that the church was no longer the sole authority on God. "Luther had invited a public disputation and nobody had come to dispute," wrote one observer. "By a stroke of magic he found himself addressing the whole world." That the world was ready to ponder Luther's ideas was a function of a changing political atmosphere in which the princes of Europe were growing eager to cast off Rome's influence in religion and nationhood was gaining ground over empire. Like the American and French revolutionaries who would follow, the loyalists in Luther's rebellion knew well how to exploit the printing press and its new readers, translating Luther's academic writings from Latin to German, illustrating them with antipapist cartoons that needed no captions. The printing press, unquestionably, was their great friend, but as great an ally of Luther's army was, ironically, the Catholic Church.

With its arrogance and dogmatism, its taxation policies and ruling hierarchy, the church not only invited opposition but provided a case study in sorry leadership in the face of a new media technology. Pope Leo X, on assuming the papacy in 1514, was quoted as saying, "God has given us the papacy. Let us enjoy it." By the end of his reign, Pope Leo had drawn down the church assets, running up a debt of 850,000 ducats, becoming the Vatican's most generous patron of the arts, commissioning embroidered tapestries spun with silver and gold. Luther's theological questions about church policies, like collecting "indulgences" from church members who thought they could buy their way out of hell or shorten their time in purgatory by greasing the papal coffers, found a ready audience among a restive congregation. Luther's timing was excellent. His questioning of authority was seized on by those of different agendas, among them politicians trumpeting German nationalism, peasants eager to revolt against the ruling class, and "beleaguered nobles enraged at the taxes of the church." It is as if the printing press had vented a torrent of words and anti-establishment feelings that until then had been kept within a small circle. The new medium delivered the word, but it was the rebels who offered a message.

What Pope Leo failed to appreciate is that the printing press, in offering a forum for debate among a larger audience, had invited a new factor into international politics. If it is too generous to attribute to the printing press a revolution in religious politics, it is not too much of an exaggeration to say that with the book came the advent of public opinion as a factor in the affairs of state. Where once the obedience of subjects was assumed, suddenly the allegiance of troops was in doubt. Royalty that had once communicated with subjects only by edict had to argue its case in print. Clearly kings needed loyalty among their troops even before Gutenberg crafted his metal letters. But from the moment soldiers could read about the strategic value of their battles, from the time debate could simmer on the wisdom of authority figures, public support was needed for any adventure of church or state. The printing press, with its authority resting on words, gave voice to people, like Martin Luther, who had a gift of phrase—and who had something to say.

In this battle for the hearts and minds of the public, the pope still held the keys to his kingdom—if he had only used the new media technology to advantage. Much has been written about Lutheranism's debt to the printing press in fomenting a revolution, but little has been said of the church's seeming inability to use the same weapon in a counteroffensive. Luther's motives may have been religious, but the Reformation, a series of wars in the fifteenth and sixteenth centuries that eventually wrestled control over religion from the Vatican, was decidedly political. Amid the moral scandals and insipid corruption of medieval Christianity, the church had been silent. And the primary response of the church to the nascent challenge posed by Luther and his followers was to spend lavish amounts on its own physical welfare, to issue denunciations of Luther without debating his ideas, to assume that if they ignored the Luther problem, it would go away. This almost never works in global politics, and certainly not when the "problem" is armed with a new weapon of media technology that can spread ideas faster than ever before.

The pope was preoccupied with geopolitics, pitting one European alliance against the next by arranging marriages, inviting invasion forces to conquer territory, and generally playing kings off against other emperors. "One must not suppose that he failed to see Luther as a challenge to papal authority," writes one of Luther's biographers. "He did." But in Leo's view, Luther had no power alone; his very existence depended upon the protection of either Maximilian, the king of Germany, or Frederick, Maximilian's predecessor and the last emperor crowned at Rome. "Maximilian had already spoken. Now Pope Leo only needed to secure Frederick's friendship for his political ends, and the Luther question would settle itself." This kind of macro thinking, the bulwark of an earlier era, might have worked, but for the printing press. It droned on and on—Luther complained at one point that he was keeping 600 printers in business—bringing the message to more and more people who used it for their own ends to strip power from Europe's oldest institution. Luther's ideas were fresher than Pope Leo's, and his printing press spread them faster than any medium known to that time.

But the real revolution was that suddenly, the audience for their debate was as vast as the population who could read. While Pope Leo dithered with chess pieces in a game of geopolitics, Luther put out the word. It is problematic to say that the church might have recovered if it had met Luther on the new playing field created by the printing press, if the pope had tried to persuade the public of his views in the new marketplace of ideas, rather than impose them from on high. Clearly, this was the very challenge to authority that Pope Leo could not tolerate. What is clear is that he did not even contemplate making the effort, and it is that failure of leadership, that inability to adjust to the new forces of the age—not the machine but the way leaders reacted to it—that settled the outcome.

Centuries later, when the printing press gave birth to the pamphlet and the printer became a figure of some political influence, the press would be seen in some quarters as a maker of revolution. Like enthusiasts who credited Gutenberg's machine for Luther's popularity and neglected to factor in the pope's hubris, these chroniclers of the American and French Revolutions felt sure that the printing press had spawned the impulse toward democracy, or at least abetted the cause. The pamphlet war in the American colonies and the newspaper editorials in the streets of Paris did underscore one new development in the history of journalism. From an eighteenth-century custom where newspapers were largely plagiarists, borrowing from other journals to fill their pages, printers and their fiery contributors found their voice. The newspaper became more than a bulletin board of community events, more than a listing of events. And the journalist became more than a chronicler of events, assuming a new role as a filter in the political process.

In the run-up to the American War for Independence, both the British and the colonialists seized on the new weapon of media technology to battle for public opinion, a war of pamphlets that has had no equal since. At the height of this campaign of ideas, literary giants like Samuel Johnson, who paid for a printing of 2,500 copies of his *Taxation No Tyranny*, were matched against savvy printers like Benjamin Franklin, who convinced English printers to issue John Dickinson's *Letters from a Farmer in Pennsylvania to the Inhabitants of the British Colonies*. Thomas Paine, writing a pamphlet called *Common Sense*, sold over 500,000 copies. Many printers were partisans, men like Isaiah Thomas, who published the *Massachusetts Spy* at half the price of other Boston newspapers to insure an audience for his diatribes against the British as monsters and tyrants. Theirs was an uphill task of persuasion. In the early years, public opinion in America was roughly divided into three groups: the Tories, who were happy as British subjects; the Patriots, who resented British rule; and the majority, who wanted some protection from the crown but also some form of self-government. Though the printers largely advocated rebellion, public opinion largely favored compromise, not war.

The most telling episode in the battle for public opinion came over Britain's Stamp Act, imposed on the American colonies in 1765 to help defray Britain's costs stemming from Europe's Seven Years' War. Britain's debt, two years after the war ended, was 130 million pounds, and Prime Minister George Grenville looked to the colonies to recoup his war losses. "Grenville saw little chance of raising much money in England," wrote one historian. "The tumults which the new cider tax provoked in the mother country convinced the ministry that the British taxpayer had about reached the limits of his willingness or ability to pay taxes, or perhaps both." His solution was a revenue law, requiring a stamp on all paper used in the colonies, in effect a blanket tax on everything from almanacs to insurance policies, from ship's papers to playing cards. Estimates were that the tax could raise 100,000 pounds, about a third of British costs in maintaining a militia in the colonies.

Those most directly affected—merchants, businessmen, lawyers, journalists—raised a cry against taxation without representation. This plea for democracy may have masked the printers' economic self-interests, but it also allowed them to claim victory when Britain repealed the tax the next year. Newly emboldened printers, thrilled at the impact of their own self-interested protests, felt vindicated. "Newspapers emerged from the contest with an exhilarated sense of their role in the community," wrote historian Arthur Schlesinger. "No longer mere purveyors of intelligence, they had become engines of opinion." The political process had acquired a referee, one whose strong opinions, expressed in the newly powerful pamphlet and the reinvigorated newspaper, could sway the debate.

In pre-Revolutionary France, the press also flourished. In 1789 alone, 130 new political newspapers came on the market, and when the Estates-General debated the issues of the day, their discourse on everything from the nature of God to the rights of private property was published whole, often in separate editions. This measure of press freedom was new for France, where censorship had until then choked free expression and lack of literacy had inhibited sales of books and pamphlets. But literacy was on the rise, and readers had tired of reading hints between the lines, the legacy of official censorship whether it is imposed in Brezhnev's Moscow or Louis XVI's Paris. "Paris reads ten times more than a century ago," journalist Louis-Sebastien Mercier observed in the 1780s. The French had long viewed their society as three estates: the clergy, the nobility, the commons. Now there was a fourth estate, the public press, and its journalists were natural heroes.

"Here I am a journalist, and it is a rather fine role," wrote Camille Desmoulins, one of the leading lights of the French Revolution. "No longer is it a wretched and mercenary profession, enslaved by the government. Today in France it is the journalist who holds the tablets." In this prewar period, the *Mercure de France* began to expand its news columns to appeal to "the commoner as well as the noble, in the salons of the aristocracy as well as the modest household of the bourgeois, delighting equally both court and Town." On the eve of the revolution in 1789, circulation stood at 20,000, and readership was estimated to be over 120,000.

It is true, as one observer wrote, that the newspapers spread "throughout France the electric fire" of rebellion. But this revolution was so fractured, its legacy so disparate, from the Rights of Man and Citizens, a declaration of democratic principles, to the Reign of Terror, where thousands were murdered by guillotine or other torture, that it is difficult to maintain the case that newspapers tipped the balance of history. What is clear is that King Louis XVI, who tried to defuse the fever for revolution, missed key opportunities to cement his authority. That he had a core constituency is clear from the record, since the French later experimented, after the first Napoleonic run, with a return to royalty. At this moment in history, the king, as Pope Leo before him, misplayed certain cards.

In the annals of insensitive sound bites, it is difficult to imagine a more inane utterance than Marie Antoinette's view that the starving masses could subsist without bread. "Let them eat cake!" may have been evidence of royal indifference, but it was hardly official policy. There is even some evidence that Antoinette was referring not to cake of French pastry fame, but to the hard, crusty residue from the baking process sometimes referred to as a cake. Apocryphal or not, the comment came to symbolize the arrogance of the crown in the eyes of its subjects. By 1792, the government had learned the importance of influencing public opinion. Interior Minister Roland was granted 100,000 livres "for the printing and the distribution in the departments and the armies of all writings fit to enlighten minds about the criminal activities of the enemies of the state and the true causes of the problems that have for too long torn the country apart." Later, a similar appropriation was granted to the minister of war to supply printed material to the troops, so that he could "enlighten and animate their patriotism." Given the fierceness of French patriotism in battle, it is tempting to wonder at the outcome if Louis had seized on the pamphlet earlier as a tool of leadership.

There were huge historical forces at work during the French Revolution, epic waves of civil order and disorder. Among these, a reinvigorated newspaper climate played a role. Louis himself, like Soviet leader Mikhail Gorbachev in a later setting, unleashed many of the reforms that turned on him. He called the Estates-General to discuss the fiscal deficit, perhaps never dreaming it would become a forum for debating democracy. He lifted the chains of censorship that had long suppressed a free press, and tried to use the new technology to stave off the foment. But, like Gorbachev too, he failed to understand that once unleashed, the new media would not be tamed. Still, he tried. When thousands of French citizens stormed the Bastille on July 14, 1789, freeing both political prisoners and the society at large from the burden of the monarchy, the country's official newspaper, *La Gazette de France*, did not report it, "in the belief that any mention of [it] might in some way condone" the event. History would not be silenced.

The printing press was a powerful new instrument in the hands of revolutionaries and loyalists, of ruffians and lords, of Jacobins and Girodins, all of them engaged in battle for the pulse of public opinion. It is too facile to say that the colonies rebelled because of the printers' outrage at the Stamp Act or that the French Revolution succeeded because of Tallyrand's eloquence in writing the Rights of Man and Citizen. It was all of those things and none. Like the revolution in communication now predicted for cyberspace, the printing press did speed communication, give the public more influence in diplomacy, and offer journalists a new role as filters of information. Without the printing press to speed delivery of the message, movements toward reform and democracy might have been slowed. But this speed in the conveyance of message did not presage the outcome of any movement in history. To revolutionaries in Luther's church, or Paine's America or Robespierre's France, the printing press was an ally to all sides, a cause for war to none.

The printing press had inspired literacy, and given power to printers. The telegraph had generated a newspaper circulation war, and stirred emotion for real combat. But these were technologies of the word. Photographs brought a new lens to war that stunned those who had read only written accounts of battlefields. They called it the first visual medium.

5

Photography and Emotion

A CENTURY AND a half after the photograph's invention, China pulled the plug on visual coverage of the student uprising in Tiananmen Square in 1989. This crackdown on satellite television came after television viewers saw a lone, unarmed demonstrator approaching an army tank who came to symbolize the movement of democracy over the forces of tyranny—at least in the West. In China, where tradition had it that a picture was worth one thousand words, a photograph of the same scene was put in a traveling exhibit to demonstrate to a domestic audience the restraint of the Chinese Army. The caption made the difference. Guardians of the image were right to worry about the impact of photographs, just as the monks had cause for concern about the coming of the printing press. Images froze impressions, put weight on passing political moments, gave credence to fleeting truths, even lent themselves to manipulation for political ends. More, they had the potential to become the icons of national memory, a road map to collective emotion.

Britain's poet laureate William Wordsworth worried at the arrival of photography, anxious that this new wonder, which in one sonnet he labeled "a dumb art," would somehow minimize the impact of "man's ablest attribute," the printed word.

Even before the photograph, leaders had reason to fear the influence of images. None had more cause to despair of the equalizing impact of the visual than King Louis XVI of France, who tried to escape the wrath of his citizens at the height of the French Revolution by disguising himself as a valet in the carriage of a nobleman. Alerted to check passing entourages for the monarch who had slipped past guards at his palace in Versailles, a local postmaster unmasked the fleeing party. The postmaster, Drouet, had never seen the king, but he recognized him from a portrait of his likeness on paper money. The portrait had done in the king, who along with his wife Marie Antoinette (she was posing as a governess) was arrested and later executed.

The idea of communication via visual image had long intrigued inventors. In 1760, the comptroller general of Paris, Étienne de Silhouette, commercialized the concept behind the shadow theater, offering clients profiles in shadow, a form that to this day bears his name. It was not until 1822 that a French landowner named Joseph-Nicéphore Niepce discovered that if he exposed lithographs treated with chemicals to light, he could produce "gradations of tone from black to white." Louis Daguerre, an artist who operated a diorama, convinced Niepce to join him in a business partnership, only to appropriate his partner's experiments, convincing the French Academy of Sciences in 1839 that the invention should be called a daguerreotype (perhaps, in the academy's defense, a niepceotype might have been too unwieldy a label). The Niepce family's attempts to prove that the daguerreotype method had been invented by its patriarch failed to produce the hoped-for financial rewards, but insured tremendous publicity for the new invention.

An American in Paris, Samuel Morse, learned to make the new pictures from Daguerre so he could add them to the offerings of his art gallery, where he painted "portraits at starvation prices" to pay for his experiments on inventions like the telegraph. With the new daguerreotypes in hand, Morse returned home in 1840 to make the first such plates in America—and to pass the secrets on to one of his pupils, Mathew Brady. Within a decade, the daguerreotype gave way to other processes for camera development, namely the making of prints from a glass-plate negative, an invention perfected by an Englishman, Frederick Scott Archer. Louis Daguerre's plates, often destroyed to make the engravings, were a thing of the past. But the lure of the photography lived on.

Brady, according to one of his biographers, may not have known how to write. If true, this intriguing fact underscores the watershed that photography represented from a world of print. The camera drew on different talents, calling for vision and borders and composition, for flattery and juxtaposition and exposure. This was a medium for those with a special eye, attuned to the needs and demands of sight. From the beginning, Brady, who with age lost his eyesight, understood the power of the photograph to leave a first, and lasting, impression. The man who pioneered the use of portrait photography knew its potential for propaganda, its vulnerability to unintended uses. "The camera is the eye of history," he told his photographers. "You must never make bad pictures."

Mathew Brady was ambitious, as eager to acquire celebrity as to photograph it. Though he died a pauper—and nearly sightless—he was in his prime a media giant, who was on familiar terms with presidents, congressmen, senators, judges, and actors. With galleries in Washington and New York, Brady's was the place to go to sit for a portrait—or to view exhibits of the rich and the famous. Portraits of Daniel Webster, John C. Calhoun, and Henry Clay, painted by artists from Brady's plates, still hang in the U.S. Capitol.

When war came, Brady thought to bring his camera to the war zone. Accompanied by newspaper correspondents Dick

McCormack and Ned House, along with sketch artist Al Waud, Brady left for Bull Run with his camera, that "mysterious and formidable instrument." As Northern troops deserted in fear when they first heard the rumbles of war, some blamed Brady for the rout, claiming the soldiers had mistaken Brady's camera for a cannon. "The runaways mistook it for the great steam gun discharging five hundred balls a minute and took to their heels when they got within focus," said one apologist.

This was the classic ritual of blaming the message on the messenger, but in any event Brady was smitten by the promise of combining photography and war. Against the advice of his wife and friends, he equipped twenty photographers and dispatched them to cover the war, using his own funds to support the venture, explaining that he felt like a newspaper publisher. "My wife and my most conservative friends had looked unfavorably upon this departure from commercial business to pictorial war correspondence with much misgiving," he told an interviewer after the war, "but, like Euphoria, a spirit in my feet said, 'Go,' and I went." Some say Brady, whose studios claimed credit for all the photographs shot by his photographers, made $12,000 a year during the Civil War. But in fact by 1862 he was in sufficient financial trouble that he was forced to give some negatives in lieu of payment to a departing star photographer, Alexander Gardner, who set up a competing gallery where at least he could get credit for his own work.

Aside from famous photographers like Brady and Gardner, thousands of photographers worked in the United States during its Civil War, and each paid a license fee of between $10 and $25 (depending on the volume of their business) to the federal government for the privilege. Photographers in the South (supply shortages made them rare) owed an annual $50 fee to the Confederacy, plus 2 ½ percent tax on total sales.

In both camps, the mission was to record army life, not to document war. Photographers trailed after the troops in large wagons where they developed their film, dubbed "whatsit" wagons by soldiers who didn't bother to name them further. Whatever they were called, these earlier photographic endeavors were hardly the stuff of journalism. Theirs were posed pictures, taken for the home front by soldiers who often pinned their portraits to their clothes so that, if they fell in battle, they could be identified and sent home to loved ones for burial.

The photograph was not at first seen as a function of journalism, but of portraiture. The battlefield was open to Brady because the danger he represented to those prosecuting war was not yet apparent. Acceptance by journalism was slow, as publishers clung to their pools of illustrators for economic and social reasons. Three years after the Spanish-American War, there were 1,000 artists still turning out more than 10,000 drawings a week for the newspapers. During World War I, "editors continued to show little enthusiasm for photographs. There was little attempt to use photographic imagery in an imaginative way." There are few great war pictures from World War I, few visual tributes to the folly of empire. There are few memorable photographs of the Russian Revolution in 1917, arguably one of the key events of the century. The technology was there, but the instinct was missing. The camera was still a stepchild to the notebook. The idea that photography could be put to the service of news was not yet clear, even to Brady, who hoped to sell his pictures to the public from his galleries. The economics of photography kept it at a distance, out of focus.

If journalism was slow to warm to the photograph, so was officialdom. It took almost a century for photography to earn a reputation for probity, to gain acceptance as a vehicle for official corroboration. In 1864, a congressional committee investigating the atrocities at the Confederate prison camp near Andersonville in Georgia included in its final report four illustrations based on photographs. The idea was to document, "lest there should be those," as Senator Lafayette Foster of Connecticut put it, "who would not believe" that cruel conditions had reduced men to skeletons. When the full Senate debated in January 1865 whether to retaliate against the South, whether to starve Rebel prisoners and subject them to the same kind of disease-infected quarters that killed up to 100 Northern men a day, some, enough to keep the Senate from passing the bill, complained that there was "no technical evidence . . . in official form" to support the charges. Politics informed this view, but somehow the pictures were not enough to override it.

Grainy pictures of victims in concentration camps after World War II shocked many who saw them, but, finally, grainy or not, seeing was believing. BRITISH ANGER DEEP AT ATROCITY PROOF, headlined the *New York Times* on April 20, 1945, PUBLICATION OF PHOTOS AROUSES THE NATION. Decades later, photographs were no longer needed to confirm the unthinkable. In 1986, photographs of Chernobyl shocked those who saw them. "It doesn't matter how many descriptions you have of the black hole where Chernobyl used to be," said Michael Bohn, the navy intelligence officer who directed the White House Situation Room when the nuclear power plant blew up. "Until you saw a picture of this stinking, smoking mass, it didn't hit you, the enormity of it." But the truth is that the real horror of Chernobyl was left to the imagination, for no camera could record the way in which nuclear radiation killed human beings. The pictures of Nazi concentration camps at war's end had served as catharsis for guilt; pictures of a hole where Chernobyl once stood carried no such emotional punch. The photograph was a mirror. The emotions belonged to the viewers.

Enthusiasts had no trouble seeing the camera's potential from the beginning. In October 1862, only weeks after the smoke had cleared from the bloody battlefield at Antietam— and that was about as instantaneous as the day's photographic technology could afford—Brady opened an exhibit on the battle at his galleries in New York. It was a sensation. "Mr. Brady has done something to bring home to us the terrible reality and earnestness of war," wrote a *New York Times* cor- respondent on October 20. "If he has not brought bodies and laid them in our dooryards and along the streets, he has done something very like it." Noting the throngs on Broadway crowding into the gallery, the *Times* commentator marveled that the photographs were so realistic that "by the aid of the magnifying glass, the very features of the slain may be distin- guished," and he worried at being in the gallery when a woman nearing a photo "should recognize a husband, a son or a brother in the still lifeless line of bodies that lie ready for the gaping trenches."

Here was the beginning of war photography. There had been photographers at the Crimea War in 1854, but they did not shoot any pictures of combat gore in that battle between Turkey and other European powers. The best known of them, Roger Fenton, was the son of a British industrialist who learned photography from Delaroche, a painter who despaired of the camera's impact on art. Financed by the Manchester publishing firm of Thomas Agnew & Son, Fenton went to the Crimea with the blessings of Prince Albert and official circles in London. But he saw his mission as less to shock than to reassure the public. Fenton took 360 photographs of the Crimean War. Not one of his photographs showed the graphic horror of war, though he was reportedly witness to several grisly scenes.

Some have argued that English Victorian society would have shunned Fenton's work if he had recorded death. Others contend that the bulky camera equipment of the day precluded war photography. Whatever the reason, the burden of bringing war to the public's front door awaited the Civil War. Antietam, the bloodiest single day in American combat, with 26,000 killed or wounded, was also the first battle whose dead were photographed as they lay, not as peaceful corpses in heavenly slumber but as bloated, gouged, twisted, grotesque figures in painful demise. "The first living room war was not Vietnam but the American Civil War," writes Vicki Goldberg in *The Power of Photography*. "[It] came into the front parlor in word and picture, even in photographs, as no war had before."

What is striking about the photographs, many taken by Gardner, is the reaction they engendered in the public. "Let him who wishes to know what war is like look at this series of illustrations," said Oliver Wendell Holmes, Sr., after viewing the exhibit. "It was so nearly like visiting the battlefield to look over these views that all the emotions excited by the actual sight of the stained and sordid scene, strewed with rags and wrecks, came back to us." A physician and amateur photographer, Holmes had gone to Antietam to look for his son, Oliver Wendell Holmes, Jr., later a Supreme Court justice, who had been wounded in battle. Though the wound was not fatal, the image of war remained powerful, like a surreal attraction. Try as he might to forget what he had seen, Holmes the elder felt the pictures would not let him bury the memories. In the end, he was grateful. "War and battles should have truth for their delineator," he said.

This is the truly stunning fact about the Antietam photographs, that instead of sending shock waves of horror they apparently had little negative impact on public opinion. Contrary to the expected connection between the camera and the emotions, there is no cache of letters to the editor in the major newspapers protesting the depiction of bloodshed in

Brady's gallery, as there would be a century later when newspapers published a picture of screaming South Vietnamese children running for their lives as napalm fire seared the skin off their bodies. Similarly, there is no pattern of protests to the Lincoln White House because of the bloodshed in Antietam, as there would be to Lyndon Johnson's White House because of battles fought in Saigon. Later in the Civil War, as casualties mounted, the peace movement in the North grew loud and numerous, its goal to seek an end to hostilities without victory. But in 1862, Quakers and other ministers who visited Lincoln came to urge him to abolish slavery. That was the cause of public protests when Brady put on his exhibit, not so much to end the war as to make it worth fighting. Perhaps too few had seen Brady's photographs to make a difference. Or perhaps photography had to instruct before it could shock; perhaps the emotional content of pictures was a learned response.

Lincoln used the Union "victory" at Antietam (most describe it more accurately as "not a loss,") to issue the Emancipation Proclamation that forever after cast the war as a fight over slavery. With this strategic move—which had little practical impact in freeing slaves in the South—Lincoln gave the cause of the North a higher calling, precluded intervention by Europe, and doomed the Confederacy to a legacy of bigotry. This was a historic milestone, a political coup, and it may have also ameliorated the shocking impact of the first war photographs to break the barrier of custom and show the dead as they lay in trenches where they fell, in the grip of battle. Antietam provided the first hint that pictures do not lead but follow public opinion, that their reception depends almost entirely on the political context in which they are received, that memory and experience frame them.

But soon enough would come signs that the photograph had the power to exaggerate weakness, that the photographer was, like a journalist, a filter of information—and not always objective. No politician since the camera's invention so feared the power of the medium to debase, with so much cause, as Franklin Delano Roosevelt. Few world leaders have ever been as protected by a new medium, news photography, as it began to earn a place in journalism. Then too, FDR was blessed with good timing, coming to power when several new technologies competed for attention, when he could excel at radio communication and hold photography at arm's length.

Crippled from an attack of polio, FDR elected to hide his affliction from the public, convinced that voters wanted their leaders in full stride, not in wheelchairs. When FDR arrived at Hyde Park Town Hall on November 6, 1928, to cast his ballot in the race for governor, newspaper and newsreel photographers greeted his car. "No movies of me getting out of the machine, boys," he said. At the 1936 Democratic National Convention, by-then President Roosevelt slipped and fell in the mud. As he struggled to his feet, CBS radio announcer Robert Trout told listeners the president was making his way slowing toward the podium. On another occasion, FDR fell on the floor in front of several photographers. None took a picture. A clear view of Roosevelt's disability is only captured in four seconds of film and three photographs that survive to this day. None were published while he was alive. In those days, photographers "voluntarily destroyed their own plates when they showed Roosevelt in poses that revealed his handicap."

The public could learn of Roosevelt's disabilities from newspaper articles like the one in the *New York Herald-Tribune* describing his entry into campaign headquarters in 1928. The candidate was "supporting himself on the left side with a crutch and on the right side with a cane, and leaning forward on these supports so that he could draw his feet after him in a sliding gait." When the reporter asked how he was feeling, FDR replied, "I told them in Poughkeepsie this afternoon that most people who are nominated for the governorship have to run, but obviously I am not in the condition to run, and therefore I am counting on my friends all over the state to make it possible for me to walk in." That is what the public knew of FDR's infirmities, that he could not run but could, with assistance, walk. No photograph contradicted this version, no paper image documented the reality, that even walking was problematic. His charming wit, good nature, and gritty cheer had something to do with this deception; his jaunty manner of holding a cigarette, perched in an upward tilt as if to convey an optimism about the future, helped in the making of his image. So did his determination to keep cameramen at bay.

This instinct that the visual was too powerful to contradict with words, that its impact could not be explained away by the best of logic, was one of the deadly legacies of the photograph. A public might have been educated to accept the disability—much as John F. Kennedy taught a 1960 public to overcome prejudice against Catholics in high office—but FDR was unwilling to risk the effort for fear that in 1932, voters wanted their leaders to look the part. Perhaps they still do. In any event, he came of age politically at a time when the media was less an adversary than a chronicler of events. In short, Franklin Roosevelt engaged in the deception because he thought he had to—and because he could.

Ironically, it was Roosevelt who freed news photography from the strict censorship that had smothered it once journalists and politicians learned to use the pictures to evoke emotion. Censorship during the First World War was based on the premise that news of any kind would destroy morale on the home front. The penalty for publishing any news stories in the United States that might be broadly defined as helping the enemy or interfering with the military during

World War I was twenty years in prison. For news photographers, the penalty for taking pictures at the front, at least at first, was death. This had a chilling effect. "Photographs seem to be the only thing the War Department is really afraid of," observed Jimmy Hare, the best-known photographer of the day.

In the decades that followed, legal scholars questioned the blanket nature of the censorship, and the U.S. government was criticized for being too restrictive, for arguing national security too often when simple fear of public opinion was a more likely cause. Even so, World War II began with the same sort of ethos, a belief that censorship in a time of war was another word for patriotism. Reporters traveled with military units, wearing the uniforms of their outfits, and the Office of War Information cleared all their stories. For photographers, corpses of dead Americans were simply off limits, though Japanese or Germans who had fallen in battle were fair game. "A message was being subtly broadcast that war was hell for the enemy but our side was faring well," wrote one critic.

By World War II, photography had come into its own as a news source, and began to impact diplomacy. Even then, the pictures were often sanitized to keep from offending the sensibilities of readers. The impulse to free the camera from censorship came from FDR, who gave his blessing to a policy that, in 1943, would finally exploit the promise of photojournalism. His rationale was domestic, and had less to do with waging war abroad than with keeping the war machine humming at home. War bond drives had been coming up short of quotas, the Red Cross blood drives were not attracting the usual numbers, and voters had been complaining of shortages. Americans wanted the war to be over.

Eyeing the dip in morale at home, Roosevelt reviewed a protest from *Life* magazine to overturn the Office of War Information's decision to ban publication of George Strock's photographs of American soldiers gunned down by Japanese artillery on Buna Beach. While the pictures were banned, censors had cleared newspaper copy about the battle. The fear was that while the words might cause a shudder and bare a concern, the pictures would horrify the public and dampen the will to fight. Sometime between Antietam and Buna Beach, the public had learned to decipher horror, had been trained to focus on grief.

Life had almost single-handedly given photography a place of honor in journalism, offering readers a weekly view of events in living color. Begun in 1936, the magazine was the brainchild of Henry Luce, who had already founded *Time* magazine and *Fortune*. Just at the time when the technology allowed worldwide dissemination of photographs by wires, *Life* meant to exploit this new medium called photojournalism. In promoting the magazine, one editor had argued, "A war, any sort of war, will be a natural promotion for a picture magazine." Now, *Life* sought to make good on that promise by arguing that the pictures of fallen American soldiers would not hurt but would actually help morale. "The job of men like Strock is to bring the war back to us, so that we who are thousands of miles removed from the danger and the smell of death may know what is at stake," *Life* wrote in its February 22 issue. "Maybe some housewives wouldn't be in such a hurry to raid the grocery stores, and John L. Lewis wouldn't feel so free to profiteer on the war—if they could see how [they] fell." Roosevelt agreed.

And so in mid-May, Army Air Force Combat Camera Units received a memo on the new policy. It was fairly straightforward, instructing army photographers "that the public be shown the grimness and hardness of war." World War II was the most photographed war in history, captured by hundreds of military cameramen and magazine photographers, but photographers still had to show restraint. "We must not pass the line beyond which the exhibition does more harm than good," said the military memo. "It is not desired that horror pictures should be released, but special effort should be made to find those photographs which accurately depict the terrible strain of wartime conditions."

As a result, war was slightly more visible, but still protected from full view. America's war dead were faceless, as censors still feared the impact of a frontal photograph, and the wounded were always being attended by medical personnel. "Photos did not depict gross mutilations or show the wounded lying between the lines, untended, thrashing in agony, bleeding to death or slowing dying of dehydration." The photographs had the desired effect at home: War bond sales topped their quotas, and grumbling about shortages quieted. They also changed the tone of news coverage. Robert Capa's telling photographs of the Italian front were included in a *Life* feature early in 1944 called "It's a Tough War," prompting one soldier to write that "the pictures clearly portray the bitterness and grimness of the battles to be fought before we reach Berlin and Tokyo." By June, *Life* was routinely publishing pictures of Americans lying dead on battlefields. In loosening the rules of censorship, FDR had abetted war photography. With it came the myth that pictures could end war.

World War II was far from the uncensored war called Vietnam, where photographers were free to roam and publish at will. But neither was it as restricted as the Persian Gulf War, where photographers were prevented often from even getting to the battlefield. Self-censorship remained a factor in journalistic decisions—to this day, editors shy from close-ups of fallen American soldiers, and CNN sat on footage from Somalia far more grisly than that shown of a corpse being dragged through the streets of Mogadishu. And technological burdens, in the lab or in transmission, remained. Capa's famous pictures from the D-Day invasion on Omaha Beach on June 6, 1944, were published by *Life* soon after the battle—despite the fact that a lab technician in London had destroyed all but eleven of his frames. This was the dawn of photojournalism, the beginning of its impact on public opinion. Not everyone was thrilled. *Newsweek* was peppered with letters from readers who were aghast, publishing some of their concerns under the dismissive title, "Realism for Breakfast." Finally, journalism had smelled the glory and the power of photojournalism, and policy makers quaked at the implications.

Generations of political figures have been nursed on the understanding that a photograph can turn public sympathy to public enmity, that the eye of the camera is as much their enemy as any battlefield opponent. No better example exists than a 1968 photograph by Associated Press photographer Eddie Adams. In the picture, which won a Pulitzer Prize, Adams captured Nguyen Ngoc Loan, chief of South Vietnam's National Police, as he held a gun to the head of a newly captured Viet Cong officer believed to have murdered a South Vietnamese major and his family. To seasoned war hands (and U.S. intelligence sources), Loan was avenging great injustices committed against his soldiers and his people. But to unschooled viewers, without knowledge of the events that led up to the execution, the picture captured the horror of war, and worse, raised doubts about the morality of the people American soldiers were dying for.

The picture haunted Loan's life. He asked to be evacuated from Saigon on one of the last U.S. helicopters out, but was rebuffed by U.S. officials. Later, he managed to escape from Vietnam and make his way to the Virginia countryside, only to have U.S. immigration officials try to deport him as a war criminal. Adams later regretted the picture's impact on Loan.

"In taking that picture, I had destroyed his life," the photographer wrote in a special feature for *Parade* magazine about his Vietnam years. "For General Loan had become a man condemned both in his country and in America because he had killed an enemy in war. People do this all the time in war, but rarely is a photographer there to record the act."

Whatever Adams's intent, his picture was soon appropriated by the antiwar forces to symbolize the horrors of American involvement in a Southeast Asian country where police chiefs serve as judge, jury, and executioner. In taking the picture, Adams had frozen a moment, exaggerated its importance, created a new cultural icon. The photograph remains raw to all those who saw it when it was news, and a cautionary tale to all those who heard of it later. What is interesting is the way it was received by the public. An electorate incensed by Viet Cong atrocities, committed to defending South Vietnam's right to democracy, supportive of Washington's methods in prosecuting the war, might have seen the photo as confirmation of its beliefs, might have responded by rallying even more loudly to the cause. But the war had already lost its constituency.

When *Life* explained why it had lobbied the War Department in 1943 to release pictures of the three dead American soldiers on Buna Beach, it editorialized that "words are never enough. Words do not exist to make us see, or know, or feel what it is like, what actually happens." In fact, words did serve precisely that function in an earlier day. The photograph's century of development from novelty to news indicates that the audience had to be trained to believe the veracity of images. Pictures may have been provocative, but they also required a context, an explanation, a caption.

In the coming age of information technology, when the photograph can be altered without fingerprints, when a camera can record pictures without film, when computer graphics can insert or delete an individual from what Mathew Brady called "the eye of history," it will fall to journalists and policy makers to guard the images. The photograph has long been manipulated by those who would use it for political ends. What is changing now is the manner of the manipulation. History suggests that political leaders, not the media or its latest technologies, have the greater influence, or anyway the first opening to sway public opinion. And like photography, public opinion is a mirror of political will.

6

Public Opinion and World War I

P UBLIC OPINION IS a fickle institution, if it is an institution at all, bowing to the latest impulses, defying the pseudoscience of pollsters, the pulse of a phantom. In few arenas is it more important, or less reliable, than in foreign policy. At few times is it more critical, or as volatile, as in war. A democratic nation cannot wage war without popular support, nor can an elected leader switch direction without regard for the voters' views. Even a dictator risks insurrection if he misreads the national mood, though Russian czar Nicholas II no doubt endeared himself to many an elected official when he remarked in 1909, "In ninety-nine cases out of a hundred, what is called 'public opinion' is mere forgery."

That technology has abetted public opinion, that it has at least invited the public to voice its opinion, is clear from the record. It is no coincidence that radio's emergence as a social force corresponded to the granting of suffrage to women in Great Britain in 1918 and in the United States in 1920. "The establishment of broadcasting coincided with the moment that the vote was finally conceded to all adult men and women," wrote early historians of the field, "and the development of mass democracy is closely connected with broadcasting's role in that process." Just at the moment when politics itself became more democratic, radio gave the audience in democracies a new way of tuning in.

Also clear is the disdain with which intellectuals greeted the new influence on policy. When the printing press and its pamphlets give new weight to public opinion, satirist Jonathan Swift warned in 1711 that "it is the folly of too many to mistake the echo of a London coffee-house for the voice of the kingdom." After the telegraph had speeded communication and, to contemporary eyes, annihilated time and space, Oscar Wilde likewise scoffed in 1891, "Public opinion, an attempt to organize the ignorance of the community, and to elevate it to the dignity of physical force." And after radio had made more information available to more people in less time than ever before, Walter Lippmann, commentator for an American century, adviser to presidents, and confidant of cabinet secretaries, could not have been more contemptuous. "Where mass opinion dominates the government, there is a morbid derangement of the true functions of power," he wrote in 1955. "This breakdown in the constitutional order is the cause of the precipitate and catastrophic decline of Western society. It may, if it cannot be arrested and reversed, bring about the fall of the West."

Lippmann and his power-brokering colleagues enjoyed a rare influence, and their distrust of the new media was in part a reaction to losing an exclusive hold on information. But the critique of those invoking the name of "public opinion" to justify policy is not misplaced. Any leader who marches to the beat of public opinion soon loses his own. Easily swayed by the latest development, public opinion is fleeting, given to a rush of passion, a hasty judgment. This is not the public's fault. A collective will is by nature a compromise of interests, a ducking of accountability. "Public opinion is always wrong," said Lippmann, "much too intransigent in war, much too yielding in peace, insufficiently informed, lacking the specialized knowledge upon which lucid judgments can be based." In short, he believed the public "has shown itself to be a dangerous master of decisions when the stakes are life and death." If there is a fault it lies with pollsters and journalists, politicians and commentators, who invoke public opinion to mask their own insecurities. The truth is that any leader who makes policy looking back over his shoulder is likely to trip over his own feet. And the public rarely applauds a clumsy performer.

Without boots or public support, few soldiers fight well. This need to summon a great cause, to explain the rationale for war, actually traces its heritage to the printing press, when the library doors of the churchmen and noblemen who oversaw the kingdoms of the day were suddenly thrown open to those who until then only heard of the news occasionally. Information left the exclusive domain of the elite and became the property of the informed. Each generation of new media technology brought a new appreciation of the senses—the speed of the telegraph, the drama of the photograph—and widened the circle of those with access to information. The public may exercise its influence only sporadically. But from the moment when informed consent became a needed adjunct to military service, leaders have always had to court public opinion. Public support is not the only requirement for war, but war is rarely won without it.

Public opinion emerged as a crucial element to battle, ironically, in World War I, the greatest tribute to the folly of empire. The War to End All Wars was also the first to acknowledge a collective will from a body politic. Even in countries without democratic traditions, even in a war that had little rationale beyond petty greed, public views mattered. The primacy of leadership, Arthur Schlesinger, Jr., has argued, began with the rise of democracy in the nineteenth century, when "ordinary people now felt entitled to a larger share in decisions that might send them out to die." Czars, kaisers, and kings were still running the globe, but by World War I they began paying lip service to the public mind.

On the eve of war, Russia's czar Nicholas II tried to rescind his own mobilization order as it was being transcribed in The central telegraph office. But he was convinced by aides that the country wanted war, wanted to defend Serbia's honor against Austria's warmongering, wanted to restore Russian military pride in the wake of defeat in the Russo-Japanese War. Enthusiastic crowds filled the streets of St. Petersburg, and the American chargé d'affaires cabled Washington: "Whole country, all classes, unanimous for war." Foreign Minister Sergey Sazonov now told the czar that he could not rescind his order without fear of a coup: "Were the government to tolerate this, there would be a revolution in the country." How ironic that three years later, a revolution there was.

Likewise in Germany, Kaiser William II had strong backing in the German newspapers for his plan to prevent a larger war by supporting a localized one, where Austria and Serbia would fight while the big powers allied with them—France, Russia, and Britain on Serbia's side; Germany on Austria's— would watch from a distance. But William had also used the newspapers to convince his public to increase its army to over 2 million men and build a navy to rival the British Royal Navy. As British public opinion chafed at this real as well as psychological affront to England's security, Germans rallied to the kaiser's grand ambitions.

A last-minute cable from Germany's ambassador to London suggested that Britain might stay out of war if France was not invaded. The kaiser asked his army chief of staff, Helmuth von Moltke, to reverse course for the troops, sending them to the eastern front in Russia rather than through the Belgian front to France. "Your Majesty," replied Moltke, "the deployment of a million men cannot be improvised." William, disappointed, cabled King George of England that "technical reasons" prevented countermanding the mobilization, and urged him to tell France to "not become nervous." Then he cabled Nicholas, urging him not to mobilize, telling him the responsibility for war or peace rested on his shoulders. Fascinated with new media technology like the telegraph and the wireless, William used them largely to foment discord among his counterparts in various world capitals. Portrayed as a man of quick action, who "always wanted it to be Sunday," he used the telegraph to bully Austria, to keep Russia at bay, to countermand his military commanders' orders on the eve of battle.

Some historians have thus blamed the inner circles in St. Petersburg and Berlin for bungling their way into war, arguing that the ruling classes were unmodern in the ways of the media that so fascinated the leaders. "Most of the aristocrats and gentlemen who made up the diplomatic corps in 1914 were of the old school in many ways," writes historian Stephen Kern. "They still counted on the ultimate effectiveness of spoken words of a decent man in face-to-face encounters but were forced to negotiate many important issues over copper wire." Kern puts the war squarely at their feet, arguing that "piles of futile telegrams (like the later rows of dead soldiers) were the tangible remains of their failure." But to suggest that the misuse of media technology led to war is to underestimate national interests and individual responsibility, as well as public opinion.

When war broke out in August of 1914 in Europe, President Woodrow Wilson faced his own public-opinion battles. Calling White House reporters to his office to admonish them about the hazards of entanglement, he argued that "of course the European world is in a highly excited state of mind, but the excitement ought not to spread to the United States."

For three years, Wilson clung to his neutrality, and his country clung to its isolationism. For three years, public opinion in the United States was informed largely by a desire to stay out of war, lead by a president who hoped that if he kept his country from the war, its combatants would look to him as the "moral arbiter" of the peace. In this hope to avoid entanglements he was aided by the country's diverse ethnic heritage, which found Russian Jews applauding the German fight against the czar and German-Americans lobbying against aiding the allies. So sanguine was Wilson about the rightness of his course, and the sureness of public sentiment behind it, that he ran for reelection in 1916 on the platform "He kept us out of war!"

While Europe went to war, Wilson showed an aptitude for exploiting the media and manipulating public opinion. He asked the State Department to find the funds to print and distribute his neutrality speech to all U.S. post offices, assuring it greater dissemination and longer currency. Hoping to sell a reluctant Congress in 1915 on the need to beef up militarily, Wilson hit the road, stumping in towns from New York to Kansas, winning national support for an expanded national defense. "A wonderful example of that opportunity for aggressive leadership which the presidency of the United States places in the hands of the bold political strategist and the effective platform speaker," wrote Herbert Croly in *The New Republic*. And when U.S. involvement in the war seemed inevitable, he agreed to Secretary of State Robert Lansing's suggestion of leaking the infamous Zimmermann cable to the Associated Press.

Arthur Zimmermann, the German foreign secretary, had written a telegram to the German ambassador in Washington, informing him of the latest German plot to keep the United States out of war. To prevent Wilson from caving in to pressures for war even as he negotiated with them for peace, Germany had hatched a plan to keep the United States preoccupied at home. It boiled down to an offer to help Mexico win back Texas, New Mexico, and Arizona. As the January 17, 1917, telegram put it, "We intend to begin unrestricted submarine warfare. We shall endeavor to keep the United States neutral. In the event of this not succeeding, we make Mexico a proposal of alliance on the following basis: Make war together, make peace together, generous financial support and an understanding on our part that Mexico is to recover the lost territory in Texas, New Mexico and Arizona."

Zimmermann did not know that the British naval intelligence had cracked the German code, and, able to pluck coded telegraphed messages out of the air, could decipher them. Seizing the opportunity, British code breakers unraveled the telegram's mysteries. Eager to protect the secret that they had broken the code, the British worked to get a purloined copy of the version of the telegram sent from the German ambassador in Washington to the Mexican authorities, confident that the Germans would blame the leak on their own embassies in Washington or Mexico.

Wilson understood that the telegram, if published by the Associated Press, would push public opinion toward war. He also grasped that the news agency would inquire of the White House whether the telegram was authentic, thus putting the president in the position of confirming his own leak, as well as assuring that the cable would be quickly and widely circulated. The story began, "The AP is enabled to reveal . . .". The impact on public opinion, as reflected in newspaper editorials, was striking. GERMANY SEEKS AN ALLIANCE AGAINST US, read the morning newspaper headlines, ASKS JAPAN AND MEXICO TO JOIN HER. Editorialized the once staunchly anti-interventionist *Detroit Times:* "It looks like war for this country." In coming days, German commanders sank several U.S.

vessels in the Atlantic, disabling them for the fight ahead, but further solidifying U.S. public opinion about the need to go to war. "It is either war or submission to oppression," one-time pacifist Elihu Root told the Union League Club of New York. "There is no question about going to war. Germany is already at war with us."

Wilson's antenna for manipulation of public opinion makes all the more remarkable his failure to win Senate rat-ification of the Versailles Treaty and a League of Nations founded on Fourteen Points of laudable ideals. Less than a month after World War I ended, Woodrow Wilson sailed out of New York Harbor aboard the presidential liner *George Washington* for peace talks in France. A buoyant Wilson gave interviews to the wire-service reporters onboard, leaving them "simply carried away with enthusiasm for his ideas and plans." Using the wireless telegraphy that Guglielmo Marconi dis-covered in the 1890s while experimenting in his father's veg-etable garden, they sent back stories that captured the moment's promise. The pacifist American president had helped win the war, and pioneer a cause: Fourteen Points of freedom and justice that all countries would agree to abide by in a new League of Nations, an international body that would protect against the bloody futility of any future wars. His grand scheme for peace was telegraphed over the wireless telegraph to a grateful Europe, and the same new technology, a forerunner of radio, helped journalists cable back home that Parisians had welcomed him as an "apostle of international justice."

Six months later, the same technology that had conveyed a sense of hope to a war-sickened world now presented a different view. Frustrated by the web of intrigue and secrecy spun by his counterparts, pained that he had been forced to compromise his principles, aware that he faced a hostile re-ception from the Senate, Wilson carried home the Treaty of

Versailles more with resolution than enthusiasm. For six months, with the exception of a brief ten-day visit back to the United States, Wilson had labored in France, working out the details of a peace treaty he had extracted as the price of war. As Americans returned to civilian life and rebuilt their communities, Wilson was "mired in the minutiae of negotiations, clinging desperately to the shards of his Fourteen Points." The same technology that brought news of Wilson's triumphant reception in Paris six months earlier now brought a sense of his obsession with the details of peace. "Wireless brought home to the nation, especially those in Washington, his failures." When finally Wilson came home to stay, the Macon [Georgia] *Telegraph* editorialized, "Just think, we will have a president all by ourselves from now on!"

By September, Wilson's cherished League of Nations was faltering. The 1916 elections had put the Republicans in charge of both the House and the Senate for the first time in years, and the GOP was still smarting over Wilson's evasiveness during treaty negotiations and his arrogant disregard for their concerns and suggested compromises on his return. Wilson, who found it unimaginable that the Senate would defeat the treaty and "break the heart of the world," vowed to take his case to "Caesar," as he called the public, scheduling a 26-city, 10,000-mile campaign across the country.

As he swept west to Los Angeles, Wilson's speeches appeared to sway opinion in favor of the treaty, and the *New York Times*'s Charles Grasty observed that Wilson was now "getting the cumulative effect of his missionary work." But there also emerged a new note of despair in his public words. Blaming the media and its new technology for the Russian Revolution and much else that was wrong in the world, Wilson told a crowd in Des Moines, "Do you not know the world is all now one single whispering gallery?" Like those now who think the fax machine fomented dissent in Beijing in 1989 or radio inspired revolution in Eastern Europe in 1989, Wilson blamed the wireless for spreading the "poison of revolt, the poison of chaos" to Russia in 1917.

"Haggard, close to the massive stroke that overcame him 19 days later, Wilson betrayed an uneasiness about the impact of the new technology," wrote radio historian Tom Lewis. To a crowd of 10,000, he lamented, "All the impulses of mankind are thrown out upon the air and reach to the ends of the earth; quietly upon steamships, silently under the cover of the Postal Service, with the tongue of the wireless and the tongue of the telegraph, all the suggestions of disorder are spread through the world." The president who fought a war to make the world safe for democracy now complained about this new medium that could democratize international relations. The former university professor who reached out to public opinion to rescue his League of Nations distrusted the new technologies, fearing they would spread not informed debate, but disinformation.

In war, most leaders enjoy a "rally round the flag" benefit when they call on the public to defend the honor of the nation, though they dare not ask too much, for too long, without risking a backlash. Wilson himself seemed to understand this. The first of his Fourteen Points, an attempt to deter large-scale war in the future, acknowledged the value of public exposure of private pacts. "Open covenants of peace, openly arrived at, after which there shall be no private international understandings of any kind but diplomacy, shall proceed always frankly and in public view," it read. That Wilson violated his own guideline in negotiating the Treaty of Versailles behind closed doors, a concession to pragmatism he saw as the price of peace, was not irrelevant to the defeat that followed.

His is a cautionary tale, testimony to those who argue that government leaders need only do their jobs, that public applause will follow. But it is also a confirmation that public applause does not always carry the day. Media technology gives public diplomacy more urgency, but any leader who ignores private negotiation will have a harder sell. Wilson, ironically, was felled by the petty angers and real concerns of men in the Senate who felt slighted by his internationalist demeanor and diffident manner. Unlike McKinley, who had shown aptitude for bureaucratic leadership and swayed public opinion by indirection, Wilson had spent his political capital on the wrong crowd, playing compromiser to the Europeans instead of the senators, banking on public opinion to deliver the votes.

The Treaty of Versailles is now a model of bad policy, a document so wracked with territorial revenge among enemies that Europe fought a second world war to overcome its perceived injustices, and border disputes left over from its provisions rage still in places like Serbia. Wilson showed less disdain for the public than he did for his foes, and his inattention to the politics of ratification, his unwillingness to compromise at home after giving away quite a bit abroad, these were likewise factors in his defeat. If public opinion were all a politician needed to succeed, then Wilson would have won his battle, as the mood was shifting in his favor when he collapsed in a stroke that paralyzed him and doomed his treaty. That public opinion was not supreme, that substance and policy and politics still mattered, suggests that the influence of public opinion, like the power of the media and its technological advances, is not an absolute.

Like diplomats today, the generation confronted by the telegraph and the wireless was convinced that the speed of the new instruments hurt due deliberation. What they actually did was speed the input of public opinion. The kaiser was more than comfortable using these new instruments of power. Perhaps if others had been as adroit at sending speedy messages, William's warmongering might have been tempered, as it was seven years earlier when an interview he gave to the *Daily Telegraph* about the likely war to come so unnerved his own countrymen that he took to his bed ill for three weeks. That contention would be put to its greatest test with the next media invention to assault the political world: the telephone. The telephone put nations in direct communication with other nations in mere minutes, giving diplomats less leeway and publics more say. Resistance, particularly among the political elite, was fierce.

7

Telephone Diplomacy

A T 4:50 P.M. on a Sunday at his dacha in the Crimea, the last president of the Union of Socialist Soviet Republics picked up the telephone, only to discover that the line was dead. Mikhail Gorbachev tried a second line, a third, a fourth—to his increasing horror, all were dead. The coup of 1991, three days in August that shook the world, began with this simple tribute to the power of the telephone.

The plotters of this coup did not pull the plug on many other weapons of modern communication, leading some observers to conclude that they were clumsy idiots and others, more conspiratorially minded, to wonder if they had acted with Gorbachev's secret consent. Perhaps in plotting his own capture he hoped to remind an unhappy citizenry of what life would be like without him. If that was the strategy, it backfired, as the coup found Muscovites only too eager to rally around a new hero for a new day, Russian president Boris Yeltsin.

Whatever their intent, these hapless plotters ignored the technology of news. They did not cut off the switch that carried all international calls to Moscow. They did not shut down Moscow's main satellite-relay station, which allowed foreign TV networks to broadcast the news. They did not cut the electrical lines needed to send faxed messages. And they did not jam radio broadcasts of the *BBC*, *Radio Liberty*, *Deutsche Welle*, and *Voice of America*, which Gorbachev was able to monitor throughout the crisis thanks to the ingenuity of a few remaining loyal guards who jury-rigged a homemade radio for his use. Even *Moscow Echo*, a local radio station shut down four times during the coup, managed to stay on the air from makeshift headquarters in cramped conditions. The coup plotters even forgot to commandeer Gorbachev's video camcorder. Angered by reports on the radio from the coup leaders describing him as ill, Gorbachev made four videotapes attesting to his health that he planned to smuggle to a waiting world.

After the coup was overturned, Yeltsin mused that the conspirators' ignorance about the new technology had been a major factor in their defeat. "The middle-age coup plotters simply could not imagine the extent and volume of the information," he wrote. "Instead of a quiet and inconspicuous coup executed party style, they suddenly had a totally public fight on their hands. The coup plotters were not prepared— especially psychologically—for an atmosphere of complete publicity."

In keeping with their halfhearted attempt to seal news, coup plotters sent troops to surround Moscow's main telephone exchange, but they did not cut the main switch that funneled all international calls. As Red Army tanks poised outside and young demonstrators began to fill the streets, James Collins, deputy chief of mission for the U.S. embassy, paid a visit to Yeltsin. In his first response to the coup, President Bush had been deliberately passive, in a misguided attempt not to offend the coup plotters for fear he might have to work with them in the future. A disappointed Yeltsin, hearing Bush's tepid remarks, knew he had to energize the White House to survive the coming assault on his front door.

He gave Collins a letter he had written to Bush in which he asked of the American president two things. One was that Bush "demand restoration of the legally elected organs of power." The other was that Bush call him.

That the telephone had come to this moment of historic application would have thrilled its inventor, Alexander Graham Bell, who even after he had mastered the technology was ridiculed for suggesting that an electrical wire could transmit the human voice. Neighbors in Boston delighted in calling him Crazy Bell. Beyond the science of the invention, critics doubted its value.

Of all the technologies under review here, the telephone inspired the most resistance from government and business leaders. Like Bell's neighbors, they undervalued its marvels. William Orton, president of Western Union, turned down a chance to buy Alexander Graham Bell's patents for $100,000, saying, "What use could this company make of an electrical toy?" This monumental gaffe in business acumen was likely caused by Orton's concern about the expense of converting from the telegraph. It had an echo abroad. The turf-conscious chief engineer of the British post office, testifying before a committee of Parliament, was equally myopic when asked if the telephone merited attention. "No sir," he said. "The Americans have need of the telephone, but we do not. We have plenty of messenger boys."

Resistance has not quieted with familiarity. In the fall of 1994, in the crucible of international neutrality, the Swiss Army announced that it was disbanding the world's last unit of military carrier pigeons. The carrier pigeons had delivered messages over Switzerland's mountainous terrain for decades. Only two years before, the Swiss Army had championed their performance. "The pigeons are immune from electronic interference, cheap to operate and after proper training can make night-time and return journeys," declared an official army brochure. Now, seeking to save money, the Defense Ministry set out to disband the unit of 7,000 staff pigeons and 23,000 reservist birds, depending instead on radio and telephones. Public emotion was intense. "We are outraged and feel betrayed," said Ulrick Frei, who fathered a referendum to spare the pigeon service. "To get rid of one of the last sympathy winners for the army is plain stupid."

That the telephone, 118 years after its invention, still inspired distrust as a method of communication is a marvelous tribute to the staying power of the pigeons—or to the unpopularity of the telephone. Such resistance makes more understandable the telephone's history at the seat of power in the White House. When it arrived at the White House in 1877, one year after U.S. patent 174,465 was granted to its inventor, the telephone was considered a crude instrument, not fit for a president's use, an intrusion on privacy, on reasoned deliberation, a useful tool perhaps for secretaries but not for men of stature. After participating in a trial telephone conversation between Washington and Philadelphia in 1876, President Rutherford B. Hayes declared, "This is an amazing invention, but who would want to use one?" While this comment may speak more to Hayes's lack of imagination than to any inherent weakness in the telephone, it posed a question that haunted Bell's invention for more than fifty years.

For half a century, the telephone remained outside the president's office in a nearby room, used by secretaries and others of the president's aides, and even some reporters when necessary. Toward the end of William Howard Taft's administration in 1912, a telephone booth was installed, designed to hold the girth of the 360-pound president, who found the whole setup inconvenient and used the phone infrequently. The phone remained "one step away from the center of power" until Herbert Hoover's administration. Hoover, an engineer with a great passion for new technologies (but, sadly, little talent for their use), ordered a telephone set placed on his desk within three weeks of his inauguration as president in March 1929. But the first president to lift up the receiver in the Oval Office and hear a dial tone, and then only because he requested it, was Bill Clinton. Until then, a bank of operators had placed the calls. Clinton wanted to eliminate the intermediary.

The telephone combined the best and worst traits of the media inventions gone before and those yet to come. It was a return to the oral tradition, favoring the narrative, challenging the imagination, and personalizing the message. As such, it threatened the written record and intruded on social customs. By the end of his life, Bell came to bristle at the invasions made by the telephone, admonishing members of his family who got up from the dinner table to answer its ring.

Political leaders had similar cause to fear the telephone, for here was an instrument that could spread information without regard for government control. Soon after the Russian Revolution, Joseph Stalin rejected a proposal from Leon Trotsky to build a modern telephone system. "It will unmake our work," he said. "I can imagine no greater instrument of counter-revolution in our time." Communism needed too many gatekeepers for the free flow of information, and technological advancements made it difficult for government agents to listen in. From Stalin's time forward, the telephone directory was unpublished in the Soviet Union. It provided a measure of freedom too tempting for the Communist regime to tolerate. Indeed, as improvements came in telephone technology, the Soviet Union and Warsaw Bloc remained on the sidelines, cut off from the pulse of modern communication. So crippling—or prescient—was Stalin's decision that the East Bloc lost a generation of technology. When political barriers came down in the 1990s, the technology that Stalin rejected had changed, and many Eastern European countries elected to leapfrog the gap in their history, rejecting the expense and labor of installing land-line phones, going straight to cellular wireless equipment.

But when the telephone was new, Stalin was not alone in his fears. "It is difficult," wrote *The Providence Press* after watching Bell demonstrate the telephone in 1877, "to resist the notion that the powers of darkness are in league with it." The world of literature was no kinder in greeting the telephone than it had been in welcoming the telegraph. Mark Twain, in an 1890 article for *The New York World*, set the tone with a sarcastic holiday greeting. "It is my heart-warm and world-embracing Christmas hope and aspiration that all of us—the high, the low, the rich, the poor, the admired, the despised, the loved, the hated, the civilized, the savage—may eventually be gathered together in a heaven of everlasting rest and peace and bliss—except the inventor of the telephone." There is reason to believe, based on later correspondent with Bell's father-in-law, Gardiner Greene Hubbard, that Mark Twain was kidding. Robert Louis Stevenson was not. The poet complained in 1889 that the telephone had invaded "our bed and board, our business and bosoms, bleating like a deserted infant." The elite preferred privacy. The telephone violated certain social norms, eliminating one of the layers of protection that kept the upper classes from dealings with the less educated. In popular culture, this equalizing power of the telephone was memorialized in hit songs like "Hello Central, Get Me Heaven." For diplomats, this ability to patch through to any source, even the rarefied home of the angels, was an invasion to be avoided.

Diplomats were wary of the new technology's impact, fearing that the telephone, like the telegraph before it, would force them to become message-carriers instead of policy makers. British diplomat Arthur Buchanan, some fifteen years before the telephone was invented, was asked to assess how the telegraph had influenced the diplomatic corps. "It reduces, to a great degree, the responsibility of the minister," he told a parliamentary committee in 1861. "For he can now ask for instructions instead of doing a thing on his own responsibility." This shift of power, from the field to the capital, from the envoy to the leader, was even more pronounced with the telephone.

To this day, it is not uncommon to hear professional diplomats lament their loss of autonomy at the end of a telegraph cable or secure telephone line. Former Secretary of State Lawrence Eagleburger, in a 1993 interview, bemoaned Washington's ability to dictate his negotiating tactics when, during the Persian Gulf War, he went to Israel to convince Prime Minister Yitzhak Shamir not to retaliate against Iraq for Scud missile attacks. Washington wanted to keep Israel out of the conflict, fearing that her direct involvement would upset the delicate coalition of Arab and Christian nations arrayed against Iraq. But Israel had a policy of retaliating, always, and if Shamir was going to break with that precedent, he needed something to show for it.

Eagleburger did not think the package he was carrying from Washington would convince Shamir. When the Israeli prime minister balked at Eagleburger's offer, the U.S. diplomat returned to the embassy and alerted Washington, urging the president's top foreign-policy advisers to sweeten the deal with pledges not only to retaliate on Israel's behalf, but to share defense intelligence. In an earlier day, Eagleburger might have been able to make that deal without conferring first with his capital. "They caved, but it took an extra twenty-four hours," he said, referring perhaps as much to the Americans as to the Israelis. It is interesting, and ironic, that in this case the speed of the new technology actually delayed the decision, in Eagleburger's view, because it allowed Washington to second-guess his moves and encroach on his autonomy.

In any event, the complaint from diplomats was not only that the new technology robbed them of autonomy over governmental decisions. The real trauma, from their point of view, was that the telephone bypassed them altogether, vesting power completely in any foreign leader who chose to dial a counterpart. In May 1940, when Winston Churchill became Britain's prime minister, Franklin Roosevelt installed a direct telephone circuit between the White House and 10 Downing Street, precisely to bypass the "traditional, time-consuming, diplomatic channels." Though it was a primitive forerunner of the more sophisticated systems to come, the FDR–Churchill line had the same effect as its successor networks. It circumvented the middleman, the diplomat, who not only lost a voice in the deliberations but suffered the further ignominy, often, of having to reconstruct conversations after the fact, for the written record on which both bureaucracy and history depended. Roosevelt and Churchill rarely used the phone, preferring to confer in person in secret visits, but the telephone was their insurance against misrepresentation by functionaries. To their aides, the phone was a fearsome instrument, one that opened the door to freelancing of policy at the top that would have to be cleaned up at the bottom.

Diplomats had another reason to resist the telephone, one that is rooted in a historic understanding of the dangers of haste. Speed—the kind of instantaneous communication made possible by the telephone—is not an advantage in diplomacy, as it is in journalism or war. Speed is the enemy, hastening decisions, locking in initial reactions, minimizing room for negotiation. In journalism and war, there is no substitute for speed. In diplomacy, there is no cure for it. Diplomats understand, as few professions outside the lawyers' bar, the strategic importance of delay. There is even an adage among diplomats, "Time is on the side of diplomacy."

No better example exists than what is known to American historians as the Trent Affair. This Civil War chapter of diplomatic success began with the arrest by Northern agents of James Mason and John Slidell, two Confederate envoys sailing aboard the British ship *Trent* to get recognition and aid from the Europeans. The British press, outraged by their arrest on the neutral territory of the high seas, clamored for Britain to enter the war against the North, a move that might well have changed the outcome of that conflict. The U.S. ambassador to Britain, Charles Francis Adams, the son of President John Quincy Adams, who was respected in London despite his support for the Northern cause, convinced government officials that the arrest of Mason and Slidell was a freelance operation, not authorized or sanctioned by Washington. In fact, sentiment ran high in the North for the two to be hanged, with Massachusetts governor John Andrew remarking that Benedict Arnold was a saint compared to Mason and Slidell. Secretary of War Edwin Stanton spoke for many when he said, "Hang Mason and Slidell first and apologize to Great Britain afterwards."

Adams knew that it would take twenty days to get a message from Washington to London through the mails, and that he could use the time to calm tempers on his side of the Atlantic. To his relief, President Lincoln used the time to similar advantage, convincing his cabinet on Christmas Day to release the pair on grounds that the Union could fight only "one war at a time." Delay had given Adams and Lincoln time for maneuvering, and they used it adroitly. The telephone would have threatened this exquisite use of delay to calm tempers. Had London been able to call Washington directly, the outrage of the moment might have changed policy. It could also, of course, have cleared the air, one reason historians have often said that if there had been an Atlantic Cable in place, the speed of a telegraph might have prevented the War of 1812. In any event, the telephone, unlike the telegraph, hastened the call of emotion. Diplomats worried at its ring.

Not so the military. To the men in uniform, delay in the delivery of messages had historically proved deadly, and the speed afforded by the telephone was especially appealing. Ground fighting continued in the Philippines for four days after a peace treaty was signed to end the Spanish-American War, in part because Commodore George Dewey had cut the telegraph cable lines from Manila to Hong Kong. He severed communication so Spanish commanders could not confer with their superiors in Madrid, but this strategic move also prevented him from cabling news of his victory at Manila for more than six days. Speed of information was the great ally of the military, which embraced the telephone as it had the telegraph. Like the runner who sped 26 miles and 385 yards to bring news that the Greeks had defeated the Persians at Marathon in 490 B.C.—only to die of exhaustion after delivering his message—the military was willing to pay dearly for quick, accurate information.

The telephone was also, of course, an elixir for journalism, which thrived on speed and was at once seized with the possibilities of this oral connection. The first newspaper to get a story by telephone was *The Boston Globe*. A stringer for the *Globe* was on hand on February 12, 1877, when Alexander Graham Bell lectured in Salem, Massachusetts. He telephoned an account of the speech to the labs in Boston, where Bell's partner, Thomas A. Watson, repeated it to another *Globe* reporter, A. B. Fletcher. Not shy about advertising its feat with this new technology, the *Globe* showcased the event in its headline: SENT BY TELEPHONE. THE FIRST NEWSPAPER

DESPATCH [*sic*] SENT BY A HUMAN VOICE OVER THE WIRES. The press was an easy convert. "The sensation felt in talking through eighteen miles . . . leaves the spiritual seance back in primeval darkness," proclaimed *The Providence Star* in one of many editorials smitten with the telephone's charms.

To unaccustomed ears, there was magic—and perhaps the devil—in hearing the human voice, much as there was in first witnessing the human image. But the novelty was short-lived. As telegraph costs mounted, savvy newspaper publishers had correspondents telephone and read their copy instead of sending it by cable. The Reuters agency in London—whose founder, Julius Reuter, began his fascination with media in the 1840s by using carrier pigeons to deliver news of Brussels stock markets to German businesses—served local newspapers in London as early as the 1880s by phoning in brief items for their use. In the United States, the Associated Press used a "pony service," where an editor at an AP bureau would read a news story at dictation speed to editors at several newspapers, all hooked up by telephone, and they wrote down the details by notes or shorthand or on a typewriter. Within a few years of its introduction, the telephone became an indispensable part of journalism, "Get me Rewrite!" becoming the battle cry of the traveling correspondent. It reached its tragic climax on November 22, 1963, when Merriman Smith of the United Press International, traveling in the front seat of a pool car provided by Southwestern Bell and equipped with a mobile radio telephone, refused to relinquish the telephone to Jack Bell of the Associated Press, who was riding in the backseat. Smith's bulletin—"Three shots were fired at President Kennedy's motorcade today in downtown Dallas"—was the world's first knowledge of the events in Dallas.

The first news of Abraham Lincoln's assassination had similarly reached Europe from the Reuters wire two hours ahead of any other source, leading many to believe the story a hoax started by stock-exchange speculators. This was the benchmark that the telephone left for history: that it took some days for news of Abraham Lincoln's assassination to travel to the remotest parts of the world, hours for news of Kennedy's death to make the same journey to all the corners of the earth. This was hardly the expected bequest, though many outsized predictions had been made for the telephone. *Scientific American*, whose masthead proclaimed it "the most popular scientific paper in the world," predicted in 1880 that the telephone would create "nothing less than a new organization of society—a state of things in which every individual, however secluded, will have at call every other individual in the community, to the saving of no end of social and business complications, of needless goings to and fro, of disappointments, delays and a countless host of those great and little evils and annoyances which go so far under present conditions to make life laborious and unsatisfactory."

For his part, Bell thought the instrument could be used for one-way speech, for entertainment, a function later provided by radio. But his motives were less to make a social revolution than to assist the deaf. Bell, a teacher of the deaf, began experimenting with what he called the harmonic telegraph at least in part to reach his mother, Eliza Grace Symonds Bell, who could hear only with the help of an ear tube. He also hoped to communicate with his pupil, Helen Keller, who dedicated her book to "Alexander Graham Bell, who has taught the deaf to speak and enabled the listening ear to hear," and with his wife, Mabel Gardiner Hubbard, who had been deaf since she fell ill at the age of five with scarlet fever. His devotion to the deaf did not, however, lessen his interest in the telephone as an instrument that could democratize everyone within its reach. "Someday all the people of the

United States will sing 'The Star-Spangled Banner' in unison by means of telephone," he remarked.

From Bell's dreams to Stalin's fears, this was the telephone's reputation, that it could bypass the ill intentions of war and spread news of peace. In terms of telephone diplomacy, Bush's conversation with Defense Secretary Dick Cheney, five days after the Iraqi invasion of Kuwait, was far more instructive. Cheney phoned in from Jedda, Saudi Arabia, to report that King Fahd had agreed to invite U.S. troops to Saudi soil to protect the kingdom, the keeper of Islam's holiest shrines, from a feared attack by Iraq. Cheney asked for formal orders to begin the massive deployment of troops, to which Bush is said to have replied, "You go it. Go."

It is hard to imagine a faster start-up for the movement of 120,000 troops some 7,000 miles in distance than the telephoned response, "You got it. Go." For a hyperactive leader, this extension of informality into the slow-moving wheels of international relations was a natural. For international relations, it was a milestone. But none of it was dictated by the telephone, only facilitated by phone communication. If Cheney had been forced to cable for instructions, and to await a reply in kind, and then relay the news to the Pentagon, the deployment might have been delayed for an hour, maybe days. But in the end, Bush's decision was political, not technological. The telephone did not dictate policy, and even Cheney's call did not force the decision. Policy was set between phone calls, in Washington, in the Cabinet Room, and the Oval Office. One reason Secretary of State James Baker rarely remained on an overseas trip for more than ten days at a time was his instinct that power flows in the halls where power resides, that command decisions are not often made at the long-distance end of a telephone. Bush gave the telephone a workout in his leader-to-leader approach to coalition building, using personal connections to press his points. But nations go to war for territory or indignation, for turf or morality, for national interest or self-interest. They rarely go to war because someone called.

When Yeltsin called out from the encircled Russian White House, he was using the fastest technology available. But there can be no doubt that if the only means of communication available were the carrier pigeon, Yeltsin would have exploited it. To be sure, messages carried by bird might have slowed the response time, and a slowed response might have given the coup plotters the upper hand for a while, perhaps even forced military intervention by NATO—something foreign ministers were reviewing in Brussels when the coup collapsed. But the intent of the players would not have changed, nor would history have judged them any differently. Political decisions, even ones as global as the life and death of an empire, were speeded by the telephone, not made by it.

In coming years, the telephone line is expected to move beyond its legacy in war to serve in cyberspace, one of the venues that will allow consumers to use their computers like television sets or their phones like computers, giving diplomats yet another tool to use or ignore. For now, the telephone has become an integral part of diplomacy and war. From an invention mocked by critics as impossible, and worse, impractical, the telephone has become a symbol of power and status, even nationhood. In the agreement on interim rule between Israel and the Palestine Liberation Organization, one little-noticed provision gave Palestinians a separate telephone area code. "It was a point of some contention," said one Israeli diplomat. "They wanted it as a symbol of statehood. For the same reason, we did not want to give it." The telephone, once an instrument of the few, feared by the elite, had become a symbol of nationhood for a wandering people in search of their roots.

The telephone, with its connection to the human voice, also promised to link the senses. Seeing the telephone in operation in Hungary in 1898, Arthur Mee, a journalist who became editor of the *Children's Encyclopedia*, predicted picture phones—and nirvana. "If, as it is said to be not unlikely in the near future, the principle of sight is applied to the telephone as well as that of sound, earth will be in truth a paradise, and distance will lose its enchantment by being abolished altogether." In recent years, in government capitals like Washington where distance can slow decisions, videoconferencing has boomed. But when Mee saw the telephone, he likely had in mind something more ethereal than a group of White House officials conferring with their counterparts in the State Department, the Pentagon, and the CIA to save the trouble of a cab ride across town. He no doubt had in mind a medium that would lift the spirits and combine the wonders of sight and sound. They called it film.

8

Film and the Global Village

I N December 1895, when Louis and Auguste Lumière first projected moving images onto the walls of the basement Salon Indien at the Paris Grand Café on Boulevard des Capucines, few were willing to pay one franc for the privilege of watching moving pictures. Within a few months, however, word of the magic spread and film became enormously popular around the world. "It was as if people were standing in line to go to the movies even before the technology of projection was developed," observed one film historian. There was something about film that appealed to the spiritual. More than a cold photograph, film conveyed the passion of movement. Less than a printed book, it filled in the places where imagination once lived alone.

Seven years before the Lumière brothers demonstrated the *cinematographe*, Thomas Alva Edison used rolls of coated celluloid to make the kinetoscope, for peep-show viewing, a forerunner of film. It is now widely believed that W.K.L. Dickson, one of Edison's employees, actually invented the kinetograph, but it is Edison who knew what they were looking for, who set out to "devise an instrument which should do for the eye what the phonograph does for the ear." Recognizing the potential of the kinetoscope—but not wanting to pay Edison's prices—Louis's father, Antoine, inventor of an early photographic plate, asked his son to create something like the American film machine. Lumière did Edison and Dickson one better, combining the camera with the projector. In the later conflicting claims and lawsuits over parenthood of this new technology (the inventor of the phonoscope sued the Lumières for having stolen his idea), Louis Lumière was characteristically blunt. "Other machines may have preceded mine," he said, "but they didn't work."

Work it did, in all the ways familiar to a new media technology. Because it was silent, film, like the photograph, at first erased national boundaries and native languages. "Lumière's *cinematographe* suddenly made the world a smaller and more ordinary place," wrote one admirer. "For a while at least it appeared as though mankind had become a Prometheus who could cheat the gods with impunity." Poets wrote of a shrinking world, commentators marveled at the speed of new fashions and trends, Sigmund Freud discovered the import of dreams. Reviewers even remarked that film allowed man to overcome death. "Now that we can photograph our loved ones, not only in stillness but as they move, as they act, as they make familiar gestures, as they speak, death ceases to be absolute." The new technology had speed and a novelty, the wonder of moving images. It seemed to transcend time and space, and reduce the world to a global village. And like the other technologies, film at first inspired resistance from those with the most to lose, in this case actors who feared its intrusion would strip business and patronage from the theater. By 1910, the German provincial town of Hildesheim reported losing 50 percent of its theater customers to the movies, and intellectuals grasped at the statistic as verification of their concerns. Theater was art, in the view of the critics, whereas this new medium, well, film was for the masses.

They were not alone in fearing the impact of the moving

pictures. Like the other technologies, film was a death knell to the middleman, a curb on incumbent political power, and a potent shaper of public opinion. Woe to the policy maker who failed to understand that film gave the audience a policy role. Czar Nicholas II, who is said to have enjoyed the movies for himself, disdained their use for his citizens. "I consider that cinematography is an empty matter, which no one needs," he said. "Only an abnormal person could place this farcical business on the level of art." Nicholas did not object when the Lumière brothers sent a cameraman, Camille Cerf, to Moscow to film the czar's coronation, but the czar banned all films showing executions of crowned subjects. He did not mind when cinematographers showed him meeting with foreign dignitaries, but he prohibited all footage of strikes and labor conditions. More than a century after Grigori Potempkin built false-front villages to please Catherine the Great as she toured the Ukraine and the Crimea, Nicholas was demanding similar obeisance from the filmmakers. Cinema verité was for the French. In Russia, Nicholas wanted a version of reality that reflected only his majesty.

Here was a classic dissonance between a leader and his subjects, an attitude of moral superiority that was one of the factors assuring that Nicholas would be the last czar of the Russian Empire. Nicholas failed to understand that film, like the other technologies, gave more voice to citizens. They voted with their eyes, electing which movies to see and which to shirk, which to belittle and which to believe. George Buchanan, the British ambassador to Moscow, urged Nicholas in January 1917 to "break down the barrier that separates you from your people and . . . regain their confidence." But Nicholas, who after the failures of World War I was forced to abdicate and who was later executed by the Bolsheviks, was an imperialist who did not understand such a democratic impulse. Staring at Buchanan dubiously, he asked, "Do you mean that I am to regain the confidence of my people, or that they are to regain my confidence?" Despite his blindness to the need to court public opinion, Nicholas might have been somewhat assuaged to know that the Bolsheviks who killed his family in the name of revolutionary justice would make the same mistake, on a far grander scale.

As a communication medium, film was sensual and serious all at once. Appealing to the senses, it gave moving reality to the visual, and heightened power to the audible. In its awesome combination of sight and sound, film posed a severe temptation for the political world. This was a medium that could lift the spirits, fool the mind, harden the heart. To those who guarded public diplomacy, film was as dangerous as it was alluring. In the history of international affairs, film has been used as one of the most potent weapons of democracies and totalitarian states alike. Film may have given the audience more of a voice, but it also gave the skilled policy maker and faithful filmmaker more power to mold reality to their own tastes. Like photography, this visual medium opened the door to manipulation of the image in the cause of swaying public opinion. In time of war, film offered the ultimate weapon. Providing entertainment with a message, it could stiffen the resolve of soldiers in combat while rallying the troops at home. Not only did film allow for wider dissemination of views, it also offered a chance to create illusion. Few could resist the allure.

And in the political world, few understood its charms as well as Adolf Hitler, who in 1938 saw that "the masses need illusion—but not only in theaters or cinemas. They've had all they can take of the serious things in life." Hitler used film to perpetuate illusion, instill loyalty, invigorate patriotism. This too was film's legacy to the democracies that fought Hitler with everything they had, including movies and newsreels. But in the battle for public opinion that is often waged alongside war, the Allies had a difficult time competing with the heavy hand of Nazi propaganda. Hollywood's illusions on-screen vied with someone else's reality in newsprint, clashed with another view expressed on radio.

Both sides enjoyed a wartime censorship that cloaked information in mystery and delay, but the Allies knew they could not guard secrets indefinitely. In the Third Reich, the penalty for listening to a BBC radio broadcast from London was death. In New York, one could regularly tune in to hear Lord Haw Haw deriding the latest Allied proclamation. In film too, the Allies were often at a disadvantage, unable to control the whole of the message, able only to influence the audience at a single screening. To Hitler, an inability to control the whole message was intolerable. "As soon as by one's own propaganda even a glimpse of right on the other side is admitted, the cause for doubting one's own right is laid," he wrote in *Mein Kampf*. To the West, the key to effective propaganda was more soft sell. "Propaganda, to be effective, must be believed," Vice President Hubert Humphrey put it many years after the war. "To be believed, it must be credible. To be credible, it must be true." This is the great divide in the history of film's intersection with diplomacy and war, whether film mirrors truth or illusion, whether filmed propaganda should be sugarcoated or force fed, whether leadership in an age of film can compete with its power to cast spells.

The first test of this new medium's influence came not in the Russian court of Czar Nicholas II but in the Soviet system that came after him. One of the founders of the Bolshevik revolution, Vladimir Ilyich Lenin, proclaimed in February 1922 that "for us, the most important of all arts is the cinema." When Lenin issued this view of film, only two out of every five adults in his nation could read. It was no accident that Lenin entrusted the job of organizing a movie industry to his wife, Nadezhda Krupskaya, and put the movie industry under the education department, believing as he did that film was key to the reeducation of a country, to converting the peasants from farmers to believers. Sending trains to the countryside with propaganda shorts called *agitki*, Lenin achieved what Nicholas could only have imagined. Within a few years, "the number of peasants who recognized Lenin and Trotsky exceeded the number of those who had ever seen a picture of the deposed czar." Film had done for Vladimir Lenin and Leon Trotsky what the photograph did for Abraham Lincoln and Theodore Roosevelt: It personalized leadership. In putting a face on revolution, film cemented the association between image and power. It gave legitimacy to those who had challenged authority.

In a 1922 letter to the film department, Lenin urged "the proper proportion of films of amusement and films of propaganda." His view was that educational films would be easier to digest if paired with entertainment. The entertainment films that Lenin envisioned could not, of course, contain obscenity or counterrevolutionary ideas, but Lenin wanted filmmakers to have "within these limitations, broad initiative." As for the propaganda itself, he believed it was at its most believable when presented as news. "The production of new films, permeated with Communist ideas, reflecting Soviet actuality, must begin with newsreels," he proclaimed. He showed a certain sophistication about methods. During the Soviet famine of 1922, Lenin thought the best propaganda would not be films with promises of bounty as a future reward for hard work, but newsreels of starvation in Berlin.

Lenin died in 1924, and his successor, Joseph Stalin, was a hard-sell man. Historian Peter Kenez writes that "the ordinary peasants and workers knew full well that collective farms and factories did not in the least look like those depicted by the directors, but Stalin did not know and did not want to know." In fact, Stalin knew well enough that his own policy of deliberate starvation for kulaks who resisted collectivization had led to the man-made famine in the Ukraine and the Caucasus. He knew well enough that his own edict had subjected Soviet citizens twelve years of age and up to eight years in a labor camp for stealing corn or potatoes. But Kenez is right about one thing: Stalin wanted to purge reality from the screen. By the late 1930s, when Stalin was ordering the execution of enemies and intellectuals and other potential troublemakers, he looked to film to validate his vision. He sided with those who favored illusion, and who thought they could make it become reality with total control over information. "The primary social role of films in the age of Stalin was not to portray reality but to help to deny it." This was the temptation for any leader, dictator or democrat, to see in the movies the justification for policy, to change the mirror to fit the times. The challenge was to manipulate the image without denying the truth, to make the visual a weapon of leadership but not an illusion.

Film also divided debate within the journalistic community, between those who saw its promise as a tool of news and those who derided its potential for illusion. In the breach came the newsreel, a stepchild of cinema and of journalism that neither community fully embraced, or much remembers. Usually aired before an entertainment movie, the newsreel in the United States was a pivotal link between the battlefields of two world wars and the home front. Critics sniffed that it was not exactly news. Re-creating scenes and filming others, producers brought viewers their vision of the San Francisco fire, the eruption of Mount Vesuvius, the Battle of San Juan Hill. Eight or nine items were spliced into a ten-minute reel, each subject separated by a title, a musical score, and a narration. American humorist Oscar Levant called the newsreel "a series of catastrophes followed by a fashion show."

For all the critics' complaints, newsreels were a power in

journalism—and a huge hit with audiences. By 1938, one observer claimed that in the United States, "the average citizen acquired most of his news through the medium of pictures." Estimates were that American newsreels were seen weekly by at least 40 million Americans and by more than 200 million worldwide. Such was the audience for moving-picture news that some theaters, like the Trans-Lux in Washington and Telenews in Cleveland, aired newsreels continuously, without any movies. And audiences trusted what they saw. Radio knew such trust before Orson Welles's *War of the Worlds* broadcast sent frightened listeners outside looking for Martians. They felt foolish in the morning, and radio lost some of its credibility. Newsreels lost some of their edge too when producer John Grierson decided, for effect, to exaggerate the one-step jig that Hitler had performed in victory after France surrendered in 1940. Grierson, who coined the term *documentary*, repeated this single step over and over through a camera loop so that it made Hitler "look like a gleeful demon dancing on the grave of his enemies." Hitler may in fact have been gleeful in victory, but manipulating the film to fit the message meant that newsreels, if ever they had aspired to news, were now just movies by another name.

One name for a newsreel was *March of Time*, the newsreel series launched in 1935 by Henry Luce to add to his arsenal of news weapons. There was the news weekly *Time*, begun in 1923; the business magazine *Fortune*, opened in 1930. Yet to come were the picture magazine *Life*, started in 1936, and *Sports Illustrated*, launched in 1954. Unlike the newsreels already in the can, the *March of Time*, borrowing a page from *Time*, offered commentary, opinion, point of view. The series, based on a radio show of the same name, also boasted an enormous acting ensemble that could impersonate political officials, military leaders, and other public figures in the re-creation of news. Exact transcripts of news events were obtained, and, whenever possible, dialogue mimicked factual conversation. One person who objected to this impersonation was President Franklin Roosevelt, who disliked statements uttered on the radio by a man sounding very much like him, statements that he had never made. From its debut, the newsreel version of *March of Time* made no pretense of depicting an objective catalog of the week's news, instead holding, like *Time*, to a distinct point of view. In this, the editors of both the newsreel and the magazine had at least one objective in common with the massive Nazi propaganda machine: to make the newsreel convincing and realistic.

In its short U.S. history, from the first broadcast in 1911 to its last in 1967, the newsreel made a big impression. Produced by five companies, shown twice a week at more than 15,000 theaters in the country, the newsreel was effectively buried by a combination of punches—a Justice Department bust of film monopolies, and a new medium called television. But the death of newsreels does not negate the important role they played in diplomacy and war. During the major wars of the twentieth century, newsreels and even the movies were instruments of power. War, more than most other adventures of government, requires the force of public will. To marshal support at home and rally the troops abroad, to instill patriotism and court sacrifice, film was ideal.

In World War I, those who emerged victorious on the battlefield had also made the best use of film and newsreels to carry public opinion through to the end. Russians saw little of their own soldiers, as private companies were banned from going to the front to film the heroics of the Russian soldiers. Of government cameramen there were only five, two of them foreigners, with the result that "Russian moviegoers had a far better visual sense of the war on the western front than on the eastern [because] British and French newsreels kept on coming." At first, patriotic movies used re-creations and dramatizations, but as the war dragged on and casualties mounted, as it became clear that the war would not end well or quickly, audience appetite for war movies sagged. Russians in World War I wanted diversionary films, crime stories, melodrama. They'd had too much of war in "real" life to want any more of it on the screen.

Americans, by contrast, grew more interested in war as their own country neared battle. With the U.S. entry into war in 1917 came also the Committee on Public Information. Known as the Creel Committee for its chairman, journalist George Creel, this $5 million ministry "mounted a propaganda campaign that remains in some ways unsurpassed in the United States." They put up posters, issued pamphlets, and, at the suggestion of Chicago businessman Donald Ryerson, sent speakers into the theaters recently sprung up around the country to boost morale. Called "four-minute men" for the length of their talks (and to evoke the patriotism of the soldiers at Concord and Lexington), these speakers urged registration for the draft ("The man who stands back now is lost, lost to the ranks of citizenship, lost to the mother who bore him, lost to the father who gave him a name, lost to the flag that protects him"), the buying of Liberty Bonds (else the kaiser's soldiers would "goose-step along Pennsylvanian Avenue"), and the importance of conserving food to share with the Allies (because "if we fail them with our grubstake, they will starve").

Though the committee prided itself on running a positive effort—Creel titled his memoirs *How We Advertised America*—the war effort unleashed a new level of hate-mongering toward Germans. Films like *The Beast of Berlin* and *My Four Years in Germany* prompted anti-German race riots in some cities. President Woodrow Wilson, who established the Creel Committee two weeks after his declaration of war, was later much criticized for its excesses. Among the challenges to constitutional rights was the government's prosecution of movie producer Robert Goldstein. His crime was to make a Revolutionary War epic in which British soldiers were seen bayoneting women and children. The judge acknowledged that the British might well have committed such offenses, but argued the film might cause the public "to question the good faith of our ally, Great Britain." Goldstein was sentenced to ten years in jail (later reduced to three) and fined $5,000 under a Sedition Act, passed in 1918, making it a crime to say anything "scornful or disrespectful" of the government, the flag, the uniform—or the Constitution.

Despite its muzzle on the artistic expression guaranteed by the Constitution, or perhaps because of it, American movie propaganda in World War I was so effective in spreading anti-German feeling that the German high command saw the urgency of replying in kind. General Erich Ludendorff ordered all German film productions merged into one company, UFA, with the intention "to advertise Germany according to government directives." In making propaganda films to order, German authorities gave no heed to public opinion, a mistake not made by Americans, in their anti-German zeal, or Russians, in their escape entertainment. "The German authorities took it for granted that public opinion could be molded into any pattern they desired." They assumed that the public would believe anything on the screen. Here was the critical mistake of leadership, to confuse film's potential to move public opinion with its ability to dictate public perceptions of reality. Films can exaggerate the truth, they can fake events, they often leave a false impression. But films are rarely viewed in a vacuum. Leadership puts the context around information, even around propaganda. The Germans could show pictures of British or French soldiers being killed in their trenches, or German forces victorious on the eastern front, but with so many soldiers not returning home, with so many in retreat, it was not an easy sell. Perhaps, by Lenin's measure, they would have been better off showing pictures of starvation—in London.

By World War II, the Germans had gotten more sophisticated. Adolf Hitler personally commissioned Leni Riefenstahl to produce an artistic film, based on the Nazi Party Convention in Nuremberg in 1934, that would inspire generations of young Germans to close rank, join the party, salute the Fuehrer. Called *Triumph of the Will*, the film is a triumph in imagery. There were huge spectacles, giant parades, faces of ecstasy. "The cameras (by one account, the young director had an unlimited budget, 130 technicians and 90 cameramen) incessantly scan faces, uniforms, arms and again faces," searching for exuberance. Each frame dramatized the contrast to a staid order. Young men in uniform were seen marching against a backdrop of ancient stone buildings and curved architecture. Speeches were delivered with hand-pounding, emotional vigor. This was a movie for the home front, as Nazi propaganda chief Joseph Goebbels put it, a film "to win the heart of a people and keep it." But it was also exported for maximum effect to occupied Europe, where obedience to Nazi imperatives was a function of learned behavior. It was even entered at the 1935 Venice Film Festival.

Goebbels understood the need, in the run-up to war, for acceptance at home and familiarity abroad. Agreeing with Lenin that propaganda was better sandwiched around entertainment, he did not nationalize the industry before the war, reasoning that he might "empty the cinemas by demanding that every German film should henceforth become a work of propaganda." Like Lenin too, he believed that the hard sell should be reserved for newsreels, "all the more effective because they were screened in well-filled theaters primarily devoted to mass entertainment." In Goebbels's Enlightenment and Propaganda Ministry, the film section was one of the largest, with several hundred employees. From script approval to recasting, from cutting to special screenings, Goebbels kept tight control of German movies, while privately screening British and French films. His was a factory for "The Big Lie," the theory that film was best suited to sweeping exaggeration.

If *Triumph of the Will* was an appeal to the heart, Goebbels's newsreels strove to convince the mind—or at least quiet the doubts that thinking people might bring to the screen. Realism was the byword of Nazi newsreels, and the Germans were perfectionists. Film crews marched with the Third Reich troops, among them some of Germany's most talented cameramen. These were "regular soldiers, doing a soldier's full duty, always in the front lines," reported one observer. "This explains the realistic pictures which we show." Realism was seen as key to effective propaganda—if the war scene seemed real, the message would too—and the Goebbels machine did everything it could to buttress the impression of real battle in its newsreels. In a minor example, German censors on April 26, 1940, allowed a *New York Times* correspondent based in Berlin to report that twenty-three of Germany's newsreel cameramen had died at the front. Speed was another ally in this deception. Footage too long delayed did not have the same impact as fresh material. So airplanes flew film from the battlefield to the studios, where editors spliced and diced and made their tributes to German heroism, their predictions of German victory. Film trucks were then dispatched throughout Germany, where, the Propaganda Ministry decreed, newsreels were released everywhere on the same day. Diplomats abroad also made use of the newsreels, showing them to counterparts in Bucharest, Oslo, Belgrade, Ankara, Sofia, all in an effort to undermine resistance of foreign governments. Realism was a ferocious weapon to the Germans, who realized after the last war that it could also be turned to their advantage.

Americans had also learned from the earlier experience with war and information. A delayed and negative reaction to the rigid control of the Creel Committee made Hollywood reluctant to submit to censorship during the Second World War. It also made Washington sensitive to the need not to use a heavy hand, either in the movies or in the movie making. Diplomats found the new medium a trauma. "The motion picture industry is potentially the most valuable ally in the conduct of our foreign relations," Assistant Secretary of State William Benton later wrote. "Conversely, it is a first-class headache."

Before the war, when many Americans hoped to remain on the sidelines, interventionists like Secretary of War Henry Stimson lobbied for a government agency to churn out inspirational movies. Vice President Henry Wallace agreed, urging Franklin Roosevelt to borrow from Goebbels the heavy use of drama and emotion. Others in the administration, including presidential press secretary Steve Early, countered with a plea for government agencies to issue not emotional appeals but simple information. Fearing that outright propaganda would backfire, Early's camp trusted that the public, and the newspapers, would come around. By 1941, the prowar sentiment was prevailing in the newspapers, in the newsreels, in the movies. Public interest and opinion had coalesced around a policy of intervening in Europe, and Roosevelt, careful never to get out too far ahead of public opinion, knew when the Japanese bombed Pearl Harbor that support for war had finally become a majority opinion. Early's side had prevailed.

As a result, the Office of War Information, one of several agencies President Roosevelt created to handle information and propaganda flow during the war, set out "to convert Hollywood, not censor it." Elmer Davis, a radio correspondent tapped to head the OWI, explained it this way: "The easiest way to inject a propaganda idea into most people's minds is to let it go in through the medium of an entertainment picture, when they do not realize that they are being propagandized." The government wanted war posters in the background of scenes that had nothing to do with war, female soldiers moving through landscapes with no purpose other than to communicate that the whole nation was united in war. But, ironically, they did not want movies, like *The Devil with Hitler*, that made evil cartoon characters out of real enemies. They wanted movies that emphasized the reasons to stamp out the evil stalking Europe, that celebrated democracy and egalitarianism and the rights of man. Davis called it a "strategy of truth." It conflicted with Hollywood's tendency for overdramatization, for trivializing, for escapism. In a seven-point memo circulated to the studios, the OWI asked, "Does the picture tell the truth, or will the young people of today have reason to say they were misled by propaganda?"

No better example exists of the use of film to boost public support for war than the Allied defeat at Dunkirk. Electing to retreat and regroup to fight another day, Winston Churchill evacuated the British Expeditionary Force by ship and boat and all manner of conveyance from the shores of Dunkirk in Belgium back to Dover in England. They called the movie *Mrs. Miniver*, and it was an emotional tribute to the fishermen of England who set sail to save their soldiers from capture or death at German hands. The reality was not quite that romantic, particularly as it involved, in the early days, deceiving French allies who defended the perimeter while the British troops escaped. But the uplifting sight of an armada of little ships rescuing doomed soldiers fit the public mood and conformed to the British pride of resolve. In reality Dunkirk represented a disaster that might have been a total catastrophe if not for the bravery of British sailors. In newspapers and books, in newsreels and in *Mrs. Miniver*, it was "forged into the main armament of Britain's moral warfare." Prime Minister Winston Churchill worried whether future generations would think it propaganda. "We must be very careful not to assign to this deliverance the attributes of a victory," he told the House of Commons after more than 335,000 British and French troops had been shipped out. "Wars are not won by evacuations."

Just before 7 P.M. on May 26, 1940, orders came from London to inaugurate Operation Dynamo. Its mission was to evacuate British troops, which after advancing into Belgium, had become hopelessly surrounded by German forces. Unbeknownst to the French, who were also battling the Germans in Belgium, British naval officials had been developing evacuation plans for almost two weeks, ordering all small boats to register with the Admiralty, even arranging 80,000 gallons of canned drinking water to be buried near the beach where cold, thirsty, hungry, demoralized troops would wait to be brought across the channel from Dunkirk to Dover. With Luftwaffe aircraft firing from above, and Royal Navy ships unable to negotiate the sandy shores, the small craft were used to ferry men to the waiting battleships. Three days into the operation, the allies had rescued 72,000 British soldiers, and 655 French. When French officials finally learned of the evacuation, and the disparate numbers being saved, they were enraged, and political pressure from above soon tipped the statistics. In the end, a majority of both armies were evacuated, but some 40,000 French troops, the defenders of the Dunkirk border whose brave conduct allowed the others to escape, were left behind. Many of the more than 100,000 French troops who escaped from Dunkirk returned to Paris just in time to surrender to German troops, which, with their heavy panzers and automatic weapons, had abandoned the fleeing Allies in Belgium to make for the more strategically important French capital.

The British public was not informed of the evacuation until after 6 P.M. on May 31. The BBC, in a broadcast approved by military censors, set the tone with a report that "all night and all day men of the undefeated British Expeditionary Force have been coming home. . . . It is clear that if they have not come back in triumph, they have come back in glory; that their morale is as high as ever; that they know they did not meet their masters; and that they are anxious only to be back again soon—as they put it—'To have a real crack at Jerry.' " But when Churchill took to the floor of the House of Commons at mission's end, he did not soft-peddle the extent of the disaster.

In what is considered one of the most masterful speeches of the century, Churchill informed the nation of its reversal. He talked of the loss of 30,000 men, of the abandonment of 1,000 weapons and the country's entire fleet of armored carriers. He looked to the "new world" to save the old, and called on his countrymen to defend their island. "We shall fight on the beaches, we shall fight on the landing grounds, we shall fight in the fields and in the streets, we shall fight in the hills, we shall never surrender." His words have become immortalized as the classic statement of a will to fight. But the most remarkable aspect of the speech is not the call to arms, it is that Churchill did not mince words about the extent of the defeat. "What has happened in France and Belgium is a colossal military disaster," he said. Because of his candor, and his eloquence, the audience was free to accept a legend that an armada of little ships with average citizens had saved the British army to fight another day. If he had underplayed the disaster, if he had oversold the rescue, distrust would have been his legacy. The legend of *Mrs. Miniver* is the ultimate tribute to those who favored the "truth strategy" in wartime propaganda. In the worlds of diplomacy and war, only those who guarded against overt exploitation of images could be sure of victory. Even then, the distance was short between reality and distortion. The public had to be willing.

The White House was thrilled with Mrs. Miniver, and FDR ordered leaflets of the movie's stirring final speech air-dropped over Europe. The administration also urged Hollywood to produce "a Mrs. Miniver of China or Russia" so that American audiences could sympathize with the burdens of China's citizens in fighting off the Japanese, the suffering of the Russian people in bearing up to German assaults. As for the film's impact abroad, Churchill said it had helped Britain more than a fleet of destroyers. The next invention would do even more, bringing war to the front room as no technology had since the invention of the daguerreotype in the last century. To a new generation, Edward R. Murrow's sign-off, "This . . . is London," chilled the heart and annihilated all the bounds of time and space. With radio, hearing was believing.

9

Radio Goes to War

In November of 1913, Lee De Forest, self-proclaimed father of radio, went on trial in New York City for fraud. Specifically, the federal government was suing the North America Wireless Company on four counts of mail and stock fraud. More than 100 witnesses "from nearly every state in the Union" testified about how they had been "duped by misleading stock offerings, deceptive claims about accomplishments and false prophesies about future achievements." Of the $1.5 million the sale of the stock generated prosecutors claimed that only $345,000 had been used for company business, the rest being distributed to the four defendants: De Forest and his lawyer, Samuel Darby, and two company officers: President James Dunlop Smith and director Elmer E. Burlingame.

At the end of the six-week trial, an impassioned federal district attorney urged that the inventor be sent to the federal penitentiary. "De Forest has said in many newspapers and over his signature that it would be possible to transmit the human voice across the Atlantic before many years," the prosecutor thundered in abject outrage. "Based on these absurd and deliberately misleading statements, the misguided public, Your Honor, has been persuaded to purchase stock in his company, paying as high as ten and twenty dollars a share for the stock." After such a summation, a jury of twelve men, remarkably, split the decision, finding the two company officials guilty of swindling money but issuing verdicts of not guilty for De Forest and his attorney. As the verdict was read, De Forest "collapsed" in his lawyer's arms. His finances were in ruin, but his invention was intact. The judge, however, was not finished with the boastful inventor. In a homily he later regretted, the judge lectured De Forest "as though he were a cheat who had narrowly escaped well-deserved punishment," instead of an inventor cheated by his business partners. Showing no understanding for the invention's import, the judge urged De Forest to "get a common garden variety of job and stick to it."

The trial verdict was page-one news in the January 2, 1914, edition of the *New York Times*. But so too was a report that the U.S. Navy had sent a New Year's greeting from its powerful radio transmitters in Arlington, Virginia, to the Eiffel Tower in Paris, France. The prosecutor could belittle such "absurd" inventions as the wireless, the judge could dismiss the inventor as an out-of-work malcontent, but the public was tantalized by the new invention. By the time De Forest's trial ended, the United States boasted 122 wireless clubs, where amateurs experimenting with homemade devices, often in their garages, communicated "in the air, on a pre-arranged wavelength." Like computer devotees who in the mid-1990s reached out to each other on the Internet, these early pioneers of two-way radio were excited by the prospect of a new invention that annihilated time and space, erased borders, and made communication faster and more direct than ever before.

Radio came into its own as a force in society and journalism when its original usage for two-way communication via the dots and dashes of Morse code was supplanted by the one-way communication called broadcasting. *The Readers' Guide to Periodic Literature* put this change to 1919, when it shifted its category heading from "Wireless" to "Radio." Others had seen it earlier. In 1906, University of Pittsburgh engineer Reginald Fessenden experimented, playing "O Holy Night" on his violin and issuing holiday greetings to see if he could transmit sound across through the airwaves, to test "the public character of the medium by sending words of a general nature to a broad audience." They called it radio, suggesting the rays of electromagnetic waves radiating from a transmitter, and borrowed from agriculture the term *broadcasting*, where it meant spreading seed wide across a field. This field was vast. It is no accident that in the computer age, when consumers can reach across the Internet to pluck information from the ether, a new term has been coined, playing off the radio's promise: *broadcatching*. But in its day, when radio was new, it was a revolution. "Radio made a huge leap beyond the coded confines of the telegraph," wrote radio historian Tom Lewis. "The telegraph and telephone were instruments for private communication between two individuals. The radio was democratic; it directed its message to the masses and allowed one person to communicate with many."

On April 14, 1912, when the *Titanic* put out a distress signal, it was picked up by the Marconi operator on the *Carpathia*, which managed to rescue some 700 passengers. The signal was also picked up by a Russian immigrant named David Sarnoff, chief operator of a Marconi station recently opened atop the Wanamaker Building at Ninth and Broadway in New York, who relayed the information to anxious relatives. Not all the ships in the area had picked up the *Titanic's* SOS, and within a week the Senate Commerce Committee held hearings on a proposal that all ships "install powerful wireless equipment and staff it with operators at all times." Radio had evolved a great deal from the wireless telegraph invented in 1896 by Guglielmo Marconi in his father's vegetable garden. Amid the squash and tomatoes, Marconi learned to flash messages, using the Morse code, at a distance of more than a mile. Sarnoff, who rose to become general manager of the Radio Corporation of America (RCA), which absorbed the American Marconi Company, acknowledged later, "The *Titanic* disaster brought radio to the front, and also me."

By the spring of 1922, a "radio boom" was sweeping America. The press called it a fever, heating everything in its way. Sales of radio sets and parts totaled $60 million. The next year sales topped $136 million; by 1924, $358 million, bringing to 3 million the number of radio sets in the United States, with an estimated audience of 20 million listeners. "In all the history of inventing," exclaimed a typical editorial in *Outlook*, "nothing has approached the rise of radio from obscurity to power." Radio was booming in other parts of the world too, in Europe and Latin America particularly, but not in China, where rulers made it a crime to own a radio set, setting a pattern their successors in Beijing would follow by banning the computer-age printer and the satellite dish.

In 1993, when the ruling regime in Beijing confronted the question of modern technology, it did not ban the computer. Instead, China's Communist rulers merely prohibited the printer that would allow users to share information, that could connect the computer to the wider marketplace of ideas. They may have underestimated the ability of a computer, coupled with a telephone line, to put Chinese citizens in touch with the world, but they understood clearly that words were far more dangerous when they were widely disseminated.

It is almost impossible to comprehend, in the shadow of cyberspace, what a revolution this new medium of radio unleashed on the politics and international relations of its day. "Nothing in history has ever caught the fancy of the American people as did radio," M. H. Aylesworth, a utility-company executive who became the first president of the National Broadcasting Company, wrote in 1929. "Indeed, radio may eventually be the means of making our country what it was theoretically supposed to be when its government was established—an ideal democracy."

Like its predecessors, radio was a megaphone for people of conviction, but it also favored those without much to say who sounded pleasant. Radio was the C-SPAN of its generation, opening the door to political discourse, stripping away one of the layers that separated political leaders from their constituents. This voice personalization of politics began in 1924, the first year both major political parties broadcast their conventions. Democrat William Jennings Bryan called radio "a gift of Providence." Unknown to Jennings, many in the audience snickered at the self-importance of the speakers. "With millions of others I had been stirred by the dramatic broadcasts of the 1924 Democratic National Convention, which, it is said, had a longer run than *Abie's Irish Rose* and *South Pacific* combined," remarked one listener—and the *Saturday Evening Post* rejoiced that exposure would force long-winded orators to desist, a general "debunking of present-day oratory and the setting of high standards in public speaking." Observing the "inanities and inefficiencies of the conventions," *Century* magazine observed, "now millions of voters, as they turn the knob on their radios, are gaining a sense of the chaos and confusion of conventions." As C-SPAN stripped away the mystery of the congressional floor, so radio unveiled the chaos of conventions. "If no man remains a hero to his valet," *Century* commented, "certainly conventions will not remain statesmanlike assemblies to listeners at the radio."

Radio's hold on politics was formalized with Commerce Secretary Herbert Hoover's 1928 campaign. Hoover, "never a dynamic radio speaker," nevertheless took a liking to radio.

Perhaps the engineer in him enjoyed the novelty, or maybe the businessman in him saw the opportunity. Whatever the reason, Hoover was one of radio's biggest advocates, calling the new medium "an instrument of beauty and learning" and describing the wireless fever as "one of the most astonishing things that [has] come under my observation of American life." Even before his nomination, Hoover elected to try a new form of electioneering, "mostly on radio and through the motion pictures." His campaign manager proclaimed personal appearances a thing of the past. "Brief, pithy statements as to the positions of the parties and candidates which reach the emotions through the minds of millions of radio listeners will play an important part in the race to the White House," agreed the *New York Times*. This was "the 1928 version of the sound bite," required because "radio was changing the attention span of listeners, who were no longer willing to suffer overly long and fulsome speeches." With radio dogging political candidates, the average length of a campaign speech in the fall of 1928 fell from an hour's normal oratory to an average of ten minutes.

Like the judge who admonished De Forest for experimenting with the audion that made modern electronics possible, doubters and critics made clear their disdain. "Why should you have your last little remnant of privacy invaded by squeaks, howls, bad music and stupid speeches from which in real life you would flee as from seven plagues?" asked Bruce Bliven in *Century*. A British colleague was equally chagrined. "During the last twenty years we have seen how much can be done by newspapers alone in regimenting a country's brains," wrote Arthur Ransome in the *Manchester Guardian* in 1924. "This new instrument will be infinitely more effective." Ransome's real objection was that "you cannot answer back" to radio. "The band may play out of tune. You hiss in private impotence. He may be doing his best, but there is no need to ask you not to shoot at the pianist. You would only damage your own furniture." Ransome's prescription was to devise a button by which the audience could release "a small electric current" to "a tender part of the performer" if his material was not to the listeners' liking. What current-day operator of the television zapper would not welcome a similar invention?

Radio's arrival may have been decades in the making, but when it burst on the scene, it made fans everywhere. Listeners regularly placed a photograph of Franklin Roosevelt next to their radio sets while listening to the president's Fireside Chats. The wartime speeches of British prime minister Winston Churchill gave new vigor to oratory. "We shall never surrender," reads like a pathetic cliché in print, but "Nevvvvvvah . . . Surrender" is an expression rich in vibrant color on the radio. Most are numb to it now, except at special moments, when they hear the cadence of a funeral procession or the wail of a child abandoned on a Rwanda roadside, but the power of radio is pure. Many are the baseball fans who prefer their sport on radio to television, who like to hear the announcer set the players and prefer their own imaginations to the harsh light of color-perfect AstroTurf under a retractable roof. During the twenty-five-year Troubles between Irish Catholics and Protestants, British officials banned the voice of Gerry Adams of Sinn Fein, the Irish Republican Army's political wing, on government airwaves. It is evocative, this medium. It makes heroes. It honors the purity of the voice, and gives power to its message.

"Radio is the miracle of the ages," wrote one early devotee. "Aladdin's Lamp, the Magic Carpet, the Seven League Boots of fable and every vision that mankind has ever entertained, since the world began, of laying hold upon the attributes of the Almighty, pale into insignificance beside the accomplished fact of radio." To transmit the human voice, that was magic. To send it around the world "in less time than it takes to pronounce the word *radio*" was nothing short of miraculous. To those keeping track of time and space, "this latest marvel of modern science" had delivered again. "From the dawn of history, men have sought to solve the problem of intercommunication between persons separated by distance." Now they had radio. Oh how the enthusiasts gushed.

They saw radio as the currency of a new global village. Unlike the telephone, which linked individuals across vast distances in private conversations, radio linked an audience to an event. "Wireless telephony means that the billion and a half people living on this planet have been virtually gathered into one room where they can listen to one man's voice," wrote the *Independent*. "The human race has snuggled together like a family about a fireside on a cold evening and can chat with one another." They saw radio as an equalizer of classes. In Britain it was a "unifying factor in national life" that would allow everyone "opportunities for cultural enjoyments, such as music and drama, which were formerly denied to the poorer sections of the population." In the United States, "initially, the fascination of radio was its magical quality, its marvelous ability to generate sound from an apparently lifeless box, its capacity to allow even the most isolated soul to listen to the very best music or the finest orator, without moving from the comfort of the fireside."

Radio also afforded journalism a new experiment in speed and novelty. James Gordon Bennett, ambitious young publisher of the *New York Herald*, the man who sent reporter Henry M. Stanley (né John Rowlands) on a three-year expedition to locate Scottish explorer David Livingstone, was excited by the new technology. An avid yachtsman and balloonist, Bennett formed the Commercial Cable Company in 1883 in one of the first attempts (there were five attempts before success came in 1866) to lay a trans-Atlantic cable on the ocean floor. In 1899, he hired Marconi to report the results of the America's Cup by sailing a news boat alongside the competitors and calling in their times. The paper was not shy about advertising how it beat the competition, telling its readers: MARCONI'S WIRELESS TELEGRAPH TRIUMPHS and WIRELESS BULLETINS WORKED LIKE MAGIC. Marconi bulletins, as they were called, were posted all over the city, and the public was only about a minute behind the actual race. Now, eyeing the International Yacht Races in New York in 1901, Bennett, along with the Associated Press, hired the Marconi Company to repeat its tour de force.

But Lee De Forest, arguing that "my fame . . . my whole future" depended on it, was determined not to cede this territory to Marconi. Selling his wireless services to the Publishers Press Association, one of the AP's competitors, De Forest set up a race for the news that was the equal of the contest on the seas. As the yachtsmen made their way up river, so did the two news tugs. Not surprisingly, interference between electrical waves on the two ships canceled each other out. Not a discernible word was received onshore. This did not deter the New York newspapers who had paid for the service, of course, and they flagged their much-delayed news as "received by wireless telegraphy from tug following the yachts." De Forest was not deterred. "We gave Marconi a blacker eye than we ourselves received," he insisted.

For journalists, radio broadcasting was a new suitor, one that required a crisper hand with news copy. The radio was too omnipresent just to blare out the news. It required a broader appeal, a bit more drama. As a result, the wire services began to write separate stories for print and radio; one for reading, one for hearing. The United Press told its newspaper clients in April 1939, "Prime Minister Neville Chamberlain announced today that Great Britain had decided to conscript all men between the ages of 20 and 21 for six months of military training." On the same day, UP put out this news for its radio clients: "Great Britain cast off centuries of tradition today in a desperate move to preserve the delicately balanced peace of Europe. Prime Minister Chamberlain announced England will expand her army by compulsory military service. A bill will be introduced at once to conscript all men between 20 and 21 years of age for six months of training." Even after the advent of television, which claimed the mantle of drama from radio scripts, anchors often delivered the news so that reporters could evoke the feeling of an event.

Print journalists feared for their jobs—an echo of the sentiment heard by the turn of the twenty-first century when online computer services again threatened the newspaper—and cast doleful looks at this new creature. The wire services, under pressure from their newspaper clients, refused to allow radio stations to use their reports. In something of a short-lived temper tantrum, many newspapers refused to carry any radio-program listings. On Capitol Hill, newspapers used their influence to lobby Congress for strong regulatory legislation against radio. And at the White House, Walter Trohan of the *Chicago Tribune* looked down his nose at CBS White House correspondent John Charles Daly, complaining that Daly seemed more an actor than a reporter because "reporters play poker when they're not working and that man is off in the woods practicing lines from Shakespeare, listening to his own voice."

This is an antecedent of the disdain and arrogance that would greet CNN's arrival at the White House in the mid-1980s, when the upstart all-news network had to file a lawsuit to gain admission to the television networks' pool coverage. CNN knocked on the door soon after Ronald Reagan arrived at the Oval Office. Wishing to cover the White House, CNN applied to be part of the "pool" rotation with the other American networks, ABC, CBS, and NBC. The Big Three refused, horrified at this upstart network from Atlanta with the audacity to attempt twenty-four-hour-a-day news, and concerned about the quality of the camera work at what they called the Chicken Noodle Network. CNN filed a lawsuit to force admission to this haughty club of Washington insiders. The White House is a stage for new media, and newcomers are perceived as a threat. Radio had a gruff reception, too.

The new medium earned its stripes—within the profession and without—during World War II. Edward R. Murrow is remembered still in newsrooms throughout the world, with his calm delivery, his poignant pauses, his ability to bring the battlefront to the home front. Radio did not win the war; it brought it home. Reuven Frank, former head of NBC News, has said often that if Murrow had been a tenor instead of a baritone, President Roosevelt might have had trouble selling his war policies to a nation intent on noninvolvement. True, there was a richness to the timber of Murrow's voice, but also in his copy. "He knew intuitively that radio was made for something beyond merely transmitting the human voice." He knew that content mattered. He believed in the message more than the medium, arguing that "the only way to judge broadcasting is by what issues forth from your receiving set."

Mostly, he believed in bringing listeners with him. "I like the House of Commons best. I like to sit in that rather dingy little room, listen to speeches and debates, then jump in a cab, go up to the studio, and try to take Americans right through the window and into the room." His attitude was best summed up by an encounter he had with J.C.W. Reith, the imposing father of the British Broadcasting Company. Receiving Murrow on his arrival in London, Reith laid down his expectations, trusting that under Murrow's stewardship CBS would become a little more intellectual. "On the contrary," replied Murrow, "I want our broadcast programs to be anything but intellectual. I want them to be down to earth, in the vernacular of the man on the street." Reith complained, "Then you will drag radio down to the level of Hyde Park Speakers' Corner." Murrow must have smiled. "Exactly," he replied, "and literally. I also plan to broadcast from English pubs."

That Murrow achieved his objectives is a tribute to his character, and his timing. Any who claim that the news media in the last years of the twentieth century have too much influence, who argue that news organizations in the satellite era are drunk on power, who lament that individual reporters have too much sway on policy decisions of state, all of these latter-day apostles of media doom would do well to listen to Edward R. Murrow describe the impact of German bombing on British morale. "As the Germans massed on the English Channel, Americans began to hear, night after night, a voice from London. Murrow—calm, never arguing, never urging an opinion—began to refer to himself as 'this reporter.' He narrated—and in so doing, had historic impact."

Murrow, on the aftermath of a bombing raid on London during the blitz: "About an hour after the 'all-clear' had sounded, people were sitting in deck chairs on their lawns, reading the Sunday papers. The girls in light, cheap dresses were strolling along the streets. There was no bravado, no loud voices, only a quiet acceptance of the situation. To me those people were incredibly brave and calm. They are the unknown heroes of this war."

Murrow, on watching bombs fall on German soil from a U.S. plane: "My mind went back to the time I had crossed that coast in 1938, in a plane that had taken off from Prague. Just ahead of me sat two refugees from Vienna, an old man and his wife. The copilot came back and told them that we were outside German territory. The old man reached out and grasped his wife's hand. Last night was a massive blow of retribution for all those who have fled from the sound of shots and blows on the stricken continent."

Murrow, on viewing the concentration camp at Buchenwald: "There was a German trailer which must have contained another fifty [bodies], but it wasn't possible to count them. The clothing was piled in a heap against the wall. It appeared that most of the men and boys had died of starvation; they had not been executed. But the manner of death seemed unimportant. Murder had been done at Buchenwald."

It may be an exaggeration to suggest, as CBS newscaster Eric Sevareid did in his memoirs, that Murrow "was of far greater influence than the American ambassador to London." What is true is that when Edward R. Murrow broadcast from London, war came closer. To listen to those broadcasts now is to know that CNN in its day has no more power to convey emotion on satellite television than Murrow did on a radio in 1943. But in neither case did the message or the messenger outweigh the actions of those duly elected. The media can impact the agenda, even steer public opinion, but wars are won by leaders.

Radio changed journalism, made it crisper and more action-oriented. After the United States entered the war, Murrow accompanied a flight crew in a bombing run over Berlin. Describing the bombs as "white cookies floating down to a velvet canvas," he interjected the visceral in ways unimaginable on television. As the plane bent its wing for a final descent, Murrow mused, "I decided that all men could be brave, as long as they left their stomachs home." There was an image that stuck to the ribs.

Like Murrow, Franklin Delano Roosevelt understood the magic and the power of radio. His language was not as mellifluous as that of Winston Churchill, whose eloquence lifted the spirits of a nation. His delivery was not as exciting as that of Father Conglin, the Midwestern preacher who inveighed against big business and "Jewish conspiracies." His resources were not as great as those afforded Goebbels, who employed a team of radio engineers to make Hitler, whose voice on its own sounded "colorless, uninteresting and at the same time overexcited" into a radio personality. Goebbels had a Nazi Propaganda Ministry that, by mid-1933, employed 500 staffers and 300 officials in 9 departments, one just for radio. Germans were prohibited by the Goebbels agency from listening to foreign radio. The penalty was death. Against such odds, what FDR had was an intuitive sense of timing, a sense of decorum. He understood that radio was an invasion into a private home, and he acted always as a polite guest who tried to earn his welcome by being engaging without being a bore. The radio networks wanted to air him every week, but he declined. He understood, as one media historian put it, that "people can't stand repetition of the highest note on the scale for very long."

Roosevelt came to radio early in his career, while he was governor of New York. In some sense, radio served to mask his disability, to hide the leg irons that were a reminder of the 1921 attack of polio that had left him partially paralyzed. In a more traditional sense, radio was for FDR what it would be for many others: a path to navigate over the heads of the elite, the opinion makers, the press, directly to the public. At first he was not masterful, speaking too quickly, and to a small audience. But from the beginning he understood the need to make simple the complex. Fighting with the state legislature in Albany in 1929 for control over the budget, Governor Roosevelt decided to issue a series of radio "reports" that were really talks advocating his position. "Speaking in simple, uncomplicated language, he persuaded his listeners of the justice of his position. A flood of letters descended upon the offending lawmakers after each talk."

By the time Roosevelt was sworn in as the thirty-second

president of the United States, he had honed his radio skills into a formula called the Fireside Chat, where he explained policy "in a way that his neighbors in Dutchess County [New York] and Warm Springs [Georgia] could understand." Happily for the jaunty Roosevelt, the country he was about to lead had come of age in radio. The great divide was 1923, when the number of households with radio sets jumped from 60,000 to 400,000. But radio had not yet become an accepted form of political communication. It took war to cement the relationship between leadership and radio. According to C. E. Hooper, whose "Hooperatings" were an early polling barometer, there was a dramatic rise in audience for fireside chats and regular speeches from June 10, 1936 (9.7 percent or 6.3 million homes listening of total homes with radios), to December 9, 1941 (79 percent or 62.1 million homes). The medium needed a message. And war always drew an audience.

The day after his inauguration, FDR declared a bank holiday, closing down the financial institutions that were in crisis. At 10 P.M. on Sunday, March 12, 1933, Americans gathered around their radio sets to hear FDR declaim on banking. To prepare, he lay on a couch and visualized the audience. He did not use language like *debits* and *foreclosures* and *the bottom line*. He said, "It is safer to keep your money in a reopened bank than it is under the mattress." The message was an appeal for a return of confidence in institutions—financial, governmental, and presidential. In many quarters, it worked. FDR "stepped to the microphone last night and knocked another home run," humorist Will Rogers wrote in the *New York Times*. "Our president took such a dry subject as banking . . . he made everybody understand it, even the bankers."

Roosevelt used radio for many things: to calm, to cajole, to criticize. He rarely used it on matters of foreign policy, devoting surprisingly few of his Fireside Chats to international

affairs, eager not to lose the audience of an intrinsically iso-
lationist nation. But when he did spotlight the world, he
made it come home. It was said that the Lend-Lease Law, a
dodge of the official Neutrality Act that allowed the United
States to "lend" needed military equipment to Britain for a
$1 lease, owed not a little to an analogy Roosevelt used to
explain the law: "Suppose my neighbor's house catches fire,
and I have a length of garden hose," he began, threading the
analogy through the speech, concluding that a loan would
not be a bad idea.

Some aides questioned the time Roosevelt spent preparing
for his radio talks. He countered that they were the most
important dates on his calendar. "Gifted with a remarkable
voice and an engaging manner, he also had the ability to
make complex issues understandable, vivid, and provocative.
No president had ever addressed so vast an audience, yet none
had ever spoken so intimately to the individual citizen." He
was personal, addressing the audience as "my friends," talking
about his dog Fala, asking for a drink of water if he was
thirsty. "Not by chance was he the first three-term and then
four-term president," writes David Halberstam. "He used radio to go over heads of party." He was repeatedly reelected
despite the steadfast opposition of most of the nation's newspapers. "He changed the nature of the presidency. From now
on it was a personalized office, less distant from the average
American." That of course is the legacy of every new media
technology, to personalize leadership. What is more important is that Roosevelt had the talents and the vision to seize
the opportunity that radio presented.

Roosevelt, who viewed the presidency as a place from
which to wield influence, saw radio as a way to increase the
audience. "The presidency is not merely an administrative
office," he told Anne O'Hare McCormick in an interview for
the *New York Times*. "It is preeminently a place of moral

leadership." He was careful never to get too far out ahead of public opinion, mindful of the cold reception afforded his 1937 speech on German aggression. Called the Quarantine Speech, the appeal to isolate Germany fell flat. "He did not want to risk his political capital in premature forays. In particular he wanted to avoid anything that looked like preparation for American intervention in the war before he was re-elected in 1940." But once war came, Roosevelt used radio to effect. So cognizant was the Third Reich of FDR's powers of persuasion that when he scheduled an important Fireside Chat on December 29, 1940, the Germans hit London with one of the heaviest bomb attacks of the war. The Germans timed the bombing runs to rob Roosevelt of his headlines in the morning newspapers, of his run at American and British public opinion.

As Europe poised for war against Hitler in October 1938, radio underestimated the importance the audience had placed in its authenticity. Orson Welles aired a radio play, a Halloween eve play, about Martians landing in Princeton, New Jersey, with death-rays capable of destroying all military might. The *War of the Worlds* broadcast, told in the form of news bulletins and eyewitness accounts, was effective drama, mistaken for news. Soon enough, there was real news. Highways were clogged by traffic of those fleeing the Martians. Hundreds of reservists in the National Guard called headquarters asking where to report for duty. Saint Michael's Hospital in Newark treated fifteen cases of shock. A church service in Indianapolis dispersed when a woman came in crying that she had heard on the radio that New York City had been destroyed. Much self-flagellation followed about "the tidal wave of terror." The lesson for radio, said one commentator, was that "a large proportion of listeners had come to rely on it, rather than on the press, for their news."

In the furor that followed, many urged Congress to regulate broadcasting, and editorialists had a field day berating radio. But public interest in news did not abate. A case could be made, in fact, that the power of the entertainment strengthened the public demand for news, ushering in the greatest period of radio reporting in history. Led by Murrow and Charles Collingwood, by Eric Sevareid and H. V. Kaltenborn, radio reporting in World War II was in a pioneer class of its own. These correspondents had power and influence and celebrity. They donned the uniforms of the units they covered, proudly, and stifled news that would hurt morale at home. They brought war into the front parlor, by the fireside, complete with the sound of gunfire and the fear in men's voices, as no other media technology had ever done before. At least until the next invention. Sarnoff, at the 1939 World's Fair in New York, said it would "add radio sight to sound." This time they called it television.

The Spanish-American War of 1898 saw the first war-time role played by the telephone. Installed by the U.S. Army Signal Corps, it is seen here on a tent used by reporters. Richard Harding Davis, whose personal fortunes benefited as much by the Spanish-American War as any other correspondent's, later lamented that the telephone and the telegraph had doomed the war correspondent by robbing him of the element of surprise. "The fall of the war correspondent," he wrote, "came about through the ease and quickness with which today news leaps from one end of the earth to the other." *(AT&T Archives)*

In the run up to World War II, Adolf Hitler personally commissioned Leni Riefenstahl to produce an artistic film, based on the Nazi Party Convention in Nuremberg in 1934, that would inspire generations of young Germans to close rank, join the party, salute the Fuehrer. Called *Triumph of the Will*, the film is a triumph in imagery. Here she is congratulated by Hitler and Nazi propaganda chief Joseph Goebbels, who viewed film as an avenue "to win the heart of a people and keep it." *(UPI/Bettmann)*

Franklin Delano Roosevelt mastered the radio as few politicians have conquered any other media technology. He understood that radio was an invasion into a private home, and he acted always as a polite guest who tried to earn his welcome by being engaging without being a bore. He used radio to mask his polio, and to go over the heads of his critics. The radio networks wanted to air him every week, but he declined. He understood, as media historian David Halberstam put it, that "people can't stand repetition of the highest note on the scale for very long." *(Signal Corp Photo)*

10

Cold War Politics in the TV Age

THE FIRST SUMMIT between television and its audience came in January of 1926, when a group of business and government leaders visited a London lab to see "an apparatus invented by John Logie Baird, who claims to have solved the problem of television." The reviews were not glowing. Noting the fuzzy image, *The Times of London* doubted the utility of the new invention. Publisher W. J. Odhams told the inventor he saw no future for "a device which only sends shadows." If the publishers were unimpressed, inventors on several continents quickly saw the promise of this invention that could apply sight to the wonders of radio. In the United States. Britain, France, Germany, Japan, and the Soviet Union, competition was keen to invent the "miracle" of television. They realized, as *Life* put it, that new technology was "more than the addition of sight to the sound of radio," that it had "a power to annihilate time and space that will unite everyone here in the immediate experience of events in contemporary life and history."

The first politician to appear on television in the United States was Herbert Hoover, commerce secretary of the United States, a leading candidate for the Republican presidential nomination in 1928. The date was April 7, 1927, and the occasion was a public demonstration of television by the American Telephone & Telegraph Company (AT&T). Broadcast from Washington and seen in New York by an invitation-only group of business officials, newspaper executives, and financiers, Hoover's speech was the top story in the next day's *New York Times*. No one bothered much with what Mr. Hoover had said. What captured the imagination was the manner in which the words were delivered. FAR-OFF SPEAKERS SEEN AS WELL AS HEARD HERE IN A TEST OF TELEVISION, read the headline. Subheads were equally enraptured: LIKE A PHOTO COME TO LIFE, HOOVER'S FACE PLAINLY IMAGED AS HE SPEAKS IN WASHINGTON, THE FIRST TIME IN HISTORY, PICTURES ARE FLASHED BY WIRE AND RADIO SYNCHRONISING WITH SPEAKER'S VOICE.

Huge expectations greeted television's arrival. Like Samuel Morse marveling at the ability of the telegraph to allow nations to communicate with each other within the hour, enthusiasts predicted an end to war, a boon to democracy, a tip of the hat to all the overblown predictions of earlier media technologies. "This was the ultimate medium, the democratic forum that would uplift and enlighten the masses," wrote one television historian, whose book was not insignificantly titled *One Nation Under Television*. "The greatest day of all will be reached when not only the human voice but the image of the speaker can be flashed through space in every direction," David Sarnoff said, predicting that television was "just around the corner." Later, the ambitious visionary of both radio and television grew even more philosophical. "It is the glory of man that he has never quailed before the apparently insurmountable obstacles of space and time," he said. "It is inconceivable that he will not make the fullest possible use of a medium of communications which bridges the distance between himself and the objects of his interest."

Sarnoff was not the only dreamer in the constellation.

Cartoonists had long assumed the inevitability of television, and scientists in the 1880s experimented with—and applied for patents on—devices transmitting pictures over the wires. The engineering needed for television's birth "existed conceptually long before technology allowed its practical achievement." Even the word *television* had entered the language by the outbreak of the First World War, underscoring that the idea of transmitting visual images was anticipated long before technology was ready.

One reason for the delay is that investors were cautious. When in 1929 Vladimir Kosma Zworykin, a Russian-born American physicist, introduced his iconoscope, the electronic eye for scanning pictures, at the Institute of Radio Engineers, the reaction was "a slight collective shrug." Industry experts sniffed at the costs of Zworykin's experiments and the RCA board of directors worried about sending millions of dollars "down the drain" after what Sarnoff called "seeing by radio." RCA would spend $50 million (some spent trying to buy other inventors' patents) before television turned its first profit. Television, wrote one commentator, "suffered as stormy a fate as ever beset a branch of the radio industry."

In the spring of 1939, the World's Fair opened at Flushing, Queens, New York. The fair was marked by many firsts: The Bell System Pavilion offered free long-distance calls to any Bell telephone in the country, and the Perisphere drew visitors from around the world. But among the biggest attractions was this new invention called television. The RCA, Westinghouse, and General Electric pavilions demonstrated their versions of the new medium, and extra security was called in to control the crowds who thronged to the exhibits. More remarkably, the National Broadcasting Company, NBC, broadcast the event, with an iconoscope camera, connected to a van by coaxial cable some fifty feet from the speakers' podium. The NBC program was broadcast to the few hundred television sets in the New York area, where it was seen by an estimated 1,000 people. Not waiting for an invitation, New York mayor Fiorello La Guardia walked up to the camera and offered his thoughts on the occasion, understanding intuitively that he could reach as many people through the lens as he could in a day of stumping on the fairgrounds. "The first real American grand master of the political photo op" saw in television a new channel to the electorate.

By the time maverick Wendell Wilkie fended off the backroom politicians at the 1940 Republican Convention to win the presidential nomination on the sixth ballot, 10,000 New Yorkers could watch his victory against the odds on television. NBC's coverage so impressed commentators that they predicted a sea change in the political world. "The sly, flamboyant or leather-lunged spellbinder has no place on the air," wrote media observer Orrin E. Dunlap, Jr. "Sincerity, dignity, friendliness and clear speech . . . are the secrets of a winning telecast." Sarnoff agreed. "Showmanship in presenting a political appeal by television will become more important than mere skill in talking of possession of a good radio voice," he said, "while appearance and sincerity will prove decisive factors with an audience which observes the candidate in close-up views." If Sarnoff and Dunlap had known of the proliferation of image consultants in politics in the wake of television's influence, one wonders if they would have been quite so cheerful. In any event, it was clear from the start that television would intersect with image to change politics from a rough verbal occupation to a smooth visual profession.

As usual, there were predictions of wonder, and worries about quality. "Television's illuminating light will go far, we hope, to drive out the ghosts that haunt the dark corners of our minds—ignorance, bigotry, fear," said FCC chairman Paul A. Porter as World War II neared its end, and television, its development stymied by war, resumed its course. "It will be able to inform, educate, and entertain an entire nation with a magical speed and vividness. . . . It can be democracy's handmaiden by bringing the whole picture of our political, social, economic and cultural life to the eyes as well as the ears." Here was the enthusiast's faith, a conviction that technology would right the wrongs of an imperfect world. Even doubters were somewhat awed by the invention's potential. E. B. White, the social commentator and author of *Charlotte's Web*, first saw television in a darkened room in 1938. "We shall stand or fall by television," he announced on emerging. "Television is going to be the test of the modern world."

The turning point for television came in 1948, after World War II rations were a matter of history and consumers registered an urge to get on with life. There was enough hype and genuine excitement on the circuit—one trade journal gushed that "John Q. America is about to receive the greatest treasury of enlightenment and education that has ever before been given to a free man"—that by the fall of 1949, 22 percent of all the families in New York and 15.5 percent in Los Angeles owned a television set. By the 1960s, the average household was watching five to six hours of television a day, and national networks were big business, with *Forbes* dubbing CBS "the money tree of Madison Avenue." By the late 1980s, there were more than 750 million TV sets in almost 160 countries, watched by an estimated 2.5 billion people—this despite efforts by some governments, like Israel and South Africa, to limit television's development out of fear it would become a tool of social instability. In the end, there were more people with access to television than to telephones. "Television is not a luxury," remarked Arthur C. Clarke, "it's a necessity."

Like other media inventions, television threatened the ones gone before. Newspapers worried that verbal communication would supplant their hold on the reading public. In one advertisement developed by a nervous radio company, Sarnoff was pictured as a "televisionary" who was shown smashing the radio industry. This concern was validated by a writer seeking advice from a columnist in May of 1930 about whether to replace an old 1925 radio set or hold out for the television set he assumed was on its way. As he put it in his letter, "Why should we get a new [radio] set now and have a television set make it obsolete in September?" By December of 1928, enough consumers were wrestling with such questions that advertisers assured Christmas shoppers that television would not supplant radio, that it was still safe to give the gift of sound. Radio devotees complained to the Federal Radio Commission after television began broadcasting, furious at the electronic interference. "Why the commission allows this purely experimental station to operate and disrupt the whole [radio] broadcast band during the hours they do is beyond me," Bostonian radio loyalist Frank W. Murphy wrote in 1931. Confirming the worst fears of the news industry, *The New Republic* predicted that television would replace newspapers, telecasting details of the daily news to every home. But other commentators dismissed the promise of television, arguing that the average family was simply too busy to spend all day and night watching programs on a small box.

If television frightened the newspapers, it also alarmed some of the politicians. Dwight D. Eisenhower, the general of World War II fame, cringed at the requirements of the new medium. When advisers suggested ways he could project himself for the camera, Eisenhower replied, "Has an old soldier come to this?" In his relations with the news media after becoming president, Eisenhower managed to hold the camera at bay, along with much of the rest of the press. Ike introduced the first televised presidential press conference, but it was not broadcast live, and journalists—print and broadcast—had to clear all quotes with Eisenhower press secretary James Hagerty.

Eisenhower may not have liked the imperatives of television, but he learned to live with them, accepting coaching from actor Robert Montgomery, even bowing as aides put a pat of powder on his bald head so that it did not shine in the camera lights. During the 1952 campaign, he made a series of one-minute advertisements showing him sitting with his family, answering questions in a casual way. The Democratic candidate would have none of it. "This is the worst thing I've ever heard of," Adlai Stevenson told an aide. "How can you talk seriously about issues with one-minute spots!" In the current political environment, a thirty-second spot is the norm, while television news offers candidates little more than a six-second sound bite.

That paradox is the invention's legacy. Television could bring nations closer together, but they had to deliver their messages in crisper terms. Television could ease communication among leaders, but briefly. This dichotomy was not new—the telegraph had a similar impact on diplomatic messages, and radio served the same function for news copy. But shortening speech for the camera influenced public debate, and may also have bred public distrust. Once the "tube" made broadcasting visual, pictures took precedence over words. In perhaps his most lasting achievement, the British inventor Baird installed a television set at 10 Downing Street. Prime Minister Ramsay MacDonald was dubious, saying, "You have put something in my room which will never let me forget how strange is this world, and how unknown."

As the other visual media inventions before it, television also personalized power, again threatening the diplomatic bureaucracy that served as a filter between world leaders and international policy. In 1959, as Vice President Richard

Nixon set out for Moscow to meet with Soviet premier Nikita Khrushchev, George V. Allen, director of the U.S. Information Agency, put television in perspective. Once upon a time, he said, diplomats "were sent abroad to various countries, sometimes supplied with a pair of striped pants and a top hat. They . . . dealt with a small group of people in the foreign office of that country, and that was the link between nations." Now, Allen continued, diplomats were no longer key players, as nations addressed one another over the ether, appealing less to each other than to public opinion. Perhaps it was nothing more complicated than the fact that the camera brought out the exhibitionist in public figures. Whatever the reason, they hammed it up for the home audience, often talking less for private elucidation than for public consumption.

Television literally set the stage for what would be dubbed the Kitchen Debate between Nixon and Khrushchev. Touring an American Exhibit in Moscow meant to display the latest in U.S. products, Nixon and Khrushchev came up on a model television studio showing off the latest development: color television. A young Ampex Company official escorted the two leaders to the front of the camera, urging them to say something on film that might be shown later to visitors at the exhibit. Khrushchev "at first seemed reluctant to say anything," Nixon wrote in one account in his *Six Crises*. "But then he saw a large crowd of Soviet workmen in the gallery overhead, and the corps of newspapermen around us, and the temptation was too much for him. He seized the opportunity as eagerly as an American politician accepts free television time." Later, when the footage was aired, viewers saw an overly aggressive Soviet leader railing against capitalism and a calm American guest politely trying to change the subject. But Nixon felt Khrushchev had gotten the better of him in the debate, and vowed not to be outgunned again.

By the time they reached a sample of a modern American

kitchen, they were in full oratorical swing. To read excerpts of the Kitchen Debate thirty-five years later brings a smile, for there is nothing particularly hotheaded in the rhetoric. Only the body language conveyed emotion. As they stood in front of a model 1950s American kitchen, Nixon poked his finger at Khrushchev's chest and warned the Soviets not to make unilateral demands at the Four Power Conference in Geneva. Khrushchev accused Nixon of threatening him. The Kitchen Debate was not recorded by television cameras, only by newspaper accounts and still photographs. Still the impression it left cemented Nixon's image as a leader who would stand up to the Communists.

For most of his career, Nixon suffered greatly at the hands of this new medium, only to make an odd peace with it in the end. During the first campaign debate with Kennedy, Nixon, recovering from the flu, looked tired, with sweat pouring from his brow and his dark suit melding into the dark backdrop. Listeners who heard the exchange on radio were sure Nixon had won. Those who saw the debates on television gave the victory to Kennedy. Later each campaign paid strict attention to matters of lighting and technique. But this moment did not represent, as some have suggested, "a seminal shift from substance to style in American political life and began the era of telepolitics in earnest." That moment had been dawning for centuries, and strutted on television's stage in 1952, when, as Eisenhower's choice to be vice president, Nixon was accused of accepting an $18,000 slush fund from GOP backers.

Contemplating how to maintain Eisenhower's confidence in the face of the slush-fund scandal, Nixon took to television airwaves as the best way of influencing public opinion. Having convinced the Republican National Committee to buy a half-hour of time on sixty-four television stations across the country, Nixon delivered one of those pathos-filled speeches that came to characterize his career. Maintaining that his wife, Pat, still wore a plain "Republican cloth coat" instead of the minks favored by unnamed, wealthier Democratic opponents, Nixon said the only gift the Nixons had received in all his years of public service was a cocker spaniel, black-and-white spotted, named Checkers. "And you know the kids love that dog, and I just want to say this right now, that regardless of what they say about it, we're going to keep it."

No leader had used his dog to mask a serious policy issue better since Franklin Roosevelt went on the defensive after reports surfaced that he sent a ship to pick up his dog Fala, after leaving the Scottie behind in the Aleutian Islands. "I am accustomed to malicious falsehoods about myself," he said, "but I deeply resent libelous statements about my little dog." Some thirty-five years later, "an astonishing number of Americans who did not remember the names of the dogs of Harry Truman, Dwight Eisenhower, and John Kennedy remembered the name of Franklin Roosevelt's dog because he had spoken with them about Fala, *my little dog Fala*, about Fala's Irish being up over Republican criticism." Now, Nixon used his dog similarly to evoke sympathy and belittle his accusers. Hundreds of thousands of telegrams rained down on Dwight Eisenhower, urging him to keep Nixon on the ticket. It was not a surprise that the speech came to be named for the dog. In the annals of American politics, the Checkers Speech is a classic, upended only by Nixon himself, a decade later when, on losing the California gubernatorial race, he angrily told reporters, "You won't have Richard Nixon to kick around anymore."

If it is difficult to see what any of this portends for diplomacy, the viewing grows easier with the presidency of John F. Kennedy. If television personalized leadership, then no one since Teddy Roosevelt was better suited to this mission than John Kennedy. Tom Wicker of the *New York Times* said at the time that under Kennedy the news conference became "more an instrument of presidential power than a useful tool of the press." If Franklin Delano Roosevelt was, as Heywood Broun once called him, "the best newspaperman who has ever been president of the United States," then Kennedy was surely the best television anchor. He came of age with the medium, used it to his electoral and leadership advantage, understanding the need for symbols and the elegance of words, without ever losing the substance that gave both symbols and words their power. On reviewing a videotape of his own television appearances, Kennedy, who won election by fewer than 100,000 votes, said, "We wouldn't have had a prayer without that gadget." His presidency was also served by that gadget.

At the height of the Cuban Missile Crisis, the cold war's most dangerous nuclear confrontation, he used television adroitly, both to convey messages to Khrushchev and to marshal public opinion. Communication between Washington and Moscow throughout the thirteen-day crisis was generally, by twenty-first-century standards, primitive, and largely dependent on intermediaries. From the time the Central Intelligence Agency first alerted Kennedy to the prospect of Soviet missiles in Cuba, through the period when he threatened military action to any Soviet ship defying a UN blockade, to the moment when Khrushchev agreed to withdraw the missiles in exchange for a later U.S. withdrawal of its missiles in Turkey, much of the diplomacy was done on paper. No satellite beamed television signals around the world, so Khrushchev's speeches had to be translated and interpreted by American diplomats in Moscow, while Kennedy's words were monitored and reported by Soviet diplomats in Washington. Radio communication likewise depended on the skills of mediators to translate and explain.

Khrushchev, frustrated by the eight-hour transmittal time

for classified notes to be coded and decoded from the Kremlin to the White House, took to using Radio Moscow to deliver his messages. Kennedy responded by calling in the news media and replying to the latest Soviet offers via the press. "The fastest way to get it there without having to go through the bureaucracy and the translation . . . was to simply get it on the air in the United States and the Soviets would pick it up," explained White House press secretary Pierre Salinger. This use of the news media to relay diplomatic messages— the Russians also floated one proposal through a luncheon date between the Soviets' Alexander Fomin and ABC correspondent John Scali—was a precursor to the role that the news media, and particularly CNN, would serve in later crises. But the function of delivering messages did not usurp the role of diplomats. If anything, it added to their load. Nor did it increase the influence of reporters. Like the technology, journalists were most often conduits.

Television not only facilitated messages between the two leaders, the new medium also gave Kennedy a stage for swaying public opinion. As Kennedy's advisers deliberated in private, they developed scenarios for action. One group favored a massive air strike. Another advocated a blockade. All of them included a televised outreach to win public sympathy. "A central role for television was so much taken for granted that each group recommended not only what should be done, but what President Kennedy should say on the air." He chose the blockade option, deciding to surround Cuba with U.S. naval ships until the Soviets withdrew their missiles. In his televised address on October 22, 1963, Kennedy painted the stakes in apocalyptic terms, using the word *nuclear* eleven times. He also warned Khrushchev to eliminate "this clandestine, reckless and provocative threat to world peace . . . to abandon this course of world domination." It may have been a skillful upping of the ante to the Kremlin, but Kennedy's rhetoric was also a ploy to win public support at home.

Attorney General Robert Kennedy, the president's brother, remained convinced afterwards that the media strategy was less important than the media silence. "The time that was available to the president and his advisers to work secretly, quietly, privately, developing a course and action and recommendations, was essential," Robert Kennedy wrote in his chronicle of the crisis, *Thirteen Days.* "If our deliberations had been publicized, if we had had to make a decision in twenty-four hours, I believe the course that we ultimately would have taken would have been quiet different and filled with far greater risks." To Bobby Kennedy, the ability to debate behind closed doors "was essential in choosing our ultimate course." Had the rush been on, he argues, those who advocated a military strike, with a possible nuclear response from Moscow, might have prevailed.

In this view he is joined by historian Michael Beschloss. "He benefited from a cocoon of time and privacy afforded by the absence of intensive television scrutiny," he wrote. "In the culture of 1962, Kennedy had the leisure, with the full consultation of his advisers, to make a thoughtful decision. A modern-day president would not be so lucky."

But there are several reasons to question this analysis. If the Cuban Missile Crisis had played out against a backdrop of satellite television, Kennedy's inner circle might have been more rushed in their deliberations, but it is not clear that their decision would have changed. Several of the participants have talked about how the debate meandered, with key aides continually changing their minds. A shortened deadline might have focused minds. Then too, in an age of real-time television where news organizations have their own satellites, Khrushchev might not have planted the missiles in the first place, knowing that his aggressions were being monitored by the news media and the Central Intelligence Agency. As it was, satellite reconnaissance photographs of the missiles in Cuba were the pictures that really mattered during the crisis, as they convinced a reluctant White House that the threat was real.

Finally, no matter whether a crisis erupts during an age of little television or saturation coverage, a White House like Kennedy's can make adroit use of leaks and lids, putting out the news it wants the public to know and sitting on the rest. Kennedy did this so well during the Cuban Missile Crisis that reporters later complained of "news management." There was plenty of precedent for managing the news. After a delegate to the Constitutional Convention of 1787 mislaid his copy of the secret proposals, George Washington warned him "to be more careful, lest our transactions get into the newspapers and disturb the public response by premature speculation." Technology makes it more difficult for leaders to manage the news, forcing them toward more sophisticated techniques, but does nothing to lessen their appetite for control. The instinct to manage the news is a function of power, not technology.

Like others before it, this new medium, television, influenced not only politics but journalism as well. During his twelve years in the White House, FDR held 998 press conferences, a record not likely to be broken. Questions were largely designed to gather information, probing the who, what, where, and when of presidential announcements. Reporters' questions averaged fourteen words in length. By the time Kennedy became the first president to air live press conferences, reporters' questions had expanded to an average of fifty words. Television had a magical lure, tempting journalists who once designed their questions to elicit information now to pontificate and filibuster and grab the camera. Journalism lost some of its standing then, when television made media stars of reporters. But glamour had long been attached to the news business, in some rough-hewn way, and there was from the beginning an audience for gossip as well as information.

Politics had lost some of its stature too, though good intentions remained. When Neil Armstrong landed on the moon in 1969, it was a television moment to remember. When he spoke the first words of a man on the moon, "That's one small step for a man, one giant leap for mankind," it evoked Samuel Morse's quotation on the telegraph's invention, "What hath God wrought?" But Richard Nixon, sitting in the Oval Office, stretched the bounds of taste in technology, picking up the telephone to call Armstrong and fellow astronaut Buz Aldrin. The caption on the television screen said, LIVE FROM MOON. Perhaps this was too much of a temptation for any world leader to resist, to be inserted by technology into one of history's grand moments, but it gave television more of a role than is healthy, or seemly. Nor was it inevitable. Several years later, while awaiting word on whether British troops had defeated Argentine forces in the battle over the Falkland Islands, British prime minister Margaret Thatcher resisted the urge to call her commanders. "I was glued to the radio for news," she wrote in her memoirs, "strictly keeping to my self-imposed rule not to telephone while the conflict was under way."

To policy makers who have grown accustomed to the fast-forward world of CNN, where microphones are thrust in the faces of policy makers as soon as an incident occurs and presidents risk public anger if they are seen recreating during a crisis, this lag of more than a week between Kennedy's first alert to Soviet missiles in Cuba and his televised address to the nation must evoke nostalgia for an earlier era, when diplomats had time to think and policy makers had time to decide. But before the advent of television, British prime minister Winston Churchill had months in secrecy to design a supply port for the Allies' invasion at Normandy. That Kennedy had barely a week to design his response to the biggest threat of nuclear war during forty years of a cold war between Washington and Moscow is hardly a luxury. Relative history requires more respect for the challenges the new medium placed on Kennedy's shoulders—and for the difficulties Churchill faced in controlling information in the age of radio.

The television news media was just beginning to test its new power during the cold war crises faced by the Kennedy administration. Kennedy's assassination ironically cemented television's domain over the public events by keeping most Americans glued to their sets for an entire weekend. The legend of Camelot was crafted in the noble posture of Jacqueline Kennedy and the graceful touches of his son John as he saluted his father good-bye. Television matured with Kennedy's death, feeling its muscle in statistics that said four of every ten television sets in the United States was tuned to the national tragedy for four days. Television's new authority was soon put to the test in civil rights clashes in the American South, in college campuses in the Ivy League North, and in the rice paddies of South Vietnam.

In all the intersections where international diplomacy has crossed paths with media technology, none has provoked the controversy of the Vietnam War. Here was a civil war that pitted North Vietnam against South Vietnam, as well as American against American. Here was a historic clash between technology and leadership, between journalism and government, between television pictures and presidential leadership, between the message and the messenger. Critics called it the first living room war, and they said it would have ended differently without the cameras.

11

Television and the War
in Vietnam

THE BATTLE OF THE Bulge in World War II was one of the most decisive battles on the western front. It was also one of the biggest military setbacks in the history of the U.S. Army. Finally, the Battle of the Bulge represented a colossal intelligence failure, as Germans charging in Adolf Hitler's last attack achieved total tactical surprise. The battle for the heart of Europe eventually proved pivotal in Nazi Germany's defeat, but the toll fell heavily on American soldiers. Some 600,000 Americans fought in that two-week battle, and when it was over, 4,000 had been killed, 17,000 were missing, and 20,000 were wounded. There were rumblings in the U.S. newspapers about why the Brits were not doing their share, and some high-brow criticism in places like the *New York Times* that the allies had, as had happened earlier in Normandy, underestimated "the capacity and will of the enemy to fight." But for the most U.S. censors refused to clear stories that might hurt morale at home. Three days after the battle began, reporters erupted in an "angry session" at Versailles, demanding that more information be released. "Everybody across hell and forty acres," knew what was going on, complained one reporter, everyone, that is, except the U.S. public.

In the face of painful losses, General Dwight D. Eisenhower exhorted the troops to continue. "By rushing out from his fixed defenses, the enemy may give us the choice to turn his great gamble into his worst defeat," Eisenhower said in a written Order of the Day. "So I call upon every man, of all the allies, to rise now to new heights of courage, or resolution of effort. Let everyone hold before him a single thought—to destroy the enemy on the ground, in the air, everywhere—destroy him."

Later, journalists and generals both would look back in wonder, marveling at the blank canvas that allowed Eisenhower to paint a compelling picture of a muscular army poised for victory. By then, a generation had soured on the realities of war it watched on television from the comfort of home. By then, Vietnam had crippled a presidency and left a legacy of doubt about national resolve. By then, a new medium had come to dominate old disciplines of diplomacy and war.

The Battle of the Bulge was much on Lyndon Johnson's mind as he prepared a speech to broadcasters in 1968, one day after he had announced that he would not seek reelection. It was a momentous declaration, a surprise, one that stunned the antiwar groups working fervently for his defeat. Now, in a bit of uncanny timing, he was scheduled to address the National Association of Broadcasters. Included in the audience were the very television executives whose nightly pictures of American GIs in Vietnam he blamed for the ebbing course of the war.

"As I sat in my office last evening, waiting to speak, I thought of the many times each week when television brings the war into the American home," he said. "No one can say exactly what effect those vivid scenes have on American opinion. Historians must only guess at the effect that television would have had during earlier conflicts on the future of this nation: during the Korean War, for example, at that time when our forces were pushed back there to Pusan; or World War II, the Battle of the Bulge, or when our men were slugging it out in Europe or when most of our Air Force was shot down that day in June 1942 off Australia." Johnson left little doubt of his own view. As he left the podium of national life, Johnson believed that television had brought war home to Americans who no longer wanted to fight communism in Southeast Asia, and that in poisoning public opinion against the Vietnam War, television had wrecked his presidency.

Lyndon Baines Johnson was perhaps the preeminent inside politician of his generation, an arm-twister who cut deals, lobbied enemies, turned votes. An accidental president, he was sworn in on *Air Force One* as the body of the young martyred president, John F. Kennedy, was being flown back to Washington. A creature of the legislative process, he had served twelve years in the House and twelve years in the Senate, six of the latter as majority leader of the Senate. He was a man of Congress, and he was determined to turn those negotiating skills on the Washington elite that disdained his southern drawl, big floppy ears, and earthy language as unworthy of succession to the Camelot imagery of the Kennedy administration. He would prove to the snobs in Washington that he could out-Kennedy Kennedy. He might not have JFK's panache, but he would deliver in hard, cold legislative reality the promises that so easily passed his predecessor's lips. Within a year, he had become a force for change. His greatest legacy still is that he personally redefined the laws of civil rights, taking the first great steps since Abraham Lincoln's Emancipation Proclamation to outlaw the consequences of racial bigotry.

But his presidency was toppled by the Vietnam War, arguably the first in which the United States retreated in defeat. Many blamed Johnson himself, for micromanaging the war, for picking bombing targets instead of leaving tactics to the

Pentagon. Some attributed the failure to his desire to be liked, a weakness that caused him to career from right to left, trying to weave compromises of policy that pleased neither hawk nor dove. Others postulated that he was afraid the Republicans would seize any opening to proclaim him weak on communism. Still others questioned how any leader facing a social revolution as well as an explosion in new media technology could have negotiated a way to victory.

How Johnson came to this moment, why he found himself picking bombing targets instead of buttonholing legislators for showdown votes on domestic legislation dear to his heart and ambition, is a story of great sadness. In private, he blamed his critics. "The only difference between the Kennedy assassination and mine is that I am alive and it has been more torturous," he told friends. In public, he faulted the media, particularly television pictures, for forcing his decision to leave office, his Great Society work largely undone by the erosion of public confidence known as Vietnam.

In this, he was not alone. Television critic Michael J. Arlen, in *Living-Room War*, argued that television had trivialized the Vietnam War by sandwiching it between commercials, soap operas, and quiz shows. Journalist Peter Braestrup, in *Big Story*, documented how the news media had misreported the Tet Offensive as a stunning military defeat for the U.S. troops and their South Vietnamese allies, when in fact it was the North Vietnamese who took a pounding. Blaming the media for the war's end was also popular in academia too, where many, like a professor named Anthony Lake who would go one to become President Clinton's national security adviser, saw antiwar protests provoked by television as a new people's power in foreign policy. Many soldiers, then and now, held the view that the media had compromised their fighting efforts and mocked their bravery by sensationalizing war crimes

and enemy gains to fit the media's own antiwar bias, drama-
tizing the agony of war without explaining its purpose.

But if some of the foot soldiers were convinced that television was the culprit, their commanding officers were less
certain. General William C. Westmoreland is no apologist for
the news media. In 1982, he sued CBS News in a $120 mil-
lion libel suit. In a documentary on the Vietnam War, CBS
had accused Westmoreland, commander of U.S. troops in
Vietnam from 1964 to 1968, of underestimating the true size
of the enemy in reports to the White House and Congress.
Though the suit was settled out of court, Westmoreland's
honor was defended by numerous Johnson administration officials as well as documents showing that the CIA and other
intelligence agencies had arrived at conflicting views on the
strength and danger of the enemy. At best, Westmoreland
had a natural enmity for reporters, and they for him. The
general often complained to Washington about skewed reporting from Vietnam, and reporters were equally exasperated
with Westmoreland's overly optimistic declarations, as when
he proclaimed that "the enemy has been defeated at every
turn."

For all the distrust in the relationship, for all his annoy-
ance at press bias, Westmoreland looked at television and saw
other causes for defeat. Ten years after he was fired from his
post in Vietnam, Westmoreland took this as the lesson of
Vietnam, that "we in this country cannot send men to the
battlefield unless the public is going to be behind them, and
it is up to the politicians to ensure that such is the case."

Having himself tried and failed to win support through
public diplomacy, Westmoreland now faulted the political
leadership for losing the war by failing to convince the public
that there was a cause to be won. This is somehow fitting,
because in Vietnam, the generals too often behaved like pol-

iticians, and the politicians too often acted like generals. It is also instructive, for it hints at the fallacy of blaming the media.

The United States lost the war in Vietnam for many reasons. The war was lost on college campuses where young men did not want to die imposing an imperialist view on an unwilling people. The war was lost by what David Halberstam called "the best and the brightest," scholars and diplomats and policy wonks who micromanaged military strategy in a desperate attempt to rescue a failed policy. But the war in Vietnam was lost not least because Lyndon Johnson decided early on not to waste political capital in selling the war to the public.

Worried that his domestic agenda would be sidetracked by a foreign conflict, Johnson tried to fight a war on the battlefield without waging it on the home front. There was plenty of evidence to buttress his fear. "History provided too many cases where the sound of the bugle put an immediate end to the hopes and dreams of the best reformers," wrote military historian Harry Summers, Jr. "The Spanish-American War drowned the populist spirit, World War I ended Woodrow Wilson's New Freedom, World War II brought the New Deal to a close." Johnson had a Great Society to legislate, a War on Poverty to wage. He did not want the nation's attention diverted to some foreign adventure that was a hand-me-down from his predecessors. He wanted to be remembered not for blundering in a swampy jungle far from home but for closing the final chapter on the Civil War.

War cannot be fought without public support. This is the heart of Westmoreland's complaint, as self-serving as it may sound, that Vietnam was a failure of political leadership. As Johnson did not delineate the reasons for war, most Americans seemed at a loss to enunciate them. In 1967, a Gallup poll showed that half of all Americans had no idea what the war in Vietnam was about. A year later, after the Tet Offensive, which became a major turning point in the public and political landscape, the chairman of the House Appropriations Committee, "genuinely seeking enlightenment," asked the army chief of staff, "Who would you say is our enemy in this conflict?" By then, Johnson knew that his worst fears had been realized, that the quagmire of Vietnam had sucked the life out of his presidency, that his legacy would forever be clouded by this unwanted war. He became obsessed with polls, stuffing them in his pockets when they validated his policy and thrusting them at dubious visitors.

Aides pressed Johnson to use the bully pulpit of the White House to sell the war. As early as 1965, when the United States first began bombing runs, James Greenfield, assistant secretary of state for public affairs, urged the administration to enunciate "the rationale for our actions." In 1966, when U.S. troop strength in Vietnam was beginning its climb from 20,000 to over a half million, Gallup polls showed that 54 percent of Americans did not favor an escalation of the conflict to a full-scale war. The U.S. ambassador to Vietnam, Henry Cabot Lodge, urged Johnson to make his case to the public: "One television fireside chat," he told Johnson, "by you personally—with all your intelligence and compassion— could tip that figure over in one evening."

Lodge was no doubt being a bit disingenuous when he suggested that Johnson could reverse public opinion by a single television address. Johnson was obsessed with television— he was the first president to line up three TV sets in his office so he could watch all the network news shows at once—but it was not kind to him. The new medium vexed him, defying his best efforts to reach the public and mocking his intentions by highlighting the hound-dog look of his face. Johnson tried, how he tried, to make television do his bidding, to earn its respect and see its honor reflected in his television image.

The president frequently tried different kinds of glasses and contact lenses to improve his physical appearance on television. But its magic eluded him.

Once, on settling a railway strike, he strode into the CBS newsroom just as Walter Cronkite was going on the air with the evening news. When Lady Bird Johnson later questioned his motives, the president explained, "I wanted to see the look on Walter Cronkite's face when I walked into the studio." But it was the look on the television screen that mattered most, and what viewers saw was no doubt a scene slightly out of control. It was a metaphor for Johnson's television presence.

Still, Lodge had a point. No matter what the physical appearance of a political leader, all benefit from the "rally around the flag" phenomenon of a crisis abroad. Richard Nixon understood this better than Johnson, and used it mercilessly, often exaggerating a foreign-policy crisis so that sympathy would accrue to his domestic-policy woes. A look at Johnson's use of television and the resulting ratings in the Gallup poll suggests that for all his reticence, LBJ did get a bounce from taking his case public. And there was a case to be made, if communism was the enemy. In July of 1965, when he spoke on television about the reasons to be in Vietnam, his popularity rating moved from 51 percent to 57 percent. Early in 1966, when Johnson announced resumption of bombing, his rating increased from 50 to 56 percent. But in each case, after about a month, the numbers dropped below where they had been before, suggesting that the content of his speeches did not match the unfolding of events. He promised a limited war, and kept calling for more troops. He offered negotiations, and kept bombing. This dissonance between words and action doomed him. They called it the credibility gap.

"During the fall of 1967, the Johnson administration had

made a special effort to persuade the public that the war was going well, that it was being won, that the end was in sight," writes scholar Michael Mandelbaum. "Tet demonstrated that there was a good deal of fight left in the enemy." Launched on January 31, 1968, Tet was the bold plan of the Communist leaders in Hanoi to win the war by attacking simultaneously in more than 100 South Vietnamese cities and towns. In this massive battle, 67,000 troops were unhurled on the enemy by the Communist North. According to official U.S. and South Vietnamese figures, the Communists lost tens of thousands of soldiers to the battle, "the best of a generation of resistance fighters." Along the way they killed more than 14,000 South Vietnamese civilians, and 4,000 U.S. soldiers. The Tet Offensive stunned a nation that "had been led to believe that success in Vietnam was just around the corner. Tet was the final blow to the sagging credibility of the Johnson administration and to the waning patience of the American people with this remote and inconclusive war."

It was not so much the pictures of bloodshed, it was the fact that the pictures did not match the optimistic chatter coming from the administration that doomed LBJ's policy. That war is hell is well understood by both soldiers and the parents who wait at home; that it has a purpose is the saving grace for both. When blood is shed without a cause, public opinion is sure to turn, even if there are no television cameras in the war zone. Lyndon Johnson's presidency was destroyed not by television pictures of the Vietnam War but by his own inability to sell the policy—on television and in other ways—to the public. Perhaps that war was unsaleable, but it is not television's fault that it was unpopular.

For the United States, the trauma of Tet, one of the highlights of early coverage by newspaper and television reporters, was the fact that twenty Vietcong had penetrated the embassy grounds. Many have criticized the media's overattention to what one American officer called a "piddling platoon action," arguing that the press exaggerated the crisis, that it suggested the VC were inside the embassy, that it left the impression of an embassy under siege. In this, they have a point. But in suggesting that reporters concentrated on the events at the embassy out of laziness to explore the countryside, critics miss a larger point. The embassy in Saigon was the psychological headquarters of the U.S. presence. If it could be so easily traversed by the enemy, if five marines were killed trying to protect its grounds, that was a story the home audience could understand. That was a major blow, and it would have been explosive news with or without television pictures.

LBJ felt the blow, and grew silent. Losing the war on the battlefield, he gave up the one on television. For forty-eight hours he maintained a virtual silence on the war, instead asking the general to play politician. Westmoreland began briefing reporters almost daily. "Standing on the blood-spattered lawn of the embassy compound, as dead Vietcong sappers were being carried away," one reporter recounted, Westmoreland put the best face on at best a dicey situation. "The enemy exposed himself and he suffered great casualties," he told incredulous reporters. "American troops went on the offensive and pursued the enemy aggressively." To Oberdorfer, Westmoreland seemed to be "standing in the ruins and saying everything was great." This impression among reporters of Alice-in-Wonderland thinking at the top had nothing to do with television. It had to do with the fact that the administration's stated goal in Vietnam, to keep the Communists from taking over the South, did not match its strategic activity, which was, as one unnamed marine put it to AP correspondent Peter Arnett, "to destroy this [Vietnamese] village in order to save it."

Television only provides a lens. Leadership provides the focus. A majority of Americans, nearly until the end of the war, backed the notion of fighting Communists. What peeled away, like an illness at the heart of the body politic, was a belief that fighting communism was in fact what U.S. troops were doing in Vietnam.

Some grew convinced that the U.S. troops were fighting local petty tyrants, others that they were fighting in circles, without strategic objectives, still others that they were trapped in a hopeless quagmire. In fact, Tet was not the defeat for America reported by its journalists. Enemy casualties were extraordinary, and U.S. forces defended major cities with great vigor against tremendous odds. But neither was it a stunning victory, as portrayed by the general and later the White House, particularly Undersecretary of State Walt Rostow, whose "Monday Group" of top administration officials battled to win the hearts and minds of the public by leaking out the optimistic and sitting on the pessimistic.

In any event, when Walter Cronkite, after visiting the war zone, issued his verdict one month later, on February 27, 1968, that "the only rational way out then will be to negotiate, not as victors, but as an honorable people who lived up to their pledge to defend democracy, and did the best they could," it marked a critical juncture. Johnson told an aide, "If I've lost Cronkite, I've lost Middle America." A few weeks later, he announced his retirement, a defeated man, defeated as much by an inability to sell his policies to the public as by any collection of cathode tubes.

There is another critical aspect to the argument that television did not doom the U.S. war in Vietnam, and it is hidden in the public-opinion polls themselves. Public opinion may be malleable, and support for war may be thin, but among the most powerful factors in the public will for war is the number of casualties. John Mueller, in his study of polls and war, found that during the Korean War, American public support fell 15 percent every time U.S. casualties increased

by a factor of 10, from 10 to 100, or from 100 to 1,000, or
from 1,000 to 10,000. This pattern he found also in Vietnam,
suggesting that public appetite for war cannot be sustained—
no matter what the rationale, no matter what the news coverage—if casualties exceed expectation. This may be another
way of saying that the military must have an end game,
something that has been clearly lacking in some of the most
brutal and senseless wars of history, like World War I. Or it
may echo the lesson drawn from Vietnam that war must have
a clearly delineated and achievable military objective, that
there is a tactical marker at which the troops can claim victory and go home. But surely this nugget from the past, this
link between public support for war and casualties, suggests
at the very least that no media technology has as much power
to sway the body politic as the reality of combat death. There
must be a reason, a reason of national interest or high moral
purpose, for young men and women to lose their lives. In the
television era, it falls to leaders to convey that reason to the
public, or risk losing their support.

The emotions generated by TV pictures did not lose the
war. The reaction to an image of a child fleeing a napalm
bomb in screams of terror is not predictable. A nation prop-
erly consulted about war, genuinely called to duty, might respond to such pictures with renewed determination, fresh
anger for the fight ahead. When the Allies in World War II
lost 4,000 men in just over two weeks of fighting in the Battle
of the Bulge, public morale did not sink. Eisenhower called
on his soldiers to turn the enemy's "greatest gamble into his
worst defeat," for "new heights of courage, of resolution and
of effort." Twenty-three years later, faced with the losses in
Tet, Westmoreland called on his troops to muster their "al-
ertness, aggressiveness, professionalism and courage" to "add
new luster to your outstanding reputation." Nothing about
God and country. Nothing about the enemy or the morality

of the cause. Television pictures may have brought the war home, and the public may not have liked what they saw, but that is hardly the fault of the pictures.

Vietnam produced more than television pictures; it produced a syndrome, a hesitancy on the part of U.S. policy makers to go to war unless there is a clear moral purpose, an overwhelming force to reduce the prospect of combat deaths, and a clear military objective that allows for an exit strategy. It is true that television, like the other media technologies, expands the audience, thus increasing the number of people who form an opinion about a war. But to say that television turns viewers against war is to attribute to the technology more than is deserved. Television cast a spotlight on Vietnam, but so did the newspapers, which throughout the war had far more influence on public opinion. Television showed pictures of Americans in combat, but they were in the background, usually, shown in film that was two or three days old, flown from Vietnam to Bangkok, from Tokyo to New York. Television dramatized the forces at work in Vietnam, no more so than when CBS correspondent Morley Safer and his crew filmed a U.S. Marine setting a Vietnamese village on fire with a Zippo lighter. This was an image with the power to inflame. It might even be said that television accentuated the visceral, giving more credence to the emotional ballast of the war than to its causes or consequences.

The Doctrine of the Picture was television's blessing, and its curse, a theory that visuals had to carry the story. For journalists, this distorted slightly the cast of their reporting, because the best pictures were by nature exaggerations. Print reporters filing from the marine base in Khe Sanh in February 1968 noted that the heaviest North Vietnamese attacks were on three outposts on hills to the west. Television correspondents could not get pictures of the outposts, settling instead on the verbal comparison to the French loss in Dien Bien

Phu, and showing pictures of wrecked planes, marines scrambling off airplanes under enemy attack, and interviews with young soldier about whether they had enough fortification.

Pictures invited explanation, but television, in this first television war, gave them platitudes. "Khe Sanh is no longer an effective roadblock against the enemy," opined CBS's Jack Laurence. Added Anchor Walter Cronkite: "Khe Sanh now is mostly a symbol. But of what? Pride, morale, bravery, or administration intransigence and military miscalculation?" For all the television hysteria, and despite the enemy shelling, marine losses at Khe Sanh were but a fraction of those suffered by U.S. troops elsewhere. Khe Sanh held, but journalism had changed. The camera seemed to encourage correspondents to look and sound more authoritative than they were, as if image could erase the need for facts. Soon enough the emotional tone would influence print journalism, inspiring a New Journalism of great writing and compelling narratives and raw drama.

Tom Wolfe was in his element at Clay Felker's *New York*, and magazine narratives were deemed a closer compass to the truth than the staccato recitation of a radio newscast. Television, shamed by the quiz scandals of the early 1960s, had expanded its nightly news shows in length from fifteen minutes to thirty minutes. War and trauma, from Vietnam and the American South, filled the time. Newspapers decided that if the public was getting its news from television, the role of the print media was to provide background. Later, after Watergate had shamed a White House press corps "scooped" by two junior reporters from the *Washington Post* metro desk, it became a badge of honor for newspaper reporters to provide the context for a politician's words, to explain the strategy behind his policy. This tendency to view government as the enemy owed something to President Nixon's use of the levers of power to engage in wiretapping, burglary, and cover-ups.

But it also coincided with a general press disdain for authority, an assumption that officials were up to no good, a mood that pervades newsrooms into the age of the Internet.

Television pictures no doubt made more graphic the scenes of Vietcong storming the U.S. embassy compound in Saigon after Tet, but even a newspaper account of enemy troops on the lawn of the U.S. embassy would have given the public pause. Military men giving inflated enemy casualty counts at what journalists came to call the Five O'clock Follies in Saigon did not help Lyndon Johnson's case. Disdain for public opinion by his cabinet officers, these "best and the brightest" of their generation, did not make his mission any easier. And social unrest by the baby boomer generation, questioning the objective of ridding a foreign land of Communists, this too complicated the hand Johnson was dealt. But the ending was not inevitable. Beyond the complications making the Vietnam War a towering dilemma, there was room at the top for political leadership. Blood was spilled in Saigon, but the war was lost in Washington. The legacy of earning public support had been learned, painfully, at a cost of over 58,000 U.S. dead, 275,000 South Vietnamese killed, perhaps 1 million Vietcong dead, a generation lost to communism in Vietnam, and a humiliating defeat on the world stage.

It was not the last. In the era that followed Vietnam, an age of satellite television and computer communication, a time of the fax and the radio, news traveled faster than ever before. From Manila to Moscow, from Beijing to Berlin, from the Palestinians in Israel to the fundamentalists in Iran, technology played a role in sparking events on the international scene. Revolutionaries crowed that the new media technology tore down national borders, gave new power to the downtrodden, and all but annihilated time and space. Sharing the stage with these new players tested the mettle leaders raised in a time of government censorship. They called it real time.

12

The Media and Revolution

T HE FIRST REAL-TIME television crisis faced by a world leader came in Tehran. Students of the revolution, angered that President Carter had allowed the shah of Iran into the United States for cancer treatments, overran the U.S. embassy, taking its diplomats and staff as hostages. Blindfolded, the Americans were paraded around the courtyard by the students, who threatened to try them as spies and kill them if there was a rescue attempt. As an American flag was burned by cheering students, the scene was recorded by television cameras. "America Held Hostage," an ABC program, would air almost every night for the next 443 days. Eventually it would spin off to become Ted Koppel's *Nightline*. At the State Department, spokesman Hodding Carter, at the request of ABC correspondent Barrie Dunsmore, allowed television cameras for the first time to record State Department briefings.

This was the first television crisis, the first screening of revolution. Satellite television was a shock to the political system, and social commentators hailed its arrival with an air of wonder—and fear. "No leader can any longer keep his people hostage using Goebbels-like propaganda," said Hubert Vedrine, national security adviser to French president François Mitterrand. "It's become technically impossible." If this greeting sounds familiar, it is the resonance of history, come to take its rightful bow on the entry of a new invention of communication technology. In this case the new medium was a satellite, orbiting the earth, that allowed transmission of voice and picture, of sound and image, in nanoseconds. It owed its existence to the technology perfected by the U.S. space program. When NASA launched *Telstar I* in 1962, FCC chairman Newton Minow told President Kennedy that launching a communication satellite was more important than launching a man into space, "because the satellite launched an idea, and ideas last longer than human beings." In this case, the idea was revolution against the "Great Satan" of U.S. foreign policy. For the most part, it angered, saddened, and frustrated Americans.

For Jimmy Carter it was more serious still. The hostage crisis was played every night like a drumbeat on national television, making the United States look like an impotent giant. Many believe it cost Carter the 1980 election. Others argue that Ronald Reagan's central question of the year, "Are you better off now than you were before?" resonated with voters because the economy, not foreign policy, decided the election. Either way, television had clearly given the student revolutionaries in Tehran a platform they would not have had without it. Every night, Walter Cronkite ended the CBS *Evening News* by reminding viewers how many days the hostages had been in captivity. Technology had again empowered dissidents, this time a visual technology that gave a face to revolution.

Carter's hostage crisis may have been the first television revolution, but it was not the last. As populations rose up in the Philippines and in the Middle East, in China and in Eastern Europe, the media and its technology functioned as they always had, to spread news and speed events. As an empire fell in the Soviet Union, the media and its technology were on hand, as they generally were, to record the dissonance between public utterances and private realities.

When these old regimes confronted dissidents, many of the revolutionaries were armed with old technologies, like the radio or the facsimile machine, which was actually invented at the time of the telephone. It was as if communication mattered more than method. Television served as the background for all of these moments of revolution in the 1980s, giving them a visual intensity that forced political leaders to face Jimmy Carter's dilemma of how to face down a mob in a television studio. But in no case did television dictate the outcome, for victory did not come uniformly to those who sought freedom from dictatorships. The deciding factor was instead the willingness of the old regimes to use force against their own people, a deadly calculation often correlated with indifference to Western public opinion. In revolution, the media technology served its traditional role of speeding events, but it was left for leaders to decide whether they were willing to kill to stay in power.

Marcos was the first to go. In an interview on ABC's *This Week with David Brinkley* on November 3, 1985, the Philippines' president looked history in the eye. Panelist George Will asked Marcos if, in light of calls from the opposition for an election, he might not call a ballot within the next eight months, to renew his mandate. Ever eager to demonstrate his belief in democracy, Marcos said he could do even better than that: He was "ready" to call an election within sixty days. ABC's Sam Donaldson wanted to know if there were "any catches," to which Marcos replied, "I'm ready. I'm ready. I'm ready."

This concession to a television query set the stage for the remarkable ascendance of "people power" rallying around Corazon Aquino, a housewife who had never held public office and widow of slain opposition leader Benigno Aquino. Marcos may have assumed that a $160 million war chest and blanket control of the official media would protect him against waves of prodemocracy emotion. Marcos supporters controlled most of the 14 major daily newspapers, 4 of the 5 major television networks, and most of the nearly 300 radio stations. But one station, *Radio Veritas*, owned by the Roman Catholic Church, and one newspaper, *Business Day*, gave play to Aquino's platform and beliefs, as well as charges from her supporters that the Marcos regime was corrupt. Foreign media played a role too, as copies of articles from U.S. newspapers and magazines on the election were widely distributed, as were videotapes of American television news shows. "Cory" swept to office despite charges of ballot fraud by the government, and Marcos and his wife, Imelda, fled for Hawaii, ending a twenty-year rule that some said had robbed the country of $5 billion. "Marcos had the media and the guns, we had the truth," Aquino said later. But Marcos may have been closer to the truth when he said, nearly a decade earlier, "It is easier to run a revolution than a government."

There is no question that the media played a role in the drama in the Philippines, as two decades of dictatorial rule ended peacefully in a new democracy. Just before the election, armed forces loyal to Marcos destroyed *Radio Veritas*'s transmitter. Moving to an alternate site, the station managed to keep broadcasting, but the message was clear. By this time, Marcos appreciated the deadly impact of this small station and the information it delivered. By this time too, Marcos may have also appreciated that he had lost the loyalty of his troops. Four days after the election, with both Marcos and Aquino declaring victory, Defense Minister Juan Ponce Enrile and Armed Forces Vice Chief of Staff Fidel Ramos withdrew their support for Marcos. They claimed the backing of only 300 soldiers, and a standoff with Marcos's men ensued. But when Marcos gave orders to his troops to attack, not everyone complied. He had lost the sense of popular will conveyed by the media, and more, he had lost command of his army.

This was the marker laid down for the revolutions to come, that regimes using force to put down dissent could survive, though at considerable cost of confidence. The barrel of the gun was still more powerful than the printing press, the transmitting station, the fascimile machine, or satellite television broadcasts. Pictures could sway public opinion, and did, as did information seeping in from once-closed borders. But any regime willing to risk public enmity for killing its own people could overcome the power of the media to foment dissent. Marcos was willing, but his army was not. Without troops willing to fire on their own, no dictatorship can survive.

The Soviet Union fell next. Though its demise came formally in Soviet leader Mikhail Gorbachev's resignation on Christmas Day 1991, the beginning of the end for the Soviet empire came several years earlier, at Chernobyl. Just after 1 P.M. on April 26, 1986, reactor number four at the Chernobyl nuclear power plant in Ukraine exploded in a fireball that spread contaminated nuclear fallout throughout Eastern Europe and Scandinavia. The reactor's cooling system had failed during a test, and its core overheated. The fire and meltdown were not brought under control for nine days. More than 600,000 workers took part in the cleanup. In their "heroic and in some cases literally suicidal" efforts, emergency crews prevented an even bigger catastrophe. Chernobyl was also the last attempt by the Kremlin to partake of the Big Lie, to confine media coverage to official policy.

For eighteen days after the accident, Gorbachev said nothing. When he did speak, Gorbachev blasted the Western media for using Chernobyl "as a jumping-off point for an unrestrained anti-Soviet campaign," condemning "a mountain of lies, the most virulent and malicious of lies . . . to discredit the Soviet Union . . . and to sow seeds of mistrust and suspicion toward the socialist countries." But Scandinavian scientists detected extreme levels of radiation. Western scientists estimated that Chernobyl had released a radioactive cloud said to be ten times more deadly than the radiation emitted at Hiroshima. Two years after the accident, the Kremlin was still in denial. Deputy Prime Minister Boris Shcherbina issued a secret decree prohibiting Soviet doctors from listing radiation as a cause of death.

Gorbachev hoped to preserve socialism by liberalizing it, to let some air out of the pressures that had been building toward social upheaval. But once the state controls were loosened, once journalists tasted the freedom to explore past wrongs, it was difficult to return again to blind obedience to government handouts. Through Stalin's purges and Khrushchev's antics, from Brezhnev's drinking to Chernenko's health, the Kremlin had long sought to keep its secrets out of public view. Whispers there may have been, but official confirmation never. Now, in the last gasps of control over information, the Kremlin maintained this unlikely denial of a major nuclear accident. The world learned of Chernobyl through a vast network of media outlets, but world opinion could neither extinguish the meltdown nor compel the Kremlin to acknowledge the obvious.

The revolution in Russia was over information. Gorbachev, who cared passionately about Western public opinion, opened the doors to his own exit by loosening the bounds of state censorship. His policies became known as "socialism with a smile," a concession to British prime minister Thatcher's instinct on first meeting Gorbachev that "we can do business with him." Basking in the West's adulation, Gorbachev ushered in a period of *glasnost*, or openness, where newspapers were suddenly free to measure the excesses and crimes of the past, and inspired a new noun, *Gorbymania,* to describe the adoring crowds who followed him like groupies at a rock concert. He was not above using force—Gorbachev unleashed a deadly assault on the radio station in Vilnius in the Baltic state of Lithuania on January 13, 1991, an attack that left fifteen dead and hundreds injured. Gorbachev understood enough about Western public opinion to understand that it was preoccupied at that moment with events in Baghdad, as the clock ticked down to war between Iraq and a coalition of thirty-four Arab and Western nations.

Still, reaction from Washington was swift and condemning. Gorbachev had made the same mistake as Louis XVI in pre-Revolutionary France, believing he could give the press more freedom and still maintain control over its utterances. Chernobyl exploded that myth, and tarnished Gorbachev's international reputation. There were too many other sources of information, too many other media influences on public opinion, for Gorbachev to be able to build any more Potempkin Villages. The unshackled Soviet press turned first to Soviet history, investigating crimes of the Stalin era and abuses from World War II. Soon enough the media turned its spotlight on contemporaneous events in the conviction that there should be no more Chernobyls. By the time Russian troops stormed into the breakaway republic of Chechnya in 1994, the first casualty of war was the Russian propaganda effort. Russian viewers saw television pictures of Chechnya that revealed all the graphic stupidity of war.

In China, pressure for democracy from students massing in Tiananmen Square played to an international audience and set off a thunderous power struggle that ended when those advocating a military response prevailed. The whole world may have been watching, but the leadership, and the army, was prepared to use force. Television may have speeded events, but it could not stop bullets. With Gorbachev on a state visit to Beijing and with CNN's cameras running, student demonstrators in China paraded a mock Statue of Liberty—the Goddess of Liberty they named her—through the square. Using fax machines, they communicated their hopes and dreams to a waiting and receptive audience abroad. In something of a return to Luther and his printing press, the students sought to receive and disseminate information by what amounted to an electronic pamphlet. Chinese students living abroad collected some 1,500 random fax numbers in China and began to distribute foreign news reports of what was happening in Beijing. Often their faxed news accounts were posted on public bulletin boards. The censors could not filter a facsimile. This was a back-channel for information, a technological solution to the dilemma of state censorship, a tool of communication so fast that even a powerful regime could not slow its arrival. Information by any means was always the first battleground of revolution.

Gorbachev's visit, rather than quieting the protests, seemed only to inspire the students, as the Soviet leader basked in the warmth of the camera lights and reveled in his international reputation as a reformer. As tens of thousands of Chinese troops took to the streets, rolling in tanks toward Tiananmen Square, one man tried to stop the advance. Wearing a white shirt, putting his hand up in an unspoken plea, the man succeeded, for a moment, in halting the procession. The photograph of his protest came to symbolize the peaceful intention of many students at Tiananmen, at least in the West. But in China, the same photograph is exhibited to demonstrate the restraint of the troops, who, it was said in exhibit captions, were humanitarian enough not to want to destroy a solitary life. But the leaders in Beijing were savvy enough to calculate the impact of pictures of bloodshed. As the army's troops poised for a crackdown on June 4, 1989, the Chinese pulled the plug on television coverage, literally telling CNN and other network crews to disconnect from the satellite uplink because they were no longer authorized to transmit pictures.

The Chinese understood that the television pictures were causing them to lose face among their own people. In the White House they were also having impact. President Bush's advisers, citing public-opinion polls, pressed him to act, to "do something" about the terrible injustice of Chinese Communists quashing student voices of democracy. Here is a vital test of the theory that the media and its technology is driving diplomacy, for Bush resisted. Having lived in the country for two years, he considered himself something of a China hand; he understood the Chinese preference for indirection. He was convinced that the best approach was a private one, without a lot of public posturing, without a lot of name-calling, a private plea for the students that would allow the leaders of China to make concessions without shame. He also doubted the utility of using television to convey a message to the Chinese, as he might to the Russians or the Cubans. The rulers in Beijing did not watch television and had little use for world opinion. For the Chinese regime, "the political consequences of not acting as far as they were concerned totally outweighed what the rest of the world thought," observed CIA director Bob Gates. "They didn't give a damn about public opinion." They cared about domestic opinion.

And so did Bush. Against his better instincts, Bush acquiesced. The administration banned high-level contacts with Beijing, cut off a few trade missions and concert tours, and designed a weak economic embargo. Press Secretary Marlin Fitzwater escalated his public rhetoric against the crackdown. These were symbolic actions, meant to calm a domestic audience rather than appeal to a foreign one, hardly a significant departure from U.S. policy, but they conceded policy to the "do something" crowd. A Gallup poll taken four days after the massacre showed that White House advisers were on target in their political assessment. Some 60 percent of all Americans, asked to grade the Bush response to China, said it was "about right." The administration's symbolic steps seemed to satisfy the public conscience. Much more of a reprisal might have occasioned public fears about creating an enemy in the world's most populous country. In any event, television again speeded delivery of the message without dictating the outcome of the event.

In Eastern Europe, the new medium played perhaps its most felicitous role in revolution. It is said of the Revolution of 1989 that it took ten years to bear fruit in Poland, ten months to leap across the border to Hungary, ten weeks to germinate in East Germany, ten days to spread like fire in Czechoslovakia, and ten hours to purge a totalitarian leader from Romania. "Satellites have no respect for political boundaries," said Newton Minow, former chairman of the Federal Communications Commission, in an address at Columbia University in 1991. "Satellites cannot be stopped by Berlin Walls, by tanks in Tiananmen Square or by dictators in Baghdad. In Manila, Warsaw and Bucharest, we saw the television station become today's Electronic Bastille."

In this view he was not alone. During the intoxicating days following the fall of the Berlin Wall on November 9, 1989, when champagne was uncorked atop the vestiges of repression, many in the West credited the media and its technology. Those who had cheered democracy from the sidelines were now convinced that media technology—television, radio, the fax machine, even the telephone—had facilitated its success on the playing field. "It was like a wave at a baseball game," recalled William Hill, former head of the *Voice of America*'s European division. "Once it started to go, the media made it impossible to stop. We heard the revolution. We saw the revolution. It was a heady fall." Ironically, the very titans being toppled from power were among the most avid listeners and viewers. The Kremlin, which often jammed *Voice of America* broadcasts through the Soviet Union, usually left one band open—so top Soviet officials could hear the news. Lech Walesa, the Solidarity Union leader who became president of Poland, left no doubt of his views. Asked about the role played by the Western media in his country's liberation, he replied, "Would there be land and earth without a sun?"

The best place to take the measure of that influence was in East Germany, where Communist ruler Erich Honecker was forced to accept the Western influences that came seeping across the border from West German radio and television broadcasts. More than other authoritarian leaders, Honecker had a special antenna for the threat posed by information. He banned Soviet leader Mikhail Gorbachev's speeches on *glasnost* and *perestroika* in East German newspapers and prohibited coverage of protests in Tiananmen Square on East German television. For a time, he even tried a Black Channel, which offered the East German view of the world. But for all his intuitive grasp of the power of information, Honecker was a prisoner of geography. Almost every home in East Germany had a radio and the ability to hear, in native German, at least six Western radio stations. By 1989, 95 percent of all East German homes had a television set—with more than 80 percent able to receive West German TV. A survey of East German homes in 1988 found that 40 percent of the women and 21 percent of the men watched the American television show *Dallas* each week. Television did not, by itself, topple Stalinist regimes, but it did provide glimpses of a society where creature comforts were common, where expression was open, where the link between a free people and a free press was assumed, and where even bad taste was given mass license to broadcast.

And in the summer of 1989, what was playing on West German TV was an exodus by East Germans, through the corridors of Central Europe, toward freedom in the West. For television, and for radio, it was a story that had everything: everyday people in search of a better life, willing to risk family and security for a better future. East Germans were voting with their feet, in an exodus that captured the imagination of the young, emboldened their parents, and frightened their politicians. Their journey went from East Germany to Czechoslovakia, across the border into Hungary, on to Austria, and then finally to West Germany. There, they could take advantage of West Germany's promise of citizenship to any East Germans who reached the West. For the television audience throughout Eastern Europe, the sense of wonder and empowerment of the East German exodus was riveting. Michal Chen, a Czechoslovakian drama student who helped forty East Germans get to the Hungary border from Prague, knew that his freedom was linked to theirs. "When we saw all those East Germans leaving, it told us anything could happen," he said.

The media, with its new speeded technology, captured the excitement of the exodus. Behind the scenes, there was a quieter triumph of steady, patient diplomacy. The exodus began in May, when Hungary started to dismantle the barbed wire on its border with Austria, what Winston Churchill called the iron curtain. When President Bush visited Budapest in July of 1989, Premier Miklos Nemeth gave him a piece of the iron curtain, a piece of barbed wire mounted on a plaque, with an inscription: "This piece of barbed wire was part of the Iron Curtain alongside the Hungarian-Austrian border. It represented the division of the European continent in two halves. Its dismantling was made possible by the will of the Hungarian people in recognition of peaceful co-existence and mutual interdependence. It is believed that the artificial, physical and spiritual walls still existing in the world someday will collapse."

The collapse of artificial walls was assured in September, when Hungary opted to let the East Germans through, to honor the Helsinki Final Act commitment to freedom of movement instead of the Warsaw Pact obligation to keep East Bloc citizens from fleeing. On its signature by Moscow and Washington and thirty-three European countries in 1975, Helsinki had been derided by some in the West as a bad deal. Critics argued that the treaty allowed the Kremlin to win the West's agreement not to rescue the once-free nations of Eastern Europe, while the West won little except a vague promise of accepting as inalienable certain human rights. And the critics were not entirely wrong. For almost fifteen years, Warsaw Pact leaders ignored the human-rights principles of Helsinki, giving lip service to ideas like freedom of movement while clamping shut the doors on emigration, in the process confirming the worst fears of the West that President Ford had given away too much geography to Soviet leader Brezhnev at Helsinki for too little tangible gain.

While it sat disdained by many in the West for nearly a generation, the Helsinki Final Act was a beacon of light to dissidents like Václav Havel in Czechoslovakia, who formed his Charter 77 dissident group based on the principles in the pact: freedom of speech, freedom of movement, freedom of the press. For almost a generation, there was an exchange of documents between dissidents and the West, advanced and speeded by the media's weapons of technology, that silently nursed the passions of revolution. The telephone, the copier, the fax machine, all aided the convergence of realities as the West sent documents on the human-rights principles embedded in Helsinki and dissidents sent back documentation that their regimes were violating those same ideals. "There was a cross-fertilization between dissidents and the West," said Jack

Maresca, U.S. ambassador to the Conference on Security and Cooperation in Europe, the Helsinki Act's institutional legacy. "We were issuing documents like crazy. There was a marriage of the final act, which recognized human rights as an interstate affair, with the explosion of communications." The information was unleashed on a population with a 98 percent literacy rate, with access to Western television and radio broadcasts, with smuggled books and a nascent underground press. Here was the case for the media as revolutionary.

But to credit the media for fomenting revolution, even in places where it may have encouraged dissent, is to minimize the courage of individuals, and of individualism. "Freedom did not come to Eastern Europe as a gift from Moscow or Washington," wrote author William Echikson. "It came from more than forty years of struggle—a daily, grinding struggle against a corrupt and evil system." Such passion for freedom was but one of the factors that tipped the balance of history in Eastern Europe in 1989. The church, for forty years, often at great risk, kept its doors open. "It was God who won in Eastern Europe," the Polish-born pope proclaimed five months after the fall of the Berlin Wall. The West, hesitant to intervene militarily, kept the pressure on with covert spy operations and overt grain embargoes. Not least among the factors that fomented revolution were the Communist leaders, who indulged in bourgeois excesses while their people lived in virtual poverty. When this hypocrisy was exposed by a newly unshackled *glasnost* generation, the only rational response was anger, anger that the few had taken so much from the many according to their greed.

Not least of the factors that made revolution possible was the Kremlin's decision not to intervene militarily, as soldiers had done to put down revolts in Hungary in 1956 and Czechoslovakia in 1968. When the Solidarity Union won overwhelming election in Poland despite a prearranged formula giving Communists a lease on power, the Soviets signaled that the Red Army would not be rolling its tanks to help the repressive regimes of Eastern Europe control a restive people. "This is entirely a matter to be decided by Poland," said Soviet envoy Yevgeny Primakov. The exodus was playing on television screens throughout the world, but Gorbachev's so-called Sinatra Doctrine, of letting Soviet Bloc nations go their own way, was more important to the outcome.

East German leader Honecker knew that Gorbachev's decision doomed his regime. As prodemocracy forces began to attract mass support for Monday night candlelight marches in Leipzig, Honecker gave the order to fire on demonstrators in Nikolai Church. "There was a written order from Honecker for a Chinese solution," said Markus Wolf, head of East Germany's spy agencies. "It could have been worse than Beijing." Instead, according to Wolf's account, Egon Krenz, Honecker's protégé, a man who thought he could preserve a reformed communism, flew to Leipzig to countermand the order. Within two weeks, Honecker resigned, Krenz succeeded him, and the infamous Black Channel was taken off the air. Within a month, on November 9, the wall that separated East from West for thirty years—a wall more than 180 East Germans had died trying to cross—was breached. The West said the wall came down, the East said it had opened. Either way, the event had been precipitated by a push for reform and sealed by the decision not to use force against the reformers. The media's role, like Mercury's, was to speed delivery of the message. It fell to the actors, in this case the citizens of Eastern Europe and the leaders who until then had dictated the terms of their existence, to write the contents.

For all the speed that satellite television afforded events on the ground, for all the impact that foreign radio had on the hearts and minds of the people of Eastern Europe, it still fell to leaders to delineate choices. The revolution that swept Eastern Europe was not a uniform march to the sea. In Czechoslovakia, reform came as a Velvet Revolution, soft as the night, virtually without violence, with enormous public support. In Romania, reform came in the form of an execution, as Nicolae Ceausescu's enemies, enraged by the brutality of his private *Securitate* forces, caught up with him. As the cold war ended in the late 1980s, and with it forty years of enmity between East and West, the media with its technology surely speeded the last crumbling vestiges of empire. But the media did not dictate the course of events in any of the places where repression gave way to democracy. If the only requirement for a successful revolution were television cameras beamed by satellite to a global audience, if the only pressure on policy makers was a drumbeat of media attention or the resulting push from a responsive public to "do something," then Tiananmen Square would have enjoyed the same result as Wenceslas Square. That they did not, that upheaval in Czechoslovakia led to a peaceful passage while the one in Beijing led to a massacre, is an indication of the latitude for leaders to counter media technology.

There are two more uprisings that called on the gifts of real-time television to convey their passions. The *Intifada*, which began in December of 1987 with women and children throwing rocks at Israeli troops in the Gaza Strip, made the evening news around the world. This is no accident, as the Palestinian leadership was among the most skilled at exploiting media technology to advance their political agenda. For much of the 1980s, when Israel banned contacts between Palestinians in the occupied territories and Yasser Arafat's exile leadership in Tunis, these revolutionaries communicated through a computer network in Cyprus or cellular phones linked through London. Within five years of the *Intifada*'s beginning, Israel and the Palestinians were in negotiations that would lead to an interim agreement ceding territory, and sovereignty, in the Gaza Strip.

Also toward the end of the decade, South Africa began waking from its forty-year obsession with apartheid, the legal attempt to segregate the races and subjugate black Africans to domination by white descendants of Britain's colonial rule. The first breakthrough came in 1977, when South Africa lifted its ban on television as morally corrupting, to say nothing of politically dangerous. ABC's Ted Koppel traveled to South Africa in 1985 for telecasts that gave the African National Congress equal billing with the Pretoria government. By 1990, when resistance leader Nelson Mandela was released from prison after more than twenty-seven years, the cameras had already broadcast his message. There was power in the cameras, but the poignancy was in Mandela's cause. And when President F. W. de Klerk asked Mandela to negotiate a political settlement that ended apartheid, it was a sign that he would not use force to dictate policy. Like the revolutions in Eastern Europe, the transition in South Africa was guaranteed by a free ballot box.

There is always a risk in reading too much into history. China's premier Zhou En Lai was asked in the 1970s to assess the significance of the French Revolution in the 1780s. His reply: "It is too soon to tell." So it may be risky to read too much into the media's role in the events of 1989, into the ability of technology to sway the outcome. But there is no question that the media speeded events, and to some extent focused the agenda of policy makers in world capitals. In the first war after the collapse of communism, the first engagement of the post–cold war era, what President Bush called the "new world order," the military establishment sought to reassert control over both agenda and timing. All the assumptions about history and technology were put to the test in the Persian Gulf War.

13

The Persian Gulf War

O N FRIDAY APRIL 2, 1982, one hour after Argentina invaded the Falkland Islands off its southeast coast, the British Ministry of Defense cabled the Royal Navy to inquire how many journalists would be allowed to sail with the task force of British sailors sent to liberate the territory, first claimed by the British in 1690 and formally colonized by England in 1733. The answer sent back from Fleet Headquarters at Norwood was succinct: none. The ministry protested that it was unthinkable to go to war without the press, so the navy reluctantly agreed to take on six journalists, then grudgingly upped the number to ten to include a television crew. After "the most violent media lobbying of No. 10 [Downing Street] in recent history," the total was raised to twenty-nine. Admiral Henry Leach groused, asking whether he was to load up his ships with "pens or bayonets?" It is a question that has long been asked of war correspondents by those waging war.

Ten weeks later Argentina surrendered, and the island retained its British allegiance. But the war had proven a model for future encounters between the military and the media. The British government had excelled at slowing and often preventing publication of news not to its liking. Correspondents sent their written copy back to London over the ships' military communications systems—available only when military needs abated. Television tapes had to be sent by ship to Ascension Island, where they were cabled or flown back to Britain. When Britain's HMS *Sheffield* was hit by an Exocet missile on May 4, British officials refused media requests to fly a photographer to the scene. When finally TV crews were permitted to record what was left of the damage, British authorities took more than two weeks to get the pictures back to London.

Officials exploited this advantage of transportation by assuring that the first spin on any story was theirs. After an Argentine air attack on British ships at Bluff Cove left fifty British troops dead, one radio reporter called it a "setback," noting, "Other survivors came off unhurt but badly shaken after hearing the cries of men trapped below." The report was held up until the graphic sentence was dropped. In the meantime, officials quickly cleared another radio report, in which the battle was described as "a day of extraordinary heroism." That was the first sound of events broadcast in Britain, evoking an image of heroism rather than of pain. The public was spared grisly details of battle, in hopes that public opinion might be spared doubts about the war.

British journalists tried to balance news from the ships with reports from the Argentinian side, but their efforts met great hostility at home, where one conservative decried "reporting live propaganda out of Buenos Aires," and a member of Parliament called the BBC's efforts to compare British and Argentinian versions of events "totally offensive and almost treasonable." Prime Minister Thatcher complained about the press's habit of giving equal weight to British and Argentine government statements. "I became very unhappy at the attempted 'even-handedness' of some of the comment, and the chilling use of the third person—talk of 'the British' and 'the Argentinians' on our news programs," she wrote in her memoirs. Defense chief of staff Terence Lewin justified the restrictions as the price of victory. "I do not see it as deceiving the press or the public, I see it as deceiving the enemy," he said. "What I am trying to do is to win. I should have thought that that was what the government and the public and the media would want too." In the Falklands, it seemed, Britain ruled not only the seas but also the story.

In Washington, the Pentagon watched closely this latest clash between the media's impulse to disclose and the military's desire for secrecy. In an article for the *Naval War College Review* in its May–June 1983 edition, Lieutenant Commander Arthur A. Humphries set the tone for coming conflicts. Among the lessons he took from Vietnam was that "if you don't want to erode the public's confidence in the government's war aims, then you cannot allow that public's sons to be wounded or maimed right in front of them via their TV sets at home." In truth, the networks had shown a certain restraint in Vietnam, eschewing close-ups of dead or maimed American soldiers, as much a concession to public sensibility as government censorship. But such distinctions were lost in the postmortems on Vietnam, when television coverage was largely viewed as a negative force. From the prism of the British experience in the Falklands, seven years after the fall of Saigon, Humphries deduced that "you must, therefore, control correspondents' access to the fighting."

The military has long sought dominance over the media during war, if only to contain the enemy's access to information. But never is this policy of censorship more important than when a new technology gives journalism additional speed. The telegraph meant that for the first time reporters could report on military battles as they were taking place, cabling news from the field, sometimes within twenty-four hours. Satellite television hastened even further the time between events and their publication, giving the public a view of battle as it occurred. It is no accident that the first war correspondents were anointed on the battlefield of the Crimea War in 1854, nor that the American Civil War saw the first full measure of government restrictions on press reporting. Nor is it any surprise that the wars from the Falklands to the Persian Gulf saw tightened restrictions on press movement.

During World War I, photographs were the new factor in diplomacy, and they were banned, on penalty of death. In World War II, radio was new, and all broadcast copy was vetted by the censor. Vietnam was an undeclared war where the new medium of television had a virtually unrestricted run of a battlefield nominally controlled by the South Vietnamese. Journalists could rent planes, drive cars, hitch a ride to the battlefield. They could also fly their news footage quickly to Bangkok or Hong Kong, where it could be processed and transmitted to headquarters in New York. In short, the jet engine was an ally of the reporters, while the jungle was no friend to the military. Without the ability to control journalists' physical travel, to limit their access to the battlefield, the military had a harder time influencing their copy. By the Persian Gulf War, satellite television had given journalism enormous speed, and military planners had no intention of letting it meander freely in the war zone.

There is a straight line from the Falklands in 1982 to the Persian Gulf War in 1991. In a series of incursions, not wars really, the American military tested the British approach to managing the media. The first was Grenada in 1983, where reporters were kept off the island for several days while American troops operated on a two-pronged mission: to restore democratic rule after Marxist hard-liners had overthrown the government, and to evacuate U.S. medical students. Journalists who did reach the island were detained. Meanwhile, U.S. troops made some embarrassing mistakes, including rushing to the college only to find that the students had been evacuated to another campus. None of this information reached the public until much later, and when it did the public tended to support the administration. Hints in the press that the administration had launched the invasion in Grenada to divert public attention from the massacre of 241 marines in a barracks bombing in Beirut a few days earlier were met with angry denials by the administration—and a cold shoulder from many in the public. "The most astounding thing about the Grenada situation," said Max Frankel of the *New York Times*, "was the quick, facile assumption by some of the public that the press wanted to get in, not to witness the invasion on behalf of the people, but to sabotage it."

Next came Panama in 1989, where U.S. forces landed to help topple strongman Manuel Noriega, then clinging to power despite democratic elections that had ousted him. President Bush had failed to support a coup effort within Noriega's army when it flared in October. Now, in December, after critics had wondered if the "wimp factor" would influence Bush's term in office, he launched a U.S. military attack.

In the aftermath of Grenada, journalists had negotiated a new system of coverage with the Pentagon. On the recommendation of the Sidle Commission, named for its author, retired Major General Winant Sidle, the press agreed to a representative "pool" of journalists and photographers, representing newspapers, magazines, wire services, radio, and television, who would report back to the rest of the media housed at a military headquarters. The Pentagon pool system saw its first test in Panama. It was not a success.

The press corps had expanded beyond the thousands that, over the course of a decade, had covered Vietnam. Now there were thousands eager to see war all at once, and the Pentagon argued that legions of reporters loosed on the battlefield would interfere with the mission. The media heavyweights countered that the public had a constitutional right to know. The Pentagon pool was the compromise. On the eve of the Panama invasion, the Pentagon decided to send the pool from Washington, rather than organize a local pool of reporters who were already covering increased tensions on the ground. As a result, the press pool arrived four hours after fighting had begun. Even as locally based reporters for CNN and other outlets raced around Panama City in search of news, the official Pentagon pool was kept at command headquarters. The Pentagon offered the journalists a lecture on Panamanian history and access to CNN television reports on Panama, largely from briefings in Washington and interviews with experts in Atlanta. "We actually watched a Bush news conference," said *Dallas Morning News* reporter Kevin Merida. "We were right there with the viewer watching CNN." Field trips were finally arranged for the pool, tours of Noriega's secret lairs of cocaine and guns, featuring a portrait of Hitler. But the fighting had long since ended. Theirs was journalism's equivalent of a cleanup mission.

In the aftermath of Panama, journalists demanded quicker access to the combat zone. But by the time U.S. forces landed in Saudi Arabia to engage Iraq in the Persian Gulf War, the field was nearly cleared of journalists. The top brass, from General Norman Schwarzkopf on down, did not want a workable pool arrangement so much as a controlled press. Veterans of Vietnam, they remembered not that war was messy but that news accounts made the military look inept. They had no intention of letting reporters have a clear view of the battlefield. And in Saudi Arabia they had a host country not accustomed to issuing visas to journalists by the thousands. Good politicians, Schwarzkopf and his allies gave lip service to the pool system, setting up arrangements that kept the number of reporters traveling with combat units to a manageable 192, charged with the responsibility of sending copy back to their 1,400 colleagues at briefing centers in Riyadh and Dhahran.

But reports first had to survive the battlefield communications systems, and then clear military censors at headquarters. Reporters called the system "Pony Express," and often it failed to meet even that lethargic mail carrier's track record for delivery. The army issued the reporters credentials, but phones were somehow less often available. Often it took three or four days for files to reach New York. One news photographer's film took thirty-six days to reach its destination. Local Pentagon officials grew tired of policing the reporters, and asked journalists to devise their own rules for selecting pool members tapped for each day's assignment. The system may not have been intended to last more than a few days into war, as the Pentagon later insisted, and a good thing too, because veteran reporters insist that the pool system was on the verge of collapse when Iraq surrendered. Had the war gone on much longer, say reporters, they would have bolted from the pool arrangement and struck out on their own. But in a 100-hour ground war, that is all the lead time Schwarzkopf and his commanders needed.

The Pentagon managed the news in other ways as well. Videotapes of successful air-bombing runs were released selectively by the Pentagon, on its own timetable. Briefings were scheduled consecutively so that reporters could be preoccupied with official words from Saudi Arabia, Europe, and the United States most of the day. Just before the start of the ground war, the military used the media to spread disinformation to the Iraqis, hoping to leave the impression that the invasion would be an amphibious attack on Kuwait from the sea. Even the decision to end the war after 100 days was made with one eye on the public-relations value of a round number, at least in the view of Saudi Arabia's top commander, General Khaled bin Sultan, who also believed that the Americans fatefully gave away too much to the Iraqis during peace talks at Safwan because they wanted "a media event" instead of a surrender.

And, unlike Vietnam, there were no photo opportunities of caskets. Bush had been deeply offended when, during the Panama invasion in December 1989, live television pictures of caskets being brought home to Dover Air Force Base were broadcast on a corner of the screen as he exchanged in some light banter with reporters in the White House briefing room, making it look as though the commander in chief were laughing at the sacrifices of his soldiers. So when troops began pouring into the Saudi desert, the Bush White House was very clear: No cameras would be allowed at Dover when bodies came home to rest. There were omissions of fact—the number of Iraqi casualties is still in contention, and years after the war a census bureau staffer was pushed out because she gave an estimate to one reporter—and there were errors of fact.

"The first casualty when war comes is truth," Hiram Johnson, a senator from California, had remarked as the United States entered World War I in 1917. In the Persian Gulf, truth suffered some. Nearly every day military briefings informed a world audience that Scud-missile launch-sites in Iraq had been destroyed, eliminating Saddam Hussein's ability to threaten Israel. Nearly every day Israelis got private intelligence that the launch sites were undamaged, having been moved during the night. Lieutenant General Thomas Kelly, director of operations for the Joint Chiefs of Staff during Panama and one of the Pentagon's key briefers on the Persian Gulf War, says there was no intent to deceive, that the Iraqis were just careful at hiding the launchers during periods when the satellite camera was orbiting. Saddam no doubt considered the reports part of a calculated disinformation strategy to showcase the coalition's military might. But anyone who thinks war can be sliced into neat summaries for press briefings has never seen it. Anyone who doubts press complicity in Pentagon management need only see the cluster of reporters who surround officials at every briefing. A news blackout at the war's beginning was justified by Kelly on grounds that "war is messy at first." Journalism and war are both messy endeavors, with victory measured an inch at a time, and truth is more often found at the front than at headquarters.

The American military had something to prove in the deserts of Saudi Arabia, a pride and confidence to reassert. Keeping journalists contained was part of the strategy. But for journalism too the Persian Gulf War was a milestone. A new technology, satellite television, brought war to an international audience, all watching at the same time. This was the elixir of all new media inventions, to bring a new dimension to the familiar, to eliminate the barriers between the audience and information, to try the patience of policy makers and exaggerate the importance of journalists, to annihilate time and space. Cable News Network, the brainchild of Atlanta entrepreneur Ted Turner, had arrived.

The vision was there. Turner told an interviewer, "I wanted to use communications as a positive force in the world, to tie the world together." But the audience was virtually nonexistent. Viewers rarely tuned in unless there was a blockbuster event, like war. Only when Saddam Hussein invaded Kuwait in August of 1990, did CNN begin to approach an audience rating of more than 1 million viewers. By the time allied troops began targeting Baghdad with nightly runs in January of 1991, CNN ranked nearly 7 million viewers, just a few million short of the other major networks. But unlike the three big American networks, the audience for CNN was worldwide. As CNN's Bernard Shaw, Peter Arnett, and John Holliman described the sights and sounds of aerial attacks outside their hotel window in Baghdad, viewers could watch war. Thatcher watched in Britain. Yeltsin watched in Moscow. Bush watched in Washington. Shamir watched in Jerusalem. Saddam watched in Baghdad. Even Libya's Muammar Qaddafi watched in his tent in Tripoli, calling the CNN control room in the days before war to say he had a plan to resolve the conflict peacefully. Staffers assumed he was a crackpot and hung up. There is simply no precedent for this experience. This was real-time war. For CNN, disdained by the older networks and dismissed by the critics, the Persian Gulf War was the ultimate redemption.

For the first time since Washington's privileged ladies brought picnic lunches down to the Battle of Bull Run to watch an early Civil War battle, an audience had witnessed war. True, satellite television did not bring war into the living room, as it had in Vietnam. This time, television brought the accoutrements of war, the sound and light and talk of war. The audience was spared the worst of it. There was no blood, no guts, no glory. Still, there were sound effects, the noise of missiles hissing through the air, and there were blazes of light in the sky, the result of Patriot missiles intercepting Scud missiles, resembling a child's Nintendo game. There were strewn tanks and blazing oil fires and surrendering troops. There were briefings from media-savvy military officers and interviews with military-wise defense experts, what the news critics called "talking heads." There were transponders and satellite dishes, laptop computers and satellite telephones. There were even enemy soldiers surrendering to American reporters.

War had become a computer game. Suddenly, thanks to Pentagon news management and CNN's blanket news format, correspondents could cover the war as easily from a television set in Washington as from a briefing room in Riyadh, and many did. Like diplomats, print reporters found that CNN could deliver the news faster than they could, leaving them the job of explaining what it meant. For better or worse, newspapers turned to analysis and policy, leaving to television the sloppier process of gathering the news. In 1935, when editors of *Time* magazine were brainstorming for a new venture, one editor advanced the idea of a photographic magazine by saying, "A war, any sort of war, is going to be a natural promotion for a picture magazine." More than fifty years later, war was a "natural promotion" for an upstart network, bringing in ratings and respect and a feeling that war would never be the same again.

Satellite television also saw the dawning of "rooftop journalism," an era of parachutist journalists jumping into unfamiliar terrain, rushing to a hotel roof and announcing that something was going on around them, sometimes before they had made a single inquiry or placed a single phone call or witnessed a single incident. With the costs of maintaining foreign bureaus out of reach, many news organizations had devolved to crisis coverage, sending their best disaster reporters to cover each breaking story, often with no knowledge of the language, customs, culture, or politics of the country they had lit down in. No matter: On television, it looked like a war zone. In reality, it might as well have been a Pentagon backdrop on a movie produced in Hollywood—lights, camera, war!

Parachutists, ultimately, are generalists, trained in crisis, not countries. They live for the anecdote that captures a sense of place. They search out the voices of victims and aggressors both that will draw the reader to the story. Interspersed with the patriots in the sky, CNN's reporters conveyed a sense of being there, even when "there" was a bed in a hotel room nine stories up from the action. In the Gulf War the parachutists shared space with the government wonks, reporters whose specialty is divining the truth from between the lines of officialspeak. Their beat is the stuff of briefings: official

Pentagon and White House briefings, official government re-action from Jerusalem or Amman, official reaction to Sad-dam's latest pronouncements, unofficial speculation from so-called experts.

The advent of live coverage of briefings and rooftop re-porting meant a real-time clock on war. But it also meant the audience could form its own views on a reporter's daring or veracity, on an expert's batting average or a Patriot missile's accuracy. Suddenly, even as the battlefield was cleared of re-porters, viewers had a rare opportunity to form their own opinions based on raw footage broadcast live. That the public sympathized in large part with Pentagon briefers attempting to win a war rather than pesky reporters asking banal ques-tions is not a surprise. What was unexpected is the depth of public anger at the press. In the Persian Gulf, reporters' ac-tions seemed to infuriate the public, which saw in questions at briefings a certain arrogance, and dullness. When it came time to parody the conflict, *Saturday Night Live*, in its first program after the war began, elected to satirize not the ribbon-bedecked generals or the bar-hopping Kuwaitis or even the bellowing Iraqis who had flavored the story, but the American reporters who in daily televised press conferences showed their ignorance of military security, operations, and objectives.

That real-time television changed diplomacy and changed the news media's direction is indisputable. Cable-news view-ers could see news as it was unfolding. Many decry this roof-top reporting as a new low for the profession. Michael Crichton, author of *Jurassic Park*, proclaimed the new state of reporting "the mediasaurus," a fossil animal due for extinc-tion, "junk food journalism." Critics like Howard Kurtz of *The Washington Post* lamented the "media circus," and scholars like Larry Sabato at the University of Virginia documented the media's "feeding frenzy." Politicians privately cursed the media's cynicism, a sort of "gotcha journalism" designed less to extract information from government officials than to skewer them for their words, their deeds, their intentions, and their histories. And the public's trust in the media dropped, as did readership and viewership of the major American news outlets.

Far from creating shoddy journalism, technology offers a showcase for communication. Like political leaders, journalists can excel or falter in its wake. Satellite communication begat tabloid television, with its insidious influences on news journalism, but it also encouraged C-SPAN, which demonstrated a new way to report the news, without a filter. Amid the satellites, talk radio had a resurgence of popularity, not because radio was new but because television had gone tabloid, creating a vacuum of debate on the issues.

The Gulf War marked the pinnacle of the "real-time" television war, where viewers could not so much see war as they could observe news-gathering in the war zone. Recalling the admonition that anyone who has respect for the law or sausage should never watch either being made, viewers might have been advised to avert their eyes. The process of gathering news is clumsy, being a series of routine questions asked of people who may or may not have the answers. To put this process on live television is to expose journalists to the ridicule of critics who prefer their news packaged neatly in thirty-minute programs.

But the Gulf War was also a wake-up call for the network news shows and all the other practitioners of news on a schedule. The videocassette recorder had given consumers more control over when they watch the news, at a time when many women, a large share of the audience, were at work, no longer housewives with time to watch the soaps. The remote control offered consumers even more choice, recalling Arthur Ransome's wish, on radio's arrival in 1924, for a button by which the audience could release "a small electric current" to "a tender part of the performer" if the performance disappointed. The hand-held zapper did not send electronic currents, but it did make waves for the news business. In the United States, Vanna White and the game show *Wheel of Fortune* became formidable competitors to the news. By contrast, CNN gave viewers news whenever they needed it.

Hours after Kuwait City was liberated by coalition forces, a CNN crew arrived, in the middle of night, and decided to set up its truck, complete with satellite dish, in the middle of a four-lane highway with tanks strewn about and street signs askew. A CBS crew, captained by tenacious producer Susan Zirinsky, had beaten them in by a few hours, and they were mildly depressed. "We turned on the lights and saw graffiti scrawled on the walls," recalled producer John Towriss. "The first three things I could see were: 'Welcome Allied Troops. George Bush Is Our Hero. We Love CNN.' And I was astonished. I thought, Wow, here I am in Kuwait City in the middle of the night in the middle of a war and here's some graffiti that says 'We Love CNN.' And we turned on the lights and started broadcasting, and Kuwaiti resistance fighters materialized out of the dark. I can't tell you how many people hugged me and kissed me and wanted to touch something that was CNN. With tears in their eyes, people told us that we were the only ones they could depend on, that they had kept their satellite dishes camouflaged and hidden, that the rest was propaganda. As light began to come over the city, and people began to realize the Iraqis had withdrawn, to find the city without Iraqis, we became the immediate point of tension—lights, cameras and soon the troops came rolling in."

CNN was able to bring to viewers the sights and sounds of war in part because its reporters were still in Baghdad when the fighting began. Baghdad had calculated that it could influence public opinion through CNN's cameras, and let them stay when the others were booted out. And one CNN reporter, a veteran of Vietnam, stayed behind when all the others had gone. Peter Arnett set a new marker for journalism, establishing a toehold in the enemy camp. In truth, he was hardly behind hostile lines, having been invited to stay by an Iraqi regime that was convinced his reports would rebound to its benefit.

Outside Iraq, public reaction to this landmark was surprising. Nearly every day CNN got hate mail, and angry calls, from viewers who did not understand why Arnett was reporting from enemy territory in Baghdad, two thousand comments a day, three-to-one against his presence. Senator Alan Simpson, a Republican from Wyoming, called Arnett "a sympathizer," provoking a huge furor within the media. Two Arnett reports in particular seemed to irk viewers. One was about the bombing of a facility the Iraqis claimed was a baby-formula factory. The Americans insisted the plant was for producing biological weapons, and when Arnett gave the Iraqi claims, White House spokesman Marlin Fitzwater called CNN "a conduit for Iraqi disinformation." The second was about civilians killed in a bomb shelter that the United States insisted was a military command headquarters.

In truth, both sides used Arnett to carry messages, stake out claims, and fight for public support, functions journalism has traditionally provided in wartime. What seemed to anger some viewers is that Arnett had pictures of the destruction, pictures of the signs, in English, that said BABY MILK FACTORY. The pictures did not make his reports more or less accurate, but they did lend them an air of authority. That is the line in the sand drawn during the Persian Gulf War, not that a reporter had crossed behind the lines—William Shirer had worked briefly from Germany in the early days of World War II—but that he had visual evidence. There was something visceral about the camera that made the audience feel uncomfortable, as if it was watching the production from behind the stage.

While Arnett was not the first journalist to visit the enemy during war—the *New York Times*'s Harrison Salisbury had toured North Vietnam in 1966 and reported on civilian damage to win the Pentagon's sobriquet: Ho Chi Salisbury of the *Hanoi Times*—no one had before this camped out on the enemy's doorstep. "War will never be the same because of what Peter Arnett did in Baghdad," said Stan Schrager, spokesman for the U.S. embassy in Haiti during the restoration of Jean-Bertrand Aristide to power. "You will never be able to conduct a war the same way again because of the influence of Peter Arnett in Baghdad." But the truth is that with international networks devoted to the fastest possible dissemination of news no matter its origin, there is no enemy territory anymore. The Iraqis invited Arnett to Baghdad to get their message to a vaster audience. Real-time reporting from behind their lines gave Iraq an enormous weapon in influencing public opinion, as well as intelligence about world reaction. It also gave real-time intelligence to U.S. military commanders, allowing them to assess damage to enemy territory. The battlefield for public acceptance has few borders.

In the five years since it ended, the Persian Gulf War has birthed several myths. One is that the war with Iraq buried the Vietnam syndrome. "It's a proud day for Americans," President Bush proclaimed on March 1, 1991, as he announced the end of the Gulf War. "By God, we've licked the Vietnam syndrome once and for all." Despite Bush's euphoria, the syndrome lives. The military generation that came of age during Vietnam resolved that war must never again be waged without an obtainable military objective, an overwhelming commitment of forces, an exit strategy, and public support. That is the Vietnam syndrome, and it is alive and well, in the Pentagon as well as the White House. Bush himself applied these guidelines to later conflicts in Bosnia and Somalia, staying out of Sarajevo largely because he could not discern a military goal, going into Mogadishu despite misgivings about how to get out. In a narrow sense, the Gulf War may have restored the American military spirit that Vietnam dampened. But in a larger sense, the Gulf War only underscored the lessons the Pentagon took from Vietnam, chief among them that a battlefield open to journalists was hostile territory.

Another delusion is that the Persian Gulf heralds an era of successful wars fought with few casualties against petty tyrants. It is unlikely that the next adversary will give the United States and its allies six months to mobilize, as Saddam did. Nor is it a given that the next war involving the United States will cost little more than 100 days and 100 lives. The only thing settled by the Persian Gulf War, argues Lieutenant General Tom Kelly, is that the military, with a strong army and a publicly supported goal, will have a winning story to tell. "The best briefer in the world could not have sold the Gulf War, any more than Vietnam, if it had gone on for ten years and left fifty-seven thousand dead and been no closer to victory at the end than at the beginning," he says.

Finally, while it may be true that the Pentagon managed the news, it is a misnomer to suggest that television changed the nature of the Persian Gulf War. Political figures like George Bush surely bowed to television's influence, timing the end of the war to give TV a neat sound bite. But that is hardly a function of real-time television. Like other media technologies before it, satellite television may have speeded the war and even supplanted the function of diplomats to carry messages, but it did not, it could not, win victory in battle. "When it comes to war, these are actually fought and won or lost not by journalists but by soldiers," said Robin

Renwick, former British ambassador to the United States. Governments, he added, "of course have to explain what we are doing, but what we are judged by is whether we win or lose. And no matter how much spin, effort, lunch or dinner you give the media, they will not fail to notice whether you have won or lost." Like other new technologies, satellite television gave advantage to those who learned how to exploit its promise.

In the history of military-media relations, it is often said that World War II was the apex. Journalists dressed in the uniforms of the units they accompanied. Reporters wore their sympathies for the allies on their sleeves. Ernie Pyle wrote home sonnets to the American fighting man. Edward R. Murrow intoned his great baritone to the cause of London's plight, describing German bombing raids with such clarity and metaphorical brilliance that Americans understood the agony of war. There were press restrictions aplenty during World War II—on photographs of Americans killed in battle, on films that gave aid and comfort to the enemy. There was a Code of Wartime Practices that required journalists to submit their stories to censors, and journalists whose work violated those rules were banished.

If World War II was the peak of media-military relations, surely Vietnam was the nadir. In the beginning reporters were respectful of government statements, giving them the currency of truth. But as the war dragged on and the pictures painted by American spokesmen no longer matched the scenes witnessed by American correspondents, as body counts of enemy dead grew inflated at regular briefings dubbed "Five O'clock Follies" by the reporters, the dissonance between the military descriptions and the eyewitness accounts played out in the copy. Relations between the press and the Pentagon had started to sour during the Kennedy administration, when Assistant Secretary of Defense Arthur Sylvester, shortly after the 1962 nuclear showdown of the Cuban Missile Crisis, proclaimed for the government "a right to lie." Now in Vietnam, reporter cooperation turned to cynicism, and some of American journalism's top names—David Halberstam, Neil Sheehan, Peter Arnett, Morley Safer—made their reputations recording the transition.

Just at that moment television arrived on the scene with its bulky equipment and demands for pictures. The Doctrine of the Picture came with the equipment, an edict that television could tell no story without images, graphic images of bloodshed or on-the-scene images of reporters in exotic places—it mattered little as long as there were pictures. As the three major networks expanded their evening news shows from fifteen minutes to a half hour, the conflict in Vietnam came to fill the screens. The images were indelible: napalmed children screaming in pain, Vietcong suspects executed on the street, American soldiers burning down Vietnamese huts with Zippo lighters, explaining that in order to save the village they had first to destroy it. So haunting were the images that many would blame television for the public's loss of will. But it was the words that brought down the curtain, words in newspaper accounts and wire-service dispatches, words that flowed from the Mai Li Massacre to the Pentagon Papers, words that conveyed a military loss of purpose. To the existential question of whether a tree has toppled in the forest if no one witnesses the fall, the military now had a real answer. From the time the last U.S. helicopters left the roof of the American embassy in Saigon in 1975 to the time when troops landed in the Saudi desert in 1990, the military nursed the wounds of defeat and contemplated its comeback. By any calculation, such a return to glory would have to survive a suspicious media, newly endowed with technological wonders, that came to war not, as in World War II, to glorify heroes and damn villains, but largely to see trees fall.

The major lesson, from Vietnam to the Falklands, that U.S. military planners brought to the Persian Gulf War was the need for public support. They fought their fiercest battle for public opinion, as they had since World War I, and so did the political leaders who sent them off to war. The morning after Saddam Hussein invaded Kuwait, reaction in Washington was muted. People filled up their tanks, and joked nervously about what the conflict would do to the price of gasoline. At the National Press Club, the ambassador to the Arab League told reporters at a previously scheduled breakfast interview that this was an inter-Arab squabble, to be resolved by the league and its members. Inside the Kuwaiti embassy, a funereal sense of doom pervaded. Ambassador Sabah al Sabah, his doleful brown eyes brimming with tears, asked for the help of the United States of America to regain his country's identity. Asked if he had talked to the American president, Sabah looked pained, as if he had been unable to get through. No, he said softly, President Bush had not called.

But if Washington and the nation it served were slow to understand the magnitude of the invasion and its ripple implications for the Middle East and the West, British prime minister Thatcher was not. Infuriated by the rank disregard for sovereignty, she told Bush at a meeting in Aspen that the West must repel the invasion. Inserting a section on Kuwait into a speech she was to deliver to the Aspen Institute, Thatcher said, "Iraq's invasion of Kuwait defies every principle for which the United Nations stands. If we let it succeed, no small country can ever feel safe again. The law of the jungle would take over from the rule of law." Giving him backbone and a critical ally, Thatcher set Bush on the course to war. Days later, to the surprise of top advisers like Colin Powell and the delight of the Saudis and Kuwaitis, he declared of Iraq's invasion of Kuwait: "This will not stand."

With this decision to draw a line in the sand, Bush had a

selling job to do, a campaign to convince the public that oil interests were enough of a national interest to risk American lives. The Bush administration was hardly artful in this campaign. At one point, Secretary of State James Baker, fumbling for some rationale that would convey the gravity of the stakes, settled on "Jobs, jobs, jobs," a line quickly abandoned by the administration as too crass. As White House press secretary Marlin Fitzwater told Bush, "American boys don't die for jobs. They die for God and country." Already, Baghdad and Washington were crowded with war talk. Saddam was holding Western hostages. U.S. troops were en route to Saudi Arabia. In America, Desert Shield hats were selling out. In Baghdad, the hot item among Westerners at the souk was a watch with a Saddam face. Amid the tensions, with Iraqis looking on, Bush had to convince Congress to go to war.

The job was complicated by the broadcasting of openly contentious congressional debates by CNN and other international networks. Bush found himself on the phone to Saudi king Fahd and other Mideast leaders explaining that the fierce rhetoric on Capitol Hill should not be read as a diminution of U.S. commitment to promises made, but as an example of democracy at work. The strategic threat, Bush knew, was real. Iraq, in capturing Kuwait, controlled 10 percent of the world's oil reserves; by continuing to Saudi Arabia, Saddam could capture almost half the world's supplies, giving him an extraordinary ability to terrorize other nations. But the Democratic argument to give economic sanctions a chance to work was gaining ground.

By late December, Bush made a rare appearance at an 8 A.M. senior staff meeting, saying he wanted a full-court press to win congressional approval of the mission. But he also told his staff that he had decided to go forward with the mission, even if Congress had rejected the resolution. This is a startling assertion from a president, that he would ignore a mandate from Congress when American lives were at stake, one that might have invited impeachment. In the end, Congress did approve the mission. And in the end, administration officials conceded that the congressional debate had proved a valuable tool, since it gave Bush and his aides a platform to make their case, and to rebut the opposition's arguments. Not the least of the debate's advantages for the White House is that it gave the president time to sway public opinion to his policy.

The battle for public opinion was joined in Baghdad as well. Hoping to show his concern for the welfare of Western "guests" held hostage by his regime in Iraq, Saddam inquired of seven-year-old British hostage Stuart Lockwood, "Did Stuart have his milk today?" The question, aired on Iraqi TV and picked up by CNN for satellite transmission around the world, chilled public opinion in Western capitals, cementing Saddam's image as a tyrant—on worldwide, satellite-driven, almost-instantaneous television. Still, the image owed something to reality. Despite a $10 million public-relations campaign by the Kuwaitis to disseminate stories of Iraqi atrocities and convince the American public to support war, Saddam himself was his own enemy, and one can only imagine how the odds will change if the next international tyrant has a better feel for public relations.

Technology unquestionably played a role in the Persian Gulf War. When Prussians invaded Austria in 1741, news of the war reached Queen Theresa and her ministers some days later, leaving them, according to the account of a British diplomat, "slumped in their chairs, looking pales as corpses." By contrast, Saddam Hussein needed no courier to tell him, in 1991, that a coalition of nations had just invaded his turf. He watched on CNN as bombs fell on Baghdad. Television had become the courier, because it could deliver a message with dispatch. This war saw the first showdown between military hardware and satellite communication, pitting global media saturation against military needs for security.

Technology can only do so much. If satellite television advanced the pace of journalism, if it speeded delivery of news and made it more potent on impact, if it traversed borders and forced agendas, if it allowed the Pentagon to news-manage a war and gave viewers an impression of combat, that was as it should be, the novelty expected of new media inventions. The sophisticated satellite dishes that brought the Persian Gulf War home would now bring pictures of misery and grief, starvation and execution, from places like Bosnia, Somalia, Rwanda, and Burundi, setting off in their wake a CNN curve that would trouble diplomats and tax policy makers. The arrival of satellite television in the Persian Gulf War was not so much a revolution as a reminder, an early warning, that the cycle of change, of speed, of influence, and finally of acceptance, was about to roll through once again, this time with a loud thunder.

14

The Satellite Spotlight

WHEN U.S. MARINES landed on the beaches of Mogadishu in December of 1992, the only resistance they encountered was the hot glare of television camera lights, blinding them despite the advantage of night-vision goggles. Some angry viewers protested, seeing media interference with military duty. "My immediate reaction was one of anger," said Defense Secretary Dick Cheney. "I cooled down." But in fact military officials had directed journalists on the beach to the best position from which to catch the action. By the time television broadcast pictures of a corpse being dragged through the streets of Mogadishu ten months later, equally angry viewers demanded an end to the Somali adventure, and chastised the media for airing such footage. "You are defiling the body of that American soldier as much as those Somalis who dragged him and spit on him," wrote one reader to the editors of the *Detroit News*. In fact, CNN and other networks did not broadcast the most graphic footage they had available, eschewing close-ups of the soldier's mutilated face in the name of decency. And the footage was not shown raw, as it came in, but processed for later viewing. Still, the impact was startling.

In assessing the influence of television on international

diplomacy in the last years of the twentieth century, Bosnia and Somalia are most often cited as proof that satellite television, its lens trained on human suffering, was driving diplomacy. The worry was that media technology had more than intruded on diplomacy's turf, that it had supplanted the very ground of sovereign nations, forcing political figures to take actions not always or precisely in their nations' interests. The news media, with its high-tech tools of trade, may well have forced these two conflicts to the top of the international agenda, though the conflict in Bosnia is likely to have drawn world attention even without television pictures. The incessant call of the television pictures to "do something" may have even distorted government responses, giving public relations equal weight to foreign relations. But neither the news media nor its new technology prescribed the outcome of these two remarkable and instructive encounters between television and war.

In Somalia, the conventional wisdom holds that pictures got the United States in, and pictures forced the United States out. Those who hold this view argue that the vivid and wrenching images of starving Somali children forced President Bush to act, and that the equally horrible pictures of the soldier's corpse compelled President Clinton to announce a departure date for U.S. troops. "Once again, television images are shaping American foreign policy," wrote the *Economist*. The result: "Damage to America's policy in Somalia, and beyond."

Those who held this view often cited public opinion as forcing the hands of policy makers. Photographs from *Life* of the starvation in Somalia were on display at the United Nations when the Security Council passed a resolution authorizing use of U.S. troops to intervene. "With the mobilization of public opinion, we have been able to obtain the resolution," said U.N. Secretary-General Boutros Boutros-

Ghali. There is some truth to the notion that still photographs and television pictures swayed the body politic to action in Somalia, but only some. For the rest, the record provides plenty of reasons to wonder.

The first problem with the assumption that television pictures alone drove policy in Somalia is the Sudan. In the early 1990s, CNN broadcast compelling and graphic stories on the starvation in the Sudan. A master list of stories shows that the network broadcast fourteen separate packages on the famine in the Sudan and related problems in 1991, four in 1992, and ten in 1993. Commentators like Roger Rosenblatt wrote arresting articles about starvation in the Sudan, in magazines as unlikely as *Vanity Fair*. Human-rights organizations warned that the coming starvation in the Sudan would dwarf anything in Ethiopia and Somalia. At the seat of power in the Clinton White House, national security adviser Anthony Lake pressed the issue on reporters and policy makers alike. In 1994, the Pulitzer Prize for feature photography was awarded to Kevin Carter, for his gripping and widely published photograph of a little Sudanese girl, collapsed from hunger, with a vulture poised a few feet away. Carter later committed suicide. For all of this media attention, nothing happened. There was no massive airlift of food, no invasion of the marines to deliver relief.

In Somalia, television pictures admittedly played some role in the decisions of two presidents, but only because they lacked the backbone to say no. For Bush, they pushed to the side his doubts about an exit strategy, the last of the four questions he had designed for military intervention. A lame-duck president defeated at the polls after having been blasted by his opponent as lacking in compassion, Bush had some personal wish to leave office a humanitarian. He was unsure of how U.S. soldiers would exit Somalia, but the pictures of starving children convinced him to quiet his doubts. It is equally clear that if the other criteria had not been met—if there was no clear military or political objective, and if the public did not support the mission—Bush would have swallowed the pain of seeing those pictures and said no. He proved that in Bosnia, and in Haiti. For Clinton, the televised pictures provided a ready excuse to pull out of a mission that he did not start but which his actions had complicated. In the wake of the death of twenty-four Pakistani peacekeepers, Clinton had turned a humanitarian relief effort into a military manhunt for one warlord, Mohamed Farah Aidid, which ended in the worst firefight in U.S. military history since Vietnam.

Much has been made of that picture of a corpse being dragged through the streets of Mogadishu, which won Paul Watson a Pulitzer Prize. It is at least arguable, however, that the public was angry not because of *pictures* of a corpse dragged through the street but *because* a corpse was dragged through the streets. TV pictures are the way information is received in the late twentieth century. The information conveyed by those pictures was this: Mohamed Farah Aidid's followers don't like Americans. Visual images are more powerful than written ones, to those living in a visual age, but that is satellite television's gift to the march of technology. The printing press was as powerful to French revolutionaries, the telegraph as remarkable to Civil War generals, the radio as powerful in Edward R. Murrow's hands, as any CNN footage is to our generation.

In Somalia, veteran diplomat George Kennan saw the dangers of emotionalism unleashed by television pictures, and the attendant risks to diplomacy. "The reaction is an emotional one, occasioned by the sight of the suffering of the starving people in question," he wrote in a critical op-ed piece in the *New York Times*. "I regard this move as a dreadful error of American policy." A few weeks later, CBS News anchor

Dan Rather replied. Rather misunderstood Kennan's point, not that television was to blame but that leaders were seemingly unwilling to fight its lure. Still, his instincts bear repeating. "To give television credit for so powerful an influence is to flatter us who toil there," he wrote. "But it's wrong."

In Bosnia-Herzegovina, after Yugoslavia imploded into its innate cultural, regional, and historic differences, there were several moments where television intersected with policy, where images influenced substance. The pictures may have moved the leadership to threaten or cajole or implement sanctions or even, finally, to strike from the air. The pictures produced a policy of humanitarian assistance—the most massive airlift of food in world history—and a euphemism called safe havens, patrolled by UN peacekeepers, meant to insure a minimal protection to innocent civilians. But never did the pictures prompt the West to enter the war on the ground.

Television pictures may have compelled the international body politic to "do something," to correct the horror seen on TV sets across the globe. But in no case did the media's spotlight of an international tragedy do more than inspire the unveiling of a new palliative. The bottom line never changed: A steady, three-year drumbeat in the news media, both in print and on the air, for intervention in Bosnia—complete with horrific images of concentration camps and bloodied civilians, of fleeing refugees and UN hostages—did not compel the West to go to war in the field. No better example of this fact exists than the city of Gorazde, a Muslim town under siege by Serbian attack in April of 1994, and again in September of 1994. In between, NATO threatened, the United Nations patrolled, the United States airlifted food, peacekeepers abandoned their posts. If television pictures swayed policy, Gorazde would have endured one massacre, not two.

Of the moments that tested television's influence, the first was the bread-line massacre of May 27, 1992, when 16 were killed and 100 injured, innocents standing in line for bread in Sarajevo, the blood and agony splattered all over television footage that was beamed out within minutes. Spurred by renewed public concern, the United Nations Security Council imposed sanctions on Serbia three days later. Even as they were voting, key players telegraphed to the Serbs that they need not fear any serious military threat. The idea that the West might respond militarily was immediately dampened by German foreign minister Klaus Kinkel, who urged time for the sanctions to work. British foreign minister Douglas Hurd weighed in with a similar line, saying Britain would be "very reluctant" to send soldiers to Bosnia to end the war. Within three days, the West had launched an economic embargo against Serbia, and later Bush authorized a humanitarian food-relief program. But Serbs continued their shelling of Sarajevo, and between 2,000 and 3,000 Muslims were killed in Brčko. By July, the International Red Cross was investigating reports of concentration camps in northern Bosnia. Vivid accounts in *Newsday* and television pictures that made viewers recoil in horror, the obvious and frightening comparison to the Nazi camps of World War II, these media influences so blithely assumed by policy critics and media experts did not oblige officials subjected to their influence to use military action to intervene in the war. Strategic national interests dominated the discussion about Bosnia, not television pictures.

The second moment when television might have galvanized the West to take action was the attack, reportedly by Serb artillery, of a busload of Bosnian children being escorted out of Sarajevo under United Nations protection. The graphic pictures of children caught in the crossfire of ethnic hatred outraged many who saw them. John Fox, an Eastern European specialist at the State Department's planning and policy office, resigned. "The images just kept mounting," he said. "The images came, they never stopped, and that's what got to people. Every now and then, even though you had to steel yourself just to get through the day . . . there would be one that you just couldn't ignore." To Fox, a particular picture of a little girl crying resonated with pain, for she looked like his own daughter. The dissonance of wanting to help end the war and working for a government that had decided not to was more than he could take. Within two years, four career State Department officers would resign in disgust. This exodus of professional diplomats is the single most eloquent testimony to the inability of television pictures to move policy.

The third graphic moment when television intersected with diplomacy in Bosnia was the February 5, 1994, massacre at the Sarajevo marketplace. Pictures of the carnage that killed sixty-eight people finally led NATO to threaten air strikes. Faced with the prospect of strikes if they did not pull back their heavy artillery, the Serbs complied. This withdrawal in effect validated the suspicion of many in the diplomatic community that a bit of military muscle, used early on, strategically placed, might have seriously derailed the Serb offensive. But it also fueled the impression that television pictures were a dangerous new player in diplomacy, that the media were now the emperors of international politics. This time the pictures had, seemingly, worked to convince a reluctant United Nations to intercede.

More than a year later, there was another Serb assault on the marketplace in Sarajevo, one that killed thirty-seven people and finally stirred the international community to respond. With a show of muscle unprecedented in its history, NATO air strikes pounded Serb targets. The warring parties moved to the negotiating table in Geneva, even as they tried to impose a kind of frontier justice, a carving out of ethnically pure regions, on the ground. But in neither case had television prevailed.

In fact, the pictures of the first Sarajevo marketplace attack were only the messenger. The message was massacre, the worst to that point in the war. That the message was delivered on television made it powerful, that it was put up on the satellite gave it instant play in world capitals. But pictures of awful bloodshed had been coming in from Bosnia for two years. Public opinion for the most part rode every wave, responding initially with outrage, calming subsequently with a sober assessment of quagmire. What distinguished these pictures is that they coincided with increasing anger by the French government about the Serb intransigence on peace talks. For weeks, France had been lobbying its European and American allies to put more pressure on Bosnian Serbs to come to the peace table. The marketplace massacre gave weight to French arguments that the Serbs should be punished. "France was pressing for action," said Assistant Defense Secretary Graham Allison. "The Sarajevo market massacre crystallized for the Clinton administration that it had to do something, that we could not do nothing. Those who wanted to do something seized on it."

But in neither case had television prevailed. Television did not lob a mortar shell into that marketplace. The antagonists did. Their action, not the pictures of it, moved policy. The media, armed with television pictures, did turn up the pressure on governments to act at every turn in the Bosnian story, prompting governments to wage a public-relations campaign alongside a private diplomatic track, encouraging the combatants to hire their own rival public-relations firms. But in the later moments that tested the world's mettle in Bosnia, when UN peacekeepers were taken hostage and UN "safe havens" were captured by Bosnian Serbs, television pictures did little to move the body politic. And one of the key factors in the ability of Washington and other world capitals to resist the pressure of the media drumbeat was a conscious decision by the Bush White House to sway the public opinion away from intervention at the beginning, when a strong military response might have deterred the Serbs without sucking the West into an impossible quagmire.

In the early years, every time emotions were roused by the sight of a bread line blown into a massacre or a child evacuated from Sarajevo for bullet wounds, the Bush administration countered the image from Bosnia with words of caution. Administration officials spoke of quagmire, of centuries-old enmities among rival ethnic groups, of the entanglements of Vietnam. "We had to keep painting the quagmire picture to make people aware of the risk," explained Fitzwater. For two years, as reports surfaced of concentration camps and mass rapes, as pictures aired of children hit by mortar fire or innocents killed trying to escape the fighting, the White House called up the ghosts of Balkan history to temper the impulse to intervene. The White House did not have the stage to itself. Haris Siladjzic, the eloquent Bosnian Muslim foreign minister, pleaded his case often and eagerly in Washington, reminding the public that the Muslims wanted the West to lift the arms embargo so they could defend themselves, that they would rather have guns than butter. "Don't feed us so we can die with fully bellies," he often said. His public diplomacy worked in spurts, until the public was reminded of the quagmire that the Balkans represented. At every turn, the Bush administration took on the job of influencing public opinion. Spin control is not the same as leadership, but it is at least a concession to public diplomacy.

Just after television pictures aired of concentration camps, Bush was asked about Bosnia during a press conference in Kennebunkport where he introduced Clarence Thomas as his Supreme Court nominee. A World War II veteran who had watched Vietnam fell Lyndon Johnson, Bush understood the poignancy of the moment. Pitching his voice higher, he said,

"I don't care how much political pressure I get, before one soldier is committed to battle, I'm gonna know how that person gets out of there. And we are not gonna get bogged down in some guerrilla warfare." The conflict in the United States between those who tended to intervention and those who cringed at the thought broke down basically between those who viewed the crisis as a war of aggression, as the Serb minority used guns to assert its influence over Bosnian independence, and those who viewed the crisis as a civil war. Bush was in the latter camp. At German insistence, he had recognized Bosnia-Herzegovina as an independent nation. But he was not about to defend its sovereignty. That was Vietnam. He remembered Johnson's, and the nation's, ordeal.

In addition to portraying Bosnia as a futile war that would only cost America lives and spirit, the Bush administration also used public relations to defend its foreign relations. But successful public-relations tactics untethered to policy can also prove a long-term hindrance to policy makers, fueling public cynicism and undermining credibility with other nations. The Bush administration and its European allies had no intention of intervening militarily in Bosnia, but Assistant Secretary of State Margaret Tutwiler was convinced that the West should at least end the suffering that was being beamed across the miles every night on satellite television. Knowing this too would be resisted by key administration figures, Tutwiler adopted the term *ethnic cleansing* to describe from her podium at the State Department the plight of Bosnian civilians. She also propelled the issue onto the agenda of a Lisbon conference on aid to the former Soviet Union by positioning Baker outside 10 Downing Street for a photo op on the day before he arrived in Portugal.

Tutwiler, a top official and aide-de-camp of James Baker as he moved from the White House to Treasury to State, had an extraordinary antenna for the winds of public opinion. It was she who masterminded the logistics of the Mideast Peace Conference in Madrid, keeping a careful eye over seating charts and speaking order, rejecting proposals to feed the delegates anything more than coffee at formal sessions for fear of offending the dietary laws of any single group. Even the timing of the event was set by Tutwiler, so as not to fall on Halloween Day and inspire a profusion of taunts about a spooked conference or a haunted process. It was Tutwiler who marched into Secretary of State Baker's office after the Persian Gulf War ended and Iraqi soldiers were killing Kurdish and Muslim rebels seeking to overthrow Saddam Hussein. She insisted to him that the administration could not sit by and watch as television pictures of starving Kurds, driven to a freezing mountaintop near Turkey in flight from the vengeful Saddam Hussein, aired on television.

For all the talk in Washington in the 1990s about how satellite television blurred the line between policy and tactics, there remained a difference. Just ask the Kurds, who came to Washington on the hope of a rescue inspired by the Bush humanitarian relief effort, only to discover that the aid was not consistent with administration policy. The administration, despite waging a successful war to expel Iraq from Kuwait, despite launching a massive public-relations campaign against Saddam Hussein, feared that a full-blown rebellion against the Saddam regime by Kurds in the north and Shi'ites in the south would destabilize Iraq and pose strategic risks for the whole region. The White House used Band-Aids to quiet public revulsion over television pictures but was unwilling to alleviate the underlying causes of discontent. The humanitarian aid program was meant not really to help the Kurds politically, but to keep them from starving to death on television.

As for the Clinton administration, its first words spelled

out why rescuing Bosnia was in U.S. national interests, raising hope among the Bosnian Muslims that genuine muscle was on the way. But soon after came words that spoke to a White House divided, unsure of its path, twisting with each development. Candidate Clinton, in the fall of 1992, told voters that "you can't allow the mass extermination of people and just watch it happen." Fifteen months later, asked about the marketplace massacre, Clinton said, "Until those folks get tired of killing each other over there, bad things will continue to happen." Secretary of State Warren Christopher, wresting Bosnian policy from predecessors he all but called cold-hearted, was aggrieved at the "mass murders, systematic beatings, the rapes of Muslims and others, prolonged shelling of innocents in Sarajevo and elsewhere, forced displacement of entire villages, inhumane treatment of prisoners in detention camps." Six weeks later, he described the war in Bosnia as a historic "problem from hell," arguing that the United States does not have the will to "make people in that region of the world like each other."

Clinton had fallen into the classic trap of policy by whiplash, a policy subject to the latest whims of television pictures and public mood, a policy without a strategic goal or consistent message. Diplomacy is one of the last fields where words matter. Messages, sent by the old-fashioned cable or the newly fashionable fax, are parsed for hidden meaning. All statements are examined between the lines. In this world, words are the coin of the realm, and disregard for the power and substance of words doomed the Clinton administration policy to ridicule. Clinton and his team showed no respect for words, throwing them around casually as if the whole world wasn't listening.

One reason for Clinton's ambivalence was that in Bosnia, the humanitarian instinct to "do something" was not matched by a political will to act, in part because of the success of the Bush policy in equating Bosnia, in the public's mind, with Vietnam. In the face of this political judgment not to intervene, television pictures tugged at the public's heart strings, but only briefly after each episode of violence. There was a half-life to public reaction, as talk about the marketplace massacre was soon replaced in television studios by analysis of the Nancy Kerrigan–Tonya Harding skating scandal.

In an interview with ABC anchor Peter Jennings in 1994, Clinton protested that his hands had been tied by the Europeans, who did not want to join him in lifting the arms embargo, leaving him unable to act unilaterally. He complained that unlike Bush in the Persian Gulf War, his options were restricted by U.S. unwillingness to fight. He could not have marshaled an international coalition against Serbia as Bush did against Iraq, he said, because he was not willing to commit "the lion's share" of troops. "I had limited leverage," he told Jennings. All of this is true, but beside the point. Anyone who sits in the Oval Office and thinks his leverage is limited has not listened to the ghosts within its walls. This is the place where symbolism and power merge, where verbal threats and military weapons dance to a deadly beat. Unless he had been willing to risk more, to lose more, Clinton was doomed to history's disregard, not because his policy was innately good or bad but because he failed to muster a consistent, compelling case for it.

Clinton's Secretary of State Warren Christopher was fond of saying that television should not be the "north star of American foreign policy." From the beginning, the north star of Clinton's policy in Bosnia was domestic politics. He sought always to prevent Bosnia from becoming an American problem. A veteran of the protests against the Vietnam War, Clinton saw in Bosnia a quagmire that could doom an American leader's presidency. When the French and the British threatened to withdraw from Bosnia, he pledged 25,000 U.S. troops to help extricate them—if they would stay on the ground as long as possible. When Congress voted to lift the arms embargo on Bosnia that kept intact the Serb military advantage, he vetoed the bill, explaining that the Europeans had vowed, otherwise, to leave the field. And when the Europeans insisted that, as *New York Times* specialist Elaine Sciolino put it, "the most promising outcome for peace was based not on ethnic blending but on ethnic division," Clinton abandoned his earlier insistence on maintaining Bosnia's multi-ethnic heritage. With his own re-election bid looming, Clinton put aside his qualms about rewarding Serb aggression and endorsed a map of a bifurcated Bosnia, one that codified the ethnically-pure neighborhoods carved out by the warring parties on the ground. If he could get the combatants to settle diplomatically, there would be no need to risk American lives because there would be no pressure to intervene.

There were plenty of fresh television pictures in 1995 to provoke public opinion, images of refugees and misery, of war and obstinacy. The so-called safe havens of Zepa and Srebrenica were overrun by Serb forces. United Nations peacekeepers were taken hostage, chained in humiliation to link fences. Fighter pilot Scott O'Grady, a U.S. captain, was shot down by Serb artillery, surviving a week on little but wits and rainwater. And three U.S. diplomats, Robert Frasure, Joseph Kruzel, and Colonel Samuel Nelson Drew, were killed in a tragic explosion of their car on the road to Sarajevo.

But it was his own pledge to deploy American soldiers, destined to be controversial at home, that sharpened Clinton's political antenna. He was worried that pictures from Bosnia of American soldiers dead or maimed would galvanize public opinion in anger, much as television pictures of a corpse dragged through Somalia's capital had aroused fury two years before. The public's anticipated rage matched his own political instincts. Clinton pressed for peace in hopes of avoiding war, as well as the images of war. How ironic that in the end he was forced to sell deployment of 25,000 American troops as a needed guarantor of a peace plan that Balkanized the Balkans and violated his own pledge not to partition Bosnia.

For all the ephemeral "do something" pull of the images from Bosnia, Clinton knew from his pollster Stan Greenberg that, as author Elizabeth Drew put it, "Bosnia was a subject on which public opinion could be shaped." But Clinton saw that the public was ambivalent about Bosnia, and elected not to use political capital to change opinion, to counter the power of the television pictures of war. In this, he may have given the images too much weight and his own ability to lead too little credit, but his was a political judgment about the antipathy of public will and the costs of marshaling support for war.

When, finally, NATO unleashed a sustained, targeted bombing campaign, it brought the Serbs to the bargaining table, validating the case of those who had argued for years that an early and robust response from the West might have tempered Serb aggression. At the end, one could only wonder what would have happened if the West had bombed at the beginning, before 200,000 lives were lost and countless others were made casualties of war, refugees and rape victims and concentration camp survivors whose collective misery added a page of shame to world history. How fitting that the West tried to close the page with a face-saving notion of splitting Bosnia in two while insisting that its borders were being preserved. That is not a deal forced on diplomacy by television, but rather one favored by leaders unwilling to risk political capital to do more.

There is simply no denying that satellite television quickens the pace of international affairs, as it does for business and sports as well. And one thing more: A medium that combines the visual and the verbal taps the emotions. Thousands of words written about concentration camps do not touch the same raw emotion as the moving picture of a concentration camp victim seen in real time or within hours after its recording. But real-time television provides a fleeting image. Television pictures "often give a quick rush, like a dose of sugar, but the rush also wears off quickly, leaving the mind with facts to sort out," said commentator Roger Rosenblatt. The first few pictures of starving children anguish the heart. After a while, the spirit becomes a bit inured to the pain, a bit callous. "People seem to understand that this is true," he added. "Otherwise all anyone would ever need to get us into a war would be a TV camera, and that has not been the case."

Those who believe that television pictures distort foreign policy argue that the visual is so potent it gives too much weight to what is depicted. Television pictures do distort the debate by giving special notice, perhaps undue notice, to what they depict. But this is the same role performed by journalism generally. International diplomacy is a stage, and journalism runs one of the spotlights. Whenever journalists spotlight an issue, they ignore the darkened area around it, giving recognition to the material that shines, neglecting the stories in the shadows. But this distortion is not any worse with satellite television pictures than it was before them. The pictures arrive faster, and they are in living color, but they are no more or less distorting than words chosen to describe events in the age of print. News stories have a life cycle of their own; they either catch the public fancy or fall from the front pages, sometimes with little regard for comparative value, having more to do with competition for attention than intrinsic importance. And the media are not the only players in the arena. Increasingly, as they did in Somalia, so-called nongovernmental organizations like *Medicins sans Frontieres* (Doctors without Borders), Save the Children, and Amnesty International have a telling impact on the international agenda. The photograph is a powerful weapon, television images even more compelling, invitations to intervention all. But none of these weapons of communicate do any more than flag a problem, or focus attention. They are a lens, not a prism.

Undeniably, there is far less pressure on the political system to respond to crises in the absence of television pictures. An oft-cited example is the Soviet invasion of Afghanistan in 1979, when no television klieg lights in Kabul brought the crisis home to Soviet citizens. But soon enough the world took notice, the legions of dissidents grew, the battle became a reminder of Vietnam. Unquestionably too, satellite television can expose hardships so graphically that people and governments are moved to intervene. A BBC report in 1984 about famine in Ethiopia, complete with graphic pictures and a poetic script, produced a harvest of charity, including an increase in the U.S. food aid budget from $23 million to $98 million. But like the sugar high that children get after eating too much junk food, television pictures are often fleeting, exposing crisis and starvation, war and famine, as blithely as they would highlight a nasty soccer match or an international banking scandal.

Already the changes represented by satellite television's intrusion into diplomacy are being absorbed by a political system more than equipped to outlast them. Bush proved that in distancing himself from the pictures from Bosnia. Even Clinton, who is clearly moved by television pictures and driven by polls, has learned to hide their toll on his thinking, so as not to give emotional weight to those who would stage photo opportunities to manipulate his policies. When he was in Tokyo for the Economic Summit in July of 1993, Clinton grew upset by televised pictures of the siege of Sarajevo. He told Christopher to prepare policy options, including military strikes. What resulted was a statement that NATO would make "immediate preparations" for "stronger measures" in Bosnia if "the strangulation of Sarajevo" continued. With White House officials warning that "the clock is ticking," the Serbs could be forgiven if they had laughed openly at the threat. Less than a year later, Clinton was equally shaken by pictures of the marketplace massacre, but he tried to disguise his emotional reaction by playing golf and speaking out on other topics. He put more muscle in the policy, and fewer words in the bluff.

And it may be true that Bosnia and Somalia represent the crises of a world uncertain of its borders, unsure in the aftermath of the cold war's end whether intervention to feed the hungry or protect the besieged is an international interest that has supplanted the national interests that once defined foreign affairs. "Empires don't collapse every day," said Francis Fukuyama, author of *The End of History and the Last Man*. "There was a lot of turmoil when the Ottoman Empire collapsed, and the Austrian-Hungarian Empire, and we're going through that period now." Perhaps too the satellite pictures have lost their impact, what some call compassion fatigue that comes of watching too many international crises on television and feeling despair that any aid can ever stop the flow of human suffering. The pictures that once tugged hearts may have lost their punch. The public may have become newly immune to the emotions provoked by image.

It is easy, in the flush of new encounters with real-time, satellite pictures, to make too much of their impact, to equate the emotional power of visual images with a heightened policy influence by the media. After Secretary of State James Baker and Iraqi foreign minister Tariq Aziz completed a fruitless day of negotiations in Geneva early in 1991, Baker told a global viewing audience that "regrettably" they had been unable to avert the Persian Gulf War. Aziz was to speak next, but Iraqi officials told CNN they were afraid that if Aziz began his remarks and President Bush began to speak in the White House briefing room, the American-based network would cut Aziz off in midsentence. CNN asked the White House if Bush would speak first. Press Secretary Marlin Fitzwater exploded, telling the network that "hell would freeze over" before Bush would give Aziz the last word. The issue dissolved when Aziz, assured that Bush would hear him out, agreed to speak first. To Fitzwater, the incident demonstrated the power of the new medium. "I'm watching this on my screen the whole time, and Saddam's watching in his office just like I am," he marveled. "That amounted to a back channel. [It] shows the magnitude of the communications change at work."

But this back channel amounted to little more than a tussle over logistics, one based on a misunderstanding of motives at that. The White House thought Aziz was positioning for the advantage of having the last word, when all the Iraqis wanted was assurance that he would not be preempted by Bush. Even if the issues involved in the back-channel negotiations had been more substantive, the idea of journalists serving as go-betweens for governments in crisis was hardly new. ABC TV's diplomatic correspondent, John Scali, was approached by Alexander Fomin, counselor of the Soviet embassy, with an offer to defuse the Cuban Missile Crisis in 1962. CBS anchor Walter Cronkite stepped right in the middle of diplomacy in 1977 when he asked Egyptian president Anwar Sadat if he would be willing to visit Jerusalem. And Ted Koppel, inviting both the foes and defenders of apartheid on *Nightline* in 1985, pushed diplomacy along, albeit with the tacit approval of the South African government, which hoped the program would showcase the wisdom of its incremental approach and found instead that television emphasized the inherent failure of that course. Every new media technology changes the balance of power between journalists and the diplomats and generals they cover. Satellite television had no greater claim on this legacy than the others—it just provided more timely anecdotes.

Rozanne Ridgway, assistant secretary of state for European affairs, recalls being delighted when, in the mid-1980s, Russian foreign minister Andrei Bessmertnyk acknowledged to the United States that the Russians watched CNN at the Foreign Ministry. Marvelous, she thought, "now we don't have to get together and argue as to what happened. Now we can argue about what we're going to do about it." When Saddam Hussein put forth a peace offering Washington viewed as specious, Fitzwater was in the White House briefing room within thirty minutes to pinpoint the plan's inadequacies, a use of satellite television to quash an idea before it could splinter the fragile coalition of Arab and Western nations battling Iraq. And Assistant Secretary of Defense Richard Perle was at Turkish president Turgot Ozal's side when Washington announced a new policy of getting food and supplies to Kurdish rebels in the hills of Iraq. This policy shift was important to Ozal, who kept a television set on his desk, because the humanitarian aid would keep Kurds from fleeing to Turkey and exacerbating the already evident ethnic tensions there. Ozal kept his television set tuned to CNN, with the Mute button on, even when he was receiving official visitors. The result was a heads-up on official policy. "Long before it was cabled from Washington, he had the essential information," recalls Perle. "He was on the phone reacting immediately."

But if these examples demonstrate anything, it is that satellite television has changed diplomacy at the margins, leaving it essentially unchanged at its core. Speeding the flow of information is of use to those who deal in policy. It may prove a burden or a gift. But either way, hastening news does not change the options for its recipients. When Greeks defeated the Persians at Marathon in 490 B.C. a runner sped across 26 miles and 385 yards to Athens to deliver the news of victory. He collapsed and died after delivering his message, making him an early martyr of the information age. Speed of delivery did not change the import of his message, though it conferred tactical advantage. Likewise, in wartime Europe in 1815, a Rothschild agent grabbed a Dutch gazette "still damp from the printer" and jumped into a boat for Britain with news that Napoleon had been defeated at Waterloo. Nathan Rothschild made a fortune by playing the British stock exchange, first selling and starting a panic as traders assumed that Rothschild knew something and surmised that Napoleon had won. Then, when the market hit bottom, Rothschild bought a bundle just before the exchange learned of the British victory over Napoleon. Speed of information did not change the essentials of either war or capitalism—the speeded flow of knowledge was but the latest method of pursuing riches or achieving military victory.

Information, for journalism as well as diplomacy, for the military as well the public, for business as well as politics, is like currency, the coin of the realm. Global politics is driven by information, delivered both in pictures and in words. Documents are culled for between-the-lines meaning. Visual images are weighed for impact on public opinion. This was true when Luther challenged the Catholic Church's hypocrisy in 1521, it was true when Mathew Brady took his pictures at Antietam in 1865, it was true when the Wilson White House leaked the Zimmermann telegram to the Associated Press in 1917, and it was true when General Loan executed a suspected Vietcong terrorist in front of cameras. The primacy of information is likely to become even more important in the face of the next media invention, which promises to marry the impact of words and pictures in an expanded volume of data. Amid predictions that the information highway will speed events, empower the powerless, join the world in peace, and annihilate time and space, the new technology announced its arrival. They call it cyberspace.

15

Cyberspace and War

IN MAY OF 1994, Polish prime minister Waldemar Pawlak sent an informal greeting to President Clinton at his E-mail address, president@whitehouse.gov. The White House computer received the message, and spit out the form letter sent to anyone contacting Clinton on the Internet. "Thank you for writing to President Clinton via electronic mail," it began. Embarrassed White House officials learned of the gaffe when they were preparing for Clinton's visit to Poland in July. By then, of course, a handshake proved a more reliable means of contact.

In the coming age of cyberspace, with computer networks leaping borders and governments competing with newspapers for the on-line audience, diplomacy and journalism face a challenge far more daunting than a failure to differentiate between casual and official letters. Digital convergence, the transfer of all forms of information to little bits, communicated at nearly the speed of light, has all the promise and peril of its predecessors.

Digital technology will carry more information than any invention gone before, a testament to the ingenuity of inventors to crash through the parameters of imagination. At first this seems an anomaly, since the telegraph, telephone, radio, television, and computer messages all travel at the same speed. But once the computer receives a message, it can download a larger quantity of material in a minute than any other medium. The speed of information relayed is the same, but the volume of information conveyed is bigger. To a generation that thought the train was a vast leap in the speed of delivering a message, the telegraph seemed unabashedly a revolution. So too for a generation that thought satellite television represented the ultimate in delivery of real-time information. Glass fibers can carry at least 150,000 times as much information as the standard copper wires now used to bring the computer into the home or office. An hour's worth of digital video can be delivered in seconds. The speeded dissemination of information has just begun.

Defenders of the status quo, as always, showed their ignorance. When Nicholas Negroponte, director of the Massachusetts Institute of Technology's Media Laboratory, predicted that 99 percent of television signals would one day travel in underground glass fibers, he was ridiculed by one CBS television executive. Testifying before a congressional committee, the dinosaur of the satellite age called forecasts of digital television nonsense, since such an invention "defies the laws of physics." Right.

Ignorance and pessimism aside, if the futurists are right, by the turn of the twenty-first century homes and offices will feature a huge monitor that can be used as a television, computer, telephone, or radio. News and entertainment, messages and mail, opportunities to interact with neighbors as well as heads of state, all of these bits of information will be coded in the ones and zeroes that define digital technology, programmed to suit the individual user.

Because digital technology represents the union of visual images and spoken words and written documents, some think its impact will be exponentially magnified. But the pattern of its arrival suggests that digital technology is little different from its ancestors. There is great excitement about the digital age and its ability to bypass the gatekeepers and censors who have long controlled information: publishers and presidents, tyrants and corporations. But it is a vanity of the on-line generation to assume that this technology will be greatly different in its impact on society from the ones gone before.

As with any new technology making its debut on the world stage, digital technology gets rave reviews in some quarters. "We stand on the verge of a great flowering of intellectual property, a true Renaissance that will unleash the creative energies of inventors, entrepreneurs, hackers, artists and dreamers," said Ray Smith, head of Bell Atlantic, one of the Baby Bells liberated from AT&T when the conglomerate was broken up in 1984. The information superhighway, with its road maps to the future, looked like gold. "I'm on the lunatic fringe of believers in this stuff," said Bill Gates, father of Microsoft, the world's largest computer-software company. "It'll change everything."

If the enthusiasts were gushing, so too were the critics in full sail. The elite worried that cyberspace would further widen the gap between rich and poor, dividing society along the informed and uninformed, insuring that the computer-literate would outpace the technologically deprived. Libraries sought to bridge the distance by putting computers next to the bookshelves, and House Speaker Newt Gingrich of Georgia suggested, to considerable ridicule, giving laptop computers to the poor. The naysayers also flagged concerns about privacy on the information highway. Oscar H. Gandy, Jr., a scholar at the University of Pennsylvania, coined a term for the primacy of technology, calling it the "panoptic sort," which he described as "an all-seeing discriminatory technology that uses information about individuals gathered from numerous sources . . . to determine the quality of options and experiences we face in our roles as citizens, employees and consumers."

Then too there was concern that an uncensored highway of information, open to anyone who could afford the toll and vulnerable to the accidents caused by erroneous, libelous, or incendiary information, would lessen the quality of public discourse and strengthen the hand of dictators. "This is a time of great danger," said Carla Hesse, a historian at the University of California at Berkeley who compared the wildness of the Internet, where individuals are talking to other individuals via computers, to the anarchy of the press during the French Revolution. This is an echo of Mark Twain discoursing on the telephone or Victor Hugo complaining about the printing press, a concern that in an age of information, with a new medium of communication, some in the newly widened audience will misuse facts. One is tempted to say, with history as an ally, "Get over it." The free flow of information inevitably entails risks. That does not lessen its appeal.

The term *cyberspace* was coined in the early 1980s by science fiction writer William Gibson, in a trilogy of novels about futuristic computers. "Gibson's cyberspace was a frontier where latter-day cowboys rode electronic steeds through a video-game landscape, breaking into and entering the vaults of corporate computers." Libertarians flocked to the Internet, sensing a kindred spirit. Cyberspace protected their privacy, while giving them unbridled freedom to search for information. And if users are not libertarians when they start, says Vic Sussman of *U.S. News & World Report*, they will be when they finish.

The Internet, created in the mid-1980s, was modeled on the Pentagon's ARPANET research network set up in the late 1960s to link scientists at universities and other various arms of the military-industrial complex. It was designed to decentralize information, to insure that in case of a nuclear attack, computer knowledge was not housed in one central locale but spread in a thousand different computers. Its legacy continued in the secular world. As commercial networks, vendors like America Online and Compuserve, contributed "millions of new users at a stroke," users found that information was fleeting. Far from creating a permanent record, cyberspace captured moments in time. The Internet was a place without an address. The prospect for misinformation, in this wild, wild West of information, hurling along on the information highway, without censors or editors, hard to trace and cumbersome to save, was a concern. "Information has now become a form of garbage," writes Neil Postman, author of *Technopoly*. "We don't know what to do with it, have no control over it, don't know how to get rid of it."

But if digital technology speeds information overload and gives new power to cowboys, it also promises to empower people who might otherwise be onlookers. Here is the potential for democracy unleashed again by a new technology, a democratic impulse to connect those who were until now disenfranchised. Already, candidates for office take to the Internet, like book authors, to converse with the public, hearing complaints and answering questions directly. This instant feedback, however unrepresentative, produces a healthy restraint in those who might be inclined to pander. Like the radio box in the age of broadcasting, like the VCR and the hand-held zapper in the age of satellite television, cyberspace offers consumers choice about when to plug in and when to tune out. And an interactive public that talks back will likely have a tempering impact on both diplomacy and journalism.

In a recent essay on the Internet's likely impact on Washington, political analyst Kevin Phillips argued that "from Hitler's mesmerizing Nuremberg rallies circa 1935 to direct mail in the 1970s to the trivializing eight-second sound bites that have marked recent campaigns, the techniques of this era have too often favored power seekers or clever interest group mobilizers while discouraging ordinary voters and making them cynical." No more, says Phillips, arguing that the advent of the computer promises an end to "this distorted top-to-bottom information cascade."

It is true, on the margins, that cyberspace gives more power to the audience, allowing an all-but-instant critique of a journalist's biases or a politician's voting record. But it is too much to put on technology's shoulders a complete restructuring of power. From either the Marxist view or the libertarian one, power has an innate structure. As with any new technology, cyberspace will ruffle the feathers of those clinging to familiar ways, only to be absorbed by the political system grown accustomed to its ways.

None of this is to suggest, however, that the digital age will not bring revolution to the ways in which information is delivered, not least to journalism. H. L. Mencken once said that the power of the press belongs to the person who owns one. But in cyberspace everyone is a publisher, everyone is a journalist, a possibility that blurs the line of professional status. If information is the currency of the Internet, then newspapers have to compete with government offices, business interests, humanitarian groups, and outraged citizens for the public's attention. Readers who prefer to get their information from specialists have little need for general news, or much appetite for reporters who pretend to be objective while pushing a deliberate if subtle ideological line. More, the audience can ignore the "professional" journalists completely. Already, chat rooms form at the drop of a crisis, as readers reach out to one another for information instead of the traditional sources of news. Already, reporters have been "flamed" by readers in on-line discussions for the mistakes or misimpressions left by their hard-copy articles.

But if history is any guide, this euphoria over the potential for choice among consumers will be temporary. To the disappointment of the digiteri, a freewheeling, unguarded cyberspace is not likely to be without middlemen for long. Given the volume of information expected to descend from cyberspace, in every vehicle from print to video to audio, intermediaries will be welcomed. Their traditional role, to bring order to a chaotic new information age, will be valued anew when time and space have again been annihilated. In an era of information overload, competent sifters of the news who know how to separate the important from the trivial and who can predict an audience's appetite for both should flourish. Public opinion is likely to play a larger role, but not a crippling one. Leaders who are adroit at fielding questions on talk radio and MTV will likely continue their prominence on computers. As always when the political system absorbs a new technology, the public may know a temporary high of influence before the balance of power returns to a shared custody over policy.

Already there is talk of "intelligence agents," computer-programmed services that will cull the broad bands of information all day for news of interest to particular groups or individual consumers. Already the U.S. government is looking at ways to inhibit freedom on the Internet, or at least to monitor it. The debate over access to information is far from over, but the battle lines are already drawn, pitting free speech against the security of federal investigations, joining an odd alliance of left-wing First Amendment absolutists with right-wing libertarians who abhor government interference in the flow of information. The Unabomber, the madman who mailed bombs to defenders of technology, who targeted university professors and public relations experts and engineers, was not the only one worried about technology's tendency to rip apart a community's social fabric. Nor was Microsoft's Bill Gates the only one eager to capitalize on technology's promise.

While the debate continues over ownership of information, journalism is already fearful that the computer age will end the newspaper age, much as Western Union, with its ability to send messages by telegram within minutes, put out of business the Pony Express, which delivered messages at the speed of a horse. The newspaper of the future will be delivered on-line, electronically, via computer, offering consumers an enormous, international menu from which to select news delivered in print, on television, with photos, or by voice. Those who prefer to get their hands dirty on Sundays with the good gray lady, the *New York Times*, will become a dwindling number. Computers that offer readers news packages customized to their own individual needs and interests—computers that download the day's activities in certain stocks on Wall Street or the latest fashions from Milan or developments from an infamous trial in Los Angeles or a preview of the Bordeaux wines—threaten the future of newspapers as they are currently produced.

With computers, customers have no risk of messy newsprint ink. They can arrange their news to avoid an editor's political bias—or reflect their own. They can ignore what reporters and editors consider news: mass starvation or exodus in Africa, terrorist hits in Israel, intrigue in the Kremlin, a bomb in Oklahoma City, or the collapse of the Mexican peso. The peril is that if few customers request stories on the water problems of the Jordan Valley, news organizations are unlikely to spend the money to deploy reporters to gather information on the topic. The bottom line came to journalism a long time ago, even before Benjamin Franklin sold his first pamphlet, but cyberspace ups the odds. For in the digital age, consumers vote with their fingers. In a way, they always have. Now their fingers are closer to the levers of power.

The news consumer of the future will make few distinctions between a newspaper and a television network, or even a government. All will merely become suppliers of news that can be called up on a screen at a moment's notice, twenty-four hours a day, competitors for the attention of an audience that will be able to customize its own news product. They will compete too against special-interest groups and even terrorists, who will go on-line to communicate their views directly, without the filter of an editor's news judgment. The trend will likely be abetted by the rising cost of newsprint. It cost *USA Today* $40 million more to publish in 1995 than the previous year because of the rising price of the paper needed to print the newspaper. Driven by the economics of publishing, news organizations will likely let consumers use their own paper to print articles for reading on a subway, or back efforts to create a portable laptop with a recyclable disk that consumers insert into their home computers each day for the latest "newspaper."

The newspaper is not dead, but it will have to reconstitute itself to survive. In fact, the multiplicity of news services are already leading to "niche" markets, where some news organizations excel in the "scoops" that once defined journalism and others carve out a market of readers interested in explanatory journalism, or trend stories. Still others may favor tabloid journalism, raw sensationalism, and gossip. It is not difficult to imagine an era of renewed sensationalism, as newspapers, no longer publishing a single edition but available on-line at all hours, flag the most spectacular happenings to lure readers and viewers to their product. But it is also possible to envision an audience for substance among readers who crave knowledge to arm them for a workday of intense global competition. Like the market for photography, there will be those who seek realism, and others who prefer flattery, titillation, or shock. "It is not technology that will kill off newspapers," wrote Max Frankel in a recent *New York Times Magazine* column. "On the contrary, technology will give them new functions and features and a global reach."

Cyberspace is a multimedia venture, and its impact will not be limited to a shake-up of the newspaper business. Television will be changed as well. Bandwidth, the amount of information channeled through a line, also brings the promise of digital video, audio, and teleconferencing. The impact of consumer freedom to arrange the visual aspects of news is even more striking than the toll of customizing print journalism. Ordering the raw footage of a war, replaying a crucial debate, interacting with political figures—this threat to television news makes CNN's preeminence in the Gulf War look tame. Like the newspapers, the television networks will likely package their news in the most compelling style possible, hoping to attract viewers by giving them lots of options to click the news on or off. The marriage of data and pictures in digital technology, where consumers can get both visual images and written words on the same medium, constitutes a revolution in information technology. It also levels the playing field, allowing the networks to compete with newspapers and even software companies like Microsoft to develop, promote, and find an audience for the most compelling news product, no matter the media features.

None of this is unprecedented, or particularly undesirable. When television arrived, it required pictures, which overwhelmed the words of earlier media technologies. Lesley Stahl's classic story has no equal, of how she aired a CBS story about the fallacies in Ronald Reagan's statements, only to be congratulated by White House officials overjoyed at the broadcasting of so many of his appearances. Television gave visual images unprecedented influence on world events, but this picture medium also pushed newspapers to a more ana-lytical tone, forcing them to use interpretation to bring con-text to events already reported by the broadcast media. Some scholars have disdained this trend toward newspaper analysis, which really began when Theodore White wrote the first of his epic portrayals of a presidential election, *The Making of the President, 1960.* In it, White detailed behind-the-scenes aspects of election strategy that made the newspaper coverage of what a candidate said or did seem superficial. So for the next campaign, newspaper reporters rushed to fill the gap, sometimes dropping coverage of what the candidate said or did in favor of reporting on what he was trying to do strate-gically. This gave news a cynical edge, a knowing sarcasm, but it also gave newspapers a purpose in an age of television. News in cyberspace will produce a similar renewal, forcing newspapers and television news organizations alike to find a function that distinguishes them from the pack.

They will have to do something, for newspaper and tele-vision news consumption is in a free fall. The Times Mirror Center for the People & the Press found in a poll that net-work news viewing had dropped from 60 percent in 1993 to 48 percent two years later, and regular newspaper reading had dropped similarly, from 58 percent in 1994 to 45 percent a year later, part of a steady 25-year drop in news consumption. The import of the Times Mirror study suggests not that the public is shifting to a new venue for news but that the au-dience is rejecting news altogether. This loss of appetite for news may owe something to an accelerated pace of life that allows little time for curiosity, or it may suggest a disaffection with the negativity of news, defined as the unusual or unex-pected occurrence, and rarely are those positive. Whatever the cause, the collapse of consumer interest in news is not the fault of technology.

If it is risky to assume that cyberspace will signal the death of journalism, it is also perilous to suppose that the new media will be universally embraced. Technology does not bestow its gifts uniformly. While Civil War generals praised the telegraph's strategic value and yellow-press journalists boasted that the telegraph allowed them to convey news as it was happening, some of the western territories were in the dark about the Battle of Gettysburg until the following year. So too with digital information. Throughout history, it was not unknown for a new technology to go unused for generations. The typewriter was invented in 1867, but did not come into general acceptance until the 1920s, when for the first time in U.S. history, numbers of urban residents exceeded those who lived in rural areas. The facsimile machine, invented at the time of the telephone, sat on the shelf for a century, until computer chips could speed the delivery time for messages, thus giving the machine a special purpose in the workplace. Cyberspace's acceptance could similarly be delayed.

But U.S. Census Bureau statistics suggest otherwise, providing a window on the relationship between new media technologies and public embrace. The key factor appears to be cost. According to the department's statistics, media inventions tend to become accepted by a majority of the public, by at least half the households in the United States, when their price drops below 2 percent of weekly household income. Radio crossed that threshold in 1929, when the price of an average radio set dipped to 1.8 percent of weekly income. Black-and-white television hit the 50 percent mark in 1955, when the price dropped from 3.3 percent to 1.8 percent of weekly income. Color television moved into half the homes in the United States by 1970, when a set cost 1.9 percent of weekly income. And the VCR passed the halfway point in 1987, when the price dropped from 3.3 percent to 1.1 percent of income. With the costs of computers falling and one in every three Americans already owning a home computer, the arrival of the digital age is hardly the stuff of science fiction. Computer footprints are already leaving their shadow.

For diplomacy and the relations between nations, cyberspace is, as it is for journalism, a mixed medium. With digital technology, the potential is enormous for global interaction, and with it common understanding—or at least more information. Already sophisticated governments and savvy political figures are making use of the Internet's global component, the World Wide Web, to reach former adversaries and attract new investors. Quick to seize the new medium's advantages, the Israeli foreign ministry has an Internet address—Ask@Israel.info.gov.il—where computer users can call up a news service that includes selected newspaper articles translated from Hebrew to English, speeches by Israeli politicians, and reports on the Tel Aviv Stock Exchange. "It's a very large discussion group in the global village," said Martin Peled-Flax, a ministry official, who estimated that 700 people browse through the service daily. "In the new realities of this world, information travels at the speed of light. And it doesn't need a passport."

Governments will not have the stage to themselves. They will be competing against all manner of interest groups and nongovernmental organizations, against newspapers and local cultural groups and corporate advertisers. For all these inherent advantages, one potential pitfall for leaders is that cyberspace, a place that does not exist but for the lines of communication between people, makes national experiences less likely. An assassination, a famine, an earthquake, a terrorist attack—these may bring viewers and readers alike to their screens to peruse the latest news. For the most part, the national experience will be the rare exception, and marshaling public opinion for national purpose like war or economic sacrifice will likely be even more difficult than it is now. Already television networks are ignoring a president's request for air time and newspapers relegate the comments of top leaders to their back pages. These are tacit acknowledgments that information is decentralizing, that national governments are less relevant, that we are, as Walt Wriston, former chairman of Citicorp, puts it, in "the twilight of sovereignty."

But if digital information and multimedia manipulation of facts make it more difficult to focus a nation, they in some sense have already spawned a new community. On-line users are fiercely loyal to their groups, as if their shared interests replicate shared borders. Conversations in cyberspace are forming virtual cities. This too is part of the pattern of media technology, to expand the bounds of community. If it is smart, the mass-market media will exploit the trend with niche-market publications and a new respect for individual tastes. The monolith of public opinion—the broad, sweeping polls that almost always exaggerate or oversimplify human views—will be as inaccessible as the power of high office. Neither has much currency in a time when everyone is searching for the road less traveled.

In the era of satellite television, the starvation in Rwanda could seem closer than the neighbor's child abuse. The challenge for leaders in the digital age will be to reach across the chat rooms and unfettered information of the Internet with a voice of authority. As radio required a pleasing voice, digital will likely demand a commanding presence. Words will still play their role, and symbols too, but leaders will no longer be able to assume the stage. With their demeanor, they will have to wrest the audience's attention from the games and wonders and distresses of the World Wide Web.

Real-time delivery of information in cyberspace, including the ability for interactive exchanges and the choice of downloading only selective data, inevitably impacts international relations. One early result at this intersection of technology and diplomacy will be to speed events beyond the realm of real time. When an hour's worth of video can be delivered in seconds through digital compression, reality loses its bearings, and the sensation that the whole world is watching gives way to a feeling that everything is a rerun. The shared history of satellite television, the idea that leaders and their publics see events unfold at the same time, may in an age of cyberspace seem a quaint chapter in technology's forward march. Such anachronisms only give credence to the larger themes of this book, that each new revolution blurs the memory of the last.

There will be war in the time of digital technology, real war that kills people and leaves battle scars among soldiers and generals both. But the military will seek more than ever to contain information about war, to restrict the length of war, the better to fight war off-screen while protecting the images and words that flash on-screen. In the computer age, the public is a group of "users," because they will use technology to ferret out information. Journalists like to gloat that digital technology will make them independent of the military in wartime, giving them an ability to broadcast live from the war zone, freeing them from the military's control over transportation and dissemination of their copy. And, unquestionably, controlling transportation is key.

But in a virtual world of computer simulations, the military enjoys the same advances as the press, and will likely use them to advantage. "In five years every journalist will have a telephone in his hip pocket," CNN war correspondent Peter Arnett boasted at the end of the Persian Gulf War. "They [policy makers] can talk tough, but time is on our side and technology is on our side." Well the five years is up and is it already clear that a telephone in the hip pocket may not be much of a passport to a battle. As Arnett knows better than most, the military can be a ferocious gatekeeper. CNN was able to broadcast from Kuwait City in the hours after the war ended from the back of a truck equipped with a satellite and phones and cameras and everything else needed to communicate with the world. But before it could drive to Kuwait City, the CNN truck had to clear military border posts.

The digital revolution will inevitably flood the public with data. Huge volumes of information will undoubtedly be shared. Whole populations will suddenly be connected. And one thing more: This new technology merges many of the inventions it succeeds. When newspapers, radio, television, film, and photographs all appear on the same screen as the sum of their bits, Marshall McLuhan and his edict that the medium is the message are moot. "Bits are bits," says MIT's Negroponte. "In a digital world, the medium is no longer the message—the message is the message."

In a way, McLuhan has always been wrong, but not until digital technology has the case against him been so clear. The message always mattered more than the medium. The Ayatollah Khomeini, living in exile in Paris, used audio cassettes to spread the message of his sermons back home to Iran. Eastern Europeans, eager for the riches and freedom of capitalism, used radio to communicate their revolution. Corazon Aquino offered videotaped messages to anyone who contributed a blank cassette to her 1986 campaign. Students hoping to escape repression in China used the fax machine to relay information about their prodemocracy movement. St. Petersburg mayor Anatoly Sobchak called out the faithful by computer to surround Boris Yeltsin's White House in a sea of human guards. Subcomandante Marcos, leader of the Zapatistas guerrilla group challenging Mexican rule in the Chiapas region, is said to write his communiqués on a laptop computer plugged into the lighter socket of an old pickup truck. Launching his uprising on the first day of implementation of the North American Free Trade Agreement, when world attention was trained on Mexico City, the guerrilla leader assured that some of the media's spotlight would shine on Chiapas.

Technology changes everything and nothing in international affairs, revolutionizing the way in which nations and peoples interact without impacting the core of their relations, influencing diplomacy and war at the margins while keeping intact their principles. In the confrontation between political leadership and media technology, there is no contest. In every age from the French Revolution of 1789 to the Soviet coup of 1991, media technology is a partner to change, not its instigator. In cyberspace too it will fall to leaders to steer the technology. Leaders who excel at a multimedia approach, who can think spatially as well as linearly, will be better equipped to handle the challenges of the digital age than those who cling to their newspapers and diplomatic cables. But technological prowess and media savvy are no substitute for character. No matter what technology defines their era, leaders who value words and exhibit backbone will find that the public and history judge them kindly. Jack Valenti, president of the Motion Picture Association of America and a White House adviser to Lyndon Johnson, remarked on this bridge between leadership and conviction. Paraphrasing Lord Macaulay, he said, "A leader without conviction is only right by accident." It is a fitting epitaph for the coming media age, when a globalized news media and international interest groups and world financial markets will compete for power with elected officials whose greatest lever will still be the bully pulpit. They call it leadership.

16

Leadership in the Information Age

I N 1923, WHEN commercial radio was two years old, the
House of Representatives began broadcasting floor action.
Within a year the experiment was abandoned, as congressmen
fled from this "pernicious influence" on House proceedings.
A half-century later, Cable Satellite Public Affairs Network
went on the air, with Brian Lamb at the helm. Lamb, who
as a young man had worked briefly in government, was fascinated by the dissonance between what he saw on his rounds
and what he could learn in the newspapers. He founded
C-SPAN, the all-government, all-the-time network funded by
the cable industry, to bridge the difference. The effect was as
revolutionary as anything unfurled by Western Union. It was
almost as if Samuel Morse were still sitting in the House
gallery, this time with a smile.

The marvel of satellite communication is that it makes
viewers feel that they are at the center of action. To see a
building explode, to witness a soldier fall in combat, this is a
breathtaking power. Watching the Russian White House
burn in the tumultuous events of September 1993, a viewer
in Los Angeles compared the experience to a feeling that
CNN had handed out guns. Thanks to C-SPAN, American
viewers could sit in virtual electronic galleries and watch

debates in Congress, the British House of Commons, the Japanese Diet, or the German Bundestag. When CNN correspondent Doug James was introduced to Iraqi information minister Latif Nasif Jassim just after Iraq invaded Kuwait in August of 1990, Jassim told the correspondent how much Saddam Hussein's government "loves the CNN." James astutely took the opportunity to suggest that if the Iraqi leadership loved the network's news so much, perhaps the regime could stop censoring CNN reports out of Baghdad. Nonsense, insisted Jassim, CNN was not censored in Baghdad. "We get it all."

Eliminating the distance between information and its audience is the greatest gift of media technology, one that has been abused, distorted, and otherwise exploited through history. Unlike Jassim, most put under the satellite spotlight were well aware of its harsh light. When C-SPAN began to televise the House debates in 1979, such arcane parliamentary procedures as the one-minute speech were turned into career makers by adept politicians like Newt Gingrich who sensed the potency of this new instrument to empower the less powerful. And the camera that beamed out of Washington convinced some viewers, like Dick Armey of Texas, to run for Congress themselves. Gingrich became speaker of the House after the 1994 elections, in an extraordinary Republican sweep to power that also installed Armey as House majority leader. Talk radio played a role in their success, as did the platform they espoused. But C-SPAN was the channel that launched their careers, peeling away the filters between viewer and Congress. Like Franklin Roosevelt using radio in 1936 to go over the heads of the 98 percent of newspapers who opposed his reelection, Gingrich in 1994 used C-SPAN to bypass a hostile media.

There is unquestionably a wonder about media technology, speeding delivery of information, democratizing the audience, erasing borders between communities. There is no question that demands on diplomacy are greater with the advent of satellite television than they were before, and that they will increase further with the arrival of cyberspace. There is a larger public, a more global audience, and information is flowing faster and in greater volume than ever before. For diplomats, the advent of modern communication—the fax machine and the computer, the cellular telephone and the Internet—has quickened the pace, favoring those who can think on their feet and gauge the impact of policy. But those attributes have, from the beginning, conferred greatness.

Beyond the constant of change in the history of technology are myths, myths about the power and the kingdom of the media giants, about the intrusions and distortions visited on international affairs by new weapons of media technology. In the era of satellite television, among the practitioners of American foreign policy, these myths amount to a conviction that diplomats have been robbed of time for due deliberation, that journalism has not only supplanted the role of the diplomat but in the process has sunk to new lows of taste while achieving record popularity, that sound bites have replaced substance. The lament is that real-time technology has made ambassadors obsolete, given new power to the uninformed, and made foreign relations an adjunct of public relations. If the core of this history is correct, if the pattern discerned in the chronology of media inventions can be applied to the future, then some things are known, and others should be discarded as aspects of techno-hysteria that serve neither history nor the future. Puncturing these myths is the last plank in the contrarian view of media history.

Of these the most telling is that television has supplanted diplomacy. That diplomacy has been changed by the speed of satellite communication and digital information is indisputable. Henry Kissinger remarked recently that diplomats seeking his advice used to ask him what they should do. "Now," he drawled in that familiar guttural monotone, "they ask me what they should say." Policy makers feel rushed to comment by the immediacy of a crisis and the mess of microphones and cameras stuck in their faces by reporters who now tread on a twenty-four-hour-a-day news cycle. As former CIA director Robert Gates put it, "The aggressiveness of moment-by-moment commentary gets policy makers in the frame of mind to answer an ambushing reporter, more than figuring out what to do." Any diplomat who resists the temptation, who declines the honor of rushing to judgment by issuing a "No comment" or a "We're studying the problem," risks an avalanche of mean-spirited editorial opinion that the government in question is inept.

But the truth is that diplomacy, the formal conversation between sovereign nations, has not so much been eliminated as driven underground. The meetings between the Israelis and the Palestine Liberation Organization in Oslo, Norway, the visits of the British to Northern Ireland, the Mexican government's negotiations with Zapatista rebels from Chiapas, all were forced into seclusion by the glare of international media attention. Even the diplomatic missions of Robert Oakley to Somalia and Jimmy Carter to North Korea and Haiti—though widely covered—were largely conducted in private. When it is important, when it is necessary, trained diplomats and even political figures can still keep secrets. Even more striking, the posturing required in front of the cameras on emergence from private talks can actually benefit the negotiations inside, forcing diplomats to think about public implications even as they are still negotiating private treaties.

Independent presidential candidate Ross Perot complained during the 1992 campaign that diplomats had been made obsolete by technological breakthroughs. "Embassies are relics of the days of sailing ships," he proclaimed. "At one time, when you had no world communications, your ambassador spoke for you in that country. But now, with instantaneous communications around the world, the ambassador is primarily in a social role." Consigned to nibble hors d'oeuvres while making small talk at vapid cocktail parties, diplomats are portrayed by critics like Perot as hapless victims of technology, dismissed as readily as used tissues. But consider the musings of U.S. Representative Samuel S. Cox, a Democrat who represented first Ohio and then New York in Congress, and who observed in 1874, "Telegraph, steam [engine], with their prompt communications, newspaper enterprise ever in advance of diplomatic dispatch—these and other elements of progress have rendered ministers abroad trifling, expensive and useless for every purpose of national comity, interest or glory."

The truth is that savvy ambassadors, then as now, have met new technology with creativity. Robin Renwick, former British ambassador to the United States, dispatched a staffer to the presidential bus in 1992 to get acquainted with candidate Bill Clinton. Renwick knew that 10 Downing Street could get news of Clinton's speeches and travels from CNN or the BBC or the wire services or copies faxed directly from Arkansas. He knew too that he needed to be able to give his leaders context, to tell them not what Clinton was saying but what he might be thinking. As an additional benefit, when Clinton was elected Renwick was one of the few ambassadors in Washington with direct access to the new White House. Far from resenting the new technology that allowed London to look over his shoulder, Renwick found ways to channel the technology to his advantage.

Likewise, Richard Burt found when he first arrived in Bonn as U.S. ambassador to Germany in the mid-1980s that Chancellor Kohl talked regularly to the Reagan White House, and that Bonn often knew of Washington's intentions before he did. His role of telling Bonn what Washington thought had been usurped by the telephone. So he set out to work public opinion. Understanding that Germany is a democracy, where public opinion bubbles up until it hardens into policy, Burt elected to give speeches. He hoped to convince the German public to let the United States house short-range missiles in Germany, on the theory that voters could then pressure their government. Despite heavy opposition from peace groups, the Kohl government did in the end accept the weapons.

The second despair of the pessimists is that technology has ruined journalism. With its widgets and gizmos, news seems less competent than ever. Clearly, in the age of satellites, at the dawn of cyberspace, some of television news has descended into tabloid journalism. But a sampling of history suggests that bad journalism is bad journalism, having little to do with the technology that speeds its way. The Civil War produced some of the most partisan, least accurate, and most irresponsible journalism of the last century. William Hearst and his yellow journalism beat the drums for war, and more. Often railing against President McKinley, Hearst wrote in one editorial, "If bad institutions and bad men can be got rid of only by killing, then the killing must be done." This invitation to kill the president was heeded, and when McKinley was felled by an assassin's bullet, the *Brooklyn Eagle* argued, "The journalism of anarchy shares responsibility."

The weaknesses of American journalism in the last years of the twentieth century are equally evident. Newspapers are closing foreign bureaus and instead sending "parachutists" abroad with no knowledge of local customs or even national trends. Journalists blessed by instant access on their television sets are becoming less reporters than transcribers. And TV cameras in search of controversy alight from crisis to crisis, from the O. J. Simpson trial to the Oklahoma City bombing, with a kind of exploitative saturation.

But none of these critiques is without precedent. Consider the words of Edwin Godkin, the first war correspondent for the *London Daily News*, who covered the Crimea War in 1854: "I knew nothing about either Greece, or the Greeks, or Constantinople, but I was possessed of that common illusion of young men, that facility in composition indicates the existence of thought." Or consider government control of information during World War I, so thorough that only after the war did Americans learn of a supply scandal that kept their troops ill equipped. Or consider the short attention span of reporters covering the Russian Revolution in 1917, where the *Manchester Guardian*'s David Soskice reported, "The Bolsheviks must fall." Or consider the bad news judgment of those who heard Abraham Lincoln's famous and eloquent speech at Gettysburg, and filed stories about Edward Everett's long keynote address. Then think of the brave reporting from war zones, the prize-winning exposés of wrongdoing, the day-in and day-out excellence of some stories, written on deadline, in daily journalism.

But if there are myths to be cleared out of the history of media technology, so too are there lessons, patterns that form along the way. For journalists, there is the sobering thought that a technologically driven trend toward sensationalism is not inevitable. One instructive model is Adolph Ochs, who bought the *New York Times* in 1896 when its circulation was down to 9,000 and it was losing $2,500 a day. Competing against the barons of yellow journalism, William Randolph Hearst and Joseph Pulitzer and, entering an era of frenzied headlines and overheated prose, Ochs took the high road. "His newspaper did not print sensational or pornographic or gaudily spiced reports of crime, sex or bloodshed. It refrained from the cartoons and comics which brought so much circulation to his competitors. His headlines were discreet. . . . His editorial page was bland and wholesome." And, after lowering the newspaper's price from three cents to one penny, he found an audience. Within six years, the *New York Times* was earning more than $200,000 a year.

For military strategists, the lessons are equally vibrant. Media technology provides new weapons to be exploited, particularly on the battlefield of public opinion, but they are of little use if the war is lost in the combat zone. For all the magic of new media technology, it is still better to win the war even if you lose the press. In the Spanish-American War, Commodore George Dewey decided to cut telegraph cable lines from Manila to Hong Kong so Spanish commanders could not confer with their political leaders in Madrid. This move also prevented Dewey from cabling victory at Manila. He sent the news by ship to Hong Kong, where it could be cabled to Washington. It took six days. For the same reason, ground fighting continued in the Philippines for four days after the peace treaty had been signed in Washington. In retrospect, the loss of life in the last days of fighting seems poignantly meaningless, but to Dewey it was the price of victory.

For diplomats, the lessons are less clear, and more painful. The diplomat's trade relies on caution, on due deliberation, and on words, and none of these skills is particularly valued by a high-speed, media-rich political system that measures policy by short-term fallout. But it is a noble undertaking, to slow the train of political expediency. Henry Stimson, Herbert Hoover's secretary of state, is best remembered for an early sound bite in diplomatic history. Deciding in 1928 to close down the State Department's code-breaking agency, Stimson explained, "Gentlemen do not read each other's mail." There was an unspoken politeness to the U.S. foreign service in Stimson's day, almost like the hush of a university library. No more. Media technology has speeded the process and made public diplomacy as important as private negotiation.

If there is one moral in this history for the field of diplomacy, it is that advocacy for public opinion is not an unworthy effort. Diplomats simply can no longer afford to ignore its imperatives. In a time of information, diplomats too must join the public debate, winning public support for their policies and even for their existence. But diplomacy should cling to its mantle of thoughtful analysis, never confusing the sound bites that are now a necessity of life with the substance that distinguishes foreign relations from public relations. Diplomats are the guardians of substance, and they should cede no territory to publicists. The media and its technology are necessary tools of the trade, but the trade depends on understanding the culture and politics of other countries, on anticipating the curves of political behavior around the world, on honoring the nuance of words whether written or spoken. Those traits are worth fighting for, publicly and privately.

Words matter too to political figures, for they are at the core of public leadership. When Ronald Reagan spoke to a nation grieving over the traumatic explosion of the shuttle *Challenger* in January of 1986, he used words, conveyed over radio and television, to temper the emotional pain of watching the explosion that killed all seven astronauts on board, including the first civilian in space, a teacher, Christa McAuliffe. "We shall never forget them nor the last time we saw them this morning as they prepared for their journey and waved good-bye," Reagan said. "They slipped the surly bonds of earth to touch the face of God." To touch the face of God, that was the kind of poetry the moment demanded and the nation needed. There is more to leadership than words, but they are at its heart. In Franklin Roosevelt's history there are chapters written around words, phrases that gave lasting value to experience. "The only thing we have to fear is fear itself," all but defined the New Deal programs that rescued a nation from the Depression. "This generation has a rendezvous with history," all but announced the U.S. entry into World War II. In communication by any means, words are the first medium.

For political leaders who are responsible to both the professional diplomats and the public at large, who are assaulted by the media technology whenever the spotlight turns in their direction, the lesson of history is that there are risks to ignoring either public policy or private politics, and that these risks are exacerbated by the glare of media attention. In the face of new technology that speeds information and a sensationalist press that tries to sell it, a leader's task is, among others, to ignore his own press clippings. No one understood this better than Abraham Lincoln, who did not have to contend with television cameras, radio broadcasts, cellular telephones, or even home movies. Lincoln's only burdens were the telegraph and the photograph, and well he wore them, though a mischievous, partisan press characterized the journalism of the day.

On being elected president in 1860 with 40 percent of the vote, most of it from the North and West, Lincoln was assailed with death threats from the South. Detective Allan Pinkerton insisted that on his way to Washington from Springfield, Illinois, Lincoln avoid Baltimore, where an assassination plot was thought to be brewing. So Lincoln, against his instincts and initial wishes, was huddled onto a less prominent train and sneaked into Washington in the middle of the night. This concession to security was mocked mightily by the Northern papers, which published scathing articles and cartoons about "the flight of Abraham." Lincoln vowed never to repeat this spectacle again, never to give his critics material for their attacks, never to duck the glare of public opinion.

He told friends he was embarrassed by the manner of his arrival, that he regretted not making an entrance into the divided Capitol with head held tall, in broad daylight. But neither did he wallow in pity over the incident. The cloistered arrival in Washington "was the beginning of a relentless smear campaign against 'this backward president' and his 'boorish' wife, particularly on the part of Democratic papers," wrote historian Stephen Oates. "Their taunts about his crudities and illiterate manner wounded Lincoln to the core, but he never replied to such journalistic abuse, tried to accept it as one of the hazards of his job." That is the forbearance required of political leaders amid a media onslaught.

There are great truths in the history of media technology, not the least of them that for all the upheaval produced by each invention, for all the new thresholds crossed, individual skills of leadership in the selling of public policy matter more. It is as if some kinds of power trump other types of power, there being no greater power than that of human beings to master the technology for their own ends. If history brings a conviction about the primacy of leadership, so too does it leave a certainty that technology is often feared or praised beyond its deserved legacy.

The marvelous thing about media history is its consistency. Whenever a new media invention intersects with the worlds of diplomacy and journalism, the same pattern recurs. The enthusiasts boast that the new medium will revolutionize the world. The critics lament that it already has. Neither is exactly wrong, nor completely right. The fax did not give victory to prodemocracy students gathered in Tiananmen Square in Beijing in 1989, though it did allow them to monitor the world's news accounts of their struggle. CNN did not end the wars in Bosnia, Rwanda, or Somalia in 1994, though reports on CNN and elsewhere did surely focus attention on those trouble spots. Too many other factors of policy and politics played a role to credit radio for the victory of citizens in Eastern Europe who tore down the Berlin Wall in 1989 or to honor television for the victory of Boris Yeltsin when he battled against a coup in Moscow in 1991.

Stripping away the awe of novelty and the excitement of invention, there is simply nothing in technology's charter to suggest that the fundamentals will change in the next generation, when diplomats communicate with the public by computer and viewers sign on to the Internet to watch history in the making. There is magic in the technology, and wonder in its results. There is speed in delivery and an information explosion. There is a new day in diplomacy, a novel outlet for public opinion and a steep test for journalism. Above all there is a challenge to leaders to exploit the new inventions. But technology gives no odds on its use. That is for people to determine, leaders and their publics, individuals all.

Acknowledgments

THERE ARE MANY to thank for helping me think through the intricacies of this topic, though any mistakes of logic or fact that remain are mine alone. I am especially indebted to Oscar Gandy, Jr., a professor at the University of Pennsylvania's Annenberg School of Communication and a colleague at the Freedom Forum, who steered me through the difficulties of organizing the book's themes, and to Michael Mandelbaum of the Council on Foreign Relations and Walter Russell Mead of the World Policy Council, who first perked my ears to the sounds of the contrarian view.

Many others are owed much thanks. My research assistants, Jerry Markon and Elizabeth Rosen, were creative, productive, and enthusiastic. I am blessed with wonderful friends—among them Florence Bank, Ralph Begleitter, Susan Bennett, Ben Bycel, Mary Curtius and Ori Nir, Alan Elsner, Zdenka Gast, Carol Giacomo, Rea and Angela Hederman, Nora Jean and Michael Levin, my sister Hildie and brother-in-law Bill Lyddan, Jack McWethy, Mike Putzel, Beverly and Stephen Schneider, Elaine Sciolino, Frank Sesno, Marc Solomon, Charlotte Ward—who offered counsel and kept my spirits from flagging.

Many thanks to the Atlantic Council, particularly Rozanne

Ridgway, Job Dittberner, and Joe Harned, for publishing, in 1991, a paper I wrote on the media's role in the revolution in Eastern Europe in 1989, the precursor to this book.

Several organizations helped financially to underwrite this project. The Freedom Forum provided a fellowship at Columbia University for the 1993–94 academic year that allowed for much of the basic research. The Annenberg Washington Program provided support for the summer of 1994 and a forum in November 1994 for a seminar on how technology has changed the role of ambassadors. *USA TODAY* provided a leave of absence and financial support. To all those who helped—Everette Dennis, Jessamyn Reich and the staff at the Freedom Forum; Yvonne Zecca and the staff of the Annenberg Washington Program; Peter Prichard, Tom McNamara, Michael Zuckerman, and Juan J. Walte at *USA Today*—many thanks.

When I taught the outlines of this book in a course at George Washington University in the spring of 1995, I had the good fortune to encounter several students who challenged my themes, and made me think anew. Several also provided insights for this book. To James Barr, P. Joy Chairusmi, Crystal Chrea, Katherine Estok, Kendra Fox, Rebecca Heruth, Katherine Holt, Daman Irby, Sara Langston, Ismat Mahmoud, Mary Beth Morgan, Maria Neve, Ben Oxley, Donald Pessin, Michael Rahill, Stephen Riffer, Roberto Rabe, Kalpana Simhan, Jennifer Stone, Ali Teymour, Cheryl Velandria, Susan Virkus, and Greg Wells, thanks for the vigor you brought to your studies. And many thanks to Maurice East, then dean of the Elliott School of International Affairs, for approving the class, with Jarol Manheim, director of the National Center for Communications Studies, and to Dean Harry Harding and Assistant Dean Peter Hill for continuing it.

This book also reunited me with an old college and family friend, Jonathan L. Kirsch, who served with efficiency and knowledge as the attorney for the contract with St. Martin's Press. There, the staff accorded me a respect and seriousness that was a delight to a first-time author. John Murphy, James Brickhouse, and Dana Albarella worked especially hard to make this book a success. And Ensley Eikenburg was the perfect editor for me. Her suggestions were insightful, yet gentle. She encouraged me to explain things I had glossed over and emphasize others I had buried. Several times she caught me in contradictions that required clarification. Always, she was positive and supportive. In sum, she was the reader's best friend.

My gratitude extends to many others, original thinkers all, who shared their views and offered their ideas, like Phil Arnold, Alan Brinkley, Michael Beschloss, John Carey, James Clad, Vary T. Coates, Lawrence Eagleburger, Marlin Fitzwater, Lewis Gould, Henry Graff, Lawrence Grossman, Stephen Hess, Ellen Hume, Robert Jervis, Brian Lamb, Francis Lohwenheim, David Malone, Edward Marks, Karl Meyer, Mike Mosettig, Robin Murphy, Harold Quan, Dan Schorr, Holly Shulman, William Slaney, Helmut Sonnenfeldt, and Bruce Weindruch.

I am also blessed with a wonderful group of aunts and uncles, who have cheered me and nurtured me, in this book as in life. A special thanks to Elaine and Leo Dozoretz, Ruth and Mickey Gribin, Dorothy and the late Alvin Leeb, Roz and Warren Steinhauser.

Several librarians and researchers were helpful as well as cheerful: Stephen Toth and William Barnard at Columbia; Tish Wells, and Christina Pino-Marina at *USA TODAY*.

Finally, I cannot imagine writing this book without the enthusiastic support of my husband, Ron Nessen, a media historian in his own right, whose pride in my work and belief in this project kept me going through many a doubt.

For years I read the author's notes of books and wondered

why, if a book is the ultimate expression of an author's voice, so many must be thanked. Now I know. To those many who helped, in Washington and in New York, in California and at Columbia, many thanks.

Johanna Neuman
Bethesda, Maryland

Endnotes

Preface

5   "I've always trembled": Newsom was quoted in Doyle McManus, "The Malta Summit," *Los Angeles Times*, (December 2, 1989).

8   "He who first": Daniel J. Boorstin, *The Discoverers* (New York, Random House, 1983), p. 516.

11   "If it rains,": John J. Fialka, *Hotel Warriors: Covering the Gulf War* (Washington, D.C.: Woodrow Wilson Center Press, 1991), p. 27.

11   Technopoly: Neil Postman, *Technopoly: The Surrender of Culture to Technology* (New York: Vintage Books, 1993).

Chapter 1: The CNN Curve Through History

13   Russian and American on the phone: Author's interview with Strobe Talbott.

14   "The people who": Quoted in Anna Quindlen, "We're Outta There," *The New York Times* (October 7, 1993).

15   "We're often forced": George Stephanopoulos quoted in Jonathan Alter, "Less Profile, More Courage," *Newsweek* (November 1, 1993).

15   "Constructive statesmanship . . . is": Boutros-Ghali speech to Fourth World Report Contributors Conference at CNN Headquarters in Altanta on May 5, 1993.

18   Luther's motivations: Charles Mee Jr., *White Robe, Black Robe* (New York: G. P. Putnam's, 1972), p. 271.

18   The pre-eminent scholar on the printing press is Elizabeth Eisenstein, *The Printing Revolution in Early Modern Europe* (Cambridge: Cambridge University Press, 1983), pp. 147–150.

Endnotes

19   "A small part": Václav Havel, *Disturbing the Peace* (London: Faber, 1990), p. 182.

19   "A lot more": Author's interview with Lawrence Eagleburger.

19   For the coming of the sound bite by telegraph, see "The Intellectual Effects of Electricity," *The Spectator* (November 9, 1889), pp. 631–632. Cited in Daniel J. Czitrom, *Media and the American Mind from Morse to McLuhan* (Chapel Hill: University of North Carolina Press, 1982), p. 19.

20   Fox comments on the impact of pictures in Bosnia: Quoted on Peter Jennings Reporting, "While America Watched, the Bosnia Tragedy," "ABC News," aired March 17, 1993.

21   CNN Library shows that CNN did fourteen stories in 1991 on the drought and refugee situation in Sudan. As world attention shifted to Somalia, CNN's coverage of the Sudan dropped to four stories in 1992, then jumped back to ten stories in 1993. CNN Library.

22   How the Ethiopia famine got on the air: Author's interview with Lawrence Grossman.

22   The food aid budget and dubious impact of television: Stephen Hess, "Crisis, TV and Public Pressure," *The Brookings Review* (Winter, 1994), p. 48.

22   Emotionalism's role in Somalia: George Kennan, "Somalia, Through a Glass Darkly," *The New York Times* (September 30, 1993), p. A23.

23   Chiding FDR for his emotionalism: George Kennan, *Memoirs, 1925–1950* (Boston: Little Brown & Co., 1967), pp. 53–54.

23   "The sixth vote": Interview with official at U.S. embassy to the United Nations.

Chapter 2: The Telegraph Annihilates Time and Space

25   The 89-83 congressional vote to fund Morris's telegraph experiment: This is the vote tally cited in the official *Congressional Globe* for February 23, 1843, but another source, James D. Reid, *The Telegraph in America* (New York: Arno Press, 1974), p. 100, puts the vote at 90-82. The vote in both cases shows the South was heavily opposed to the bill, which later passed the Senate.

26   Morse's troubles with Congress: See Robert Luther Thompson, *Wiring a Continent, The History of the Telegraph Industry in the United States, 1832–1866* (Princeton: Princeton University Press, 1947), p. 17; Carleton Mabee, *The American Leonardo: A Life of Samuel F. B. Morse* (New York: Alfred A. Knopf, 1943); and Edward Lind Morse, editor, *Samuel F. B. Morse, His Letters and Journals* (Boston: Houghton Mifflin Company, 1914).

Endnotes

PAGE

26   Political convention: Reid, p. 107.

26   The remorse of one-time critics of the telegraph: Morse, pp. 224–225.

26   Speed of various technologies: Tom Lewis, *Empire of the Air: The Men Who Made Radio* (New York: HarperCollins, 1991), p. 32.

27   "Time and space": Mabee, p. 207.

27   "Man may instantly": Reid, p. 92.

27   "The wonderful fact": Czitrom, p. 7.

27   "Space will be,": *House Commerce Committee Report # 753*, April 6, 1838.

27   "The Great Highway": Harold A. Williams, *The Baltimore Sun, 1837–1987* (Baltimore: Johns Hopkins University Press, 1987), p. 23.

27   "Slender bridges": Menahim Blondheim, *News Over the Wires, The Telegraph and the Flow of Public Information in America, 1844–1897* (Cambridge: Harvard University Press, 1994), p. 34.

27   Loring's remarks: Reid, p. 736.

28   "The whooping cough": Henry David Thoreau, *Walden* (New York: Collier Books, 1962), p. 48.

28   "Just imagine what": Ithiel de Sola Pool, ed., *The Social Impact of the Telephone* (Cambridge: MIT Press, 1977), p. 99.

28   Nicholas fear of telegraph: Mabee, p. 225.

29   Early Russian negotiations with Morse: Thompson, p. 15.

29   Russian scientists had actually preceded Morse, laying the world's first practical electrical telegraph line from St. Petersburg to Kronstadt in 1835. But their military advance was wiped out by the czar's politics.

29   Strategic blunder for Russians: Anthony Livesey, *Great Battles of World War I* (New York: Macmillan, 1989), pp. 26–37.

30   "Of the invention": Reid, p. 889.

30   "Both are gone": Author's interview with Marvin Kalb, 1994.

31   First message sent from Baltimore: Williams, p. 22.

31   "Have you any news?": Blondheim, p. 33.

31   Financial constraints on publishers in 1860: Czitrom, pp. 15–16.

32   Telegraph operators: William R. Plum, *The Military Telegraph During the Civil War in the United States, Vol. 1* (Chicago: Jansen, McClurg & Company, 1882).

33   Bribing military telegraph operators: Ibid., p. 14.

33   The byline wars: Michael Schudson, *Discovering the News: A Social History of American Newspapers* (New York: BasicBooks, 1978), p. 68.

34   Reporter boycott impact on Meade's political ambitions: Phillip Knightley, *The First Casualty, From the Crimea to Vietnam: The War Correspondent as Hero, Propagandist and Myth Maker* (New York, Harcourt Brace Jovanovich, 1975), p. 27.

Endnotes

PAGE

34 Lee's use of Philadelphia newspaper for sources on enemy: William M. Hammond, *The Military and the Media, 1962–1968* (Washington, D.C.: U.S. Army Center of Military History, 1988), p. 3.

34 Russell's early years: Alan Hankinson, *Man of Wars: William Howard Russell* (London: Heinemann, 1982); Hammond, p. 3.

35 Russell at the Battle of Bull Run: Knightley, pp. 35–36.

35 "Entire human existence": Simon N. Patten, *Product and Climax* (New York: B. W. Heubsch, 1909), pp. 18–19. Cited in Czitrom, p. 19.

35 Russell's style: Knightley, p. 10.

36 On learning of the fall of Vera Cruz from the *Baltimore Sun*: Allan Nevins, ed. *Polk: The Diary of a President, 1845–1849* (London: Longmans, Green and Co., 1929), p. 211.

36 On the Trist mission: Nevins, p. 219.

36 Sherman on the telegraph: Quoted in Plum, p. 140.

36 By the end: Lewis Coe, *The Telegraph: A History of Morse's Invention and Its Predecessors in the United States* (Jefferson, North Carolina: McFarland & Co., Inc., 1993), p. 61.

37 Grant's view of telegraph: Coe, p. 58.

37 The South depended: Coe, p. 61.

37 "Estimated in money": Plum, p. 35.

37 Rebel spy operator: Ulysses S. Grant, *Memoirs and Selected Letters* (New York: Library of America, 1990), p. 219.

37 Intercept of forty-day food supply by Lee: Plum, pp. 265–266.

38 "Under the influence": Ibid., p. 31.

38 Four years and took 617,548 lives: Richard B. Morris, ed., *Encyclopedia of American History, The Bicentennial Edition* (New York: Harper & Row, 1976), p. 292.

38 "Of this one": John W. Schildt, *Four Days in October: Lincoln and McClellan* (self-published, 1978), p. 40.

39 Stanton's war diary: Knightley, p. 27.

39 History of the Associated Press: Blondheim, p. 49; see also Czitrom, p. 16.

39 "The opinion of": Plum, vol. 1, p. 11.

39 "The greatest possible": Robert M. Hughes, *General Johnston* (New York: D. Appleton and Company, 1893), p. 273; Carl Sandburg, *Abraham Lincoln: The War Years* (New York: Harcourt Brace & Company, 1939), vol. 4, p. 343.

Endnotes

Chapter 3: A Splendid Little War

PAGE

41 "Loves the brave": Frank Freidel, *The Splendid Little War* (Boston: Little Brown and Company, 1958), p. 3.

41 Sensationalist reporting got the name yellow journalism because one of its practioners, the *New York World*, used a yellow-ink cartoon strip on its front page, "The Yellow Kid," which was copied by the *World's* main competitor in sensationalism, the *New York Journal*. Since both featured "The Yellow Kid," they came to be viewed as the "yellow press," pioneers of "yellow journalism."

42 Journal headlines and reports: W. A Swanberg, *Citizen Hearst* (New York: Collier Books, 1961), pp. 130–131.

42 The Rothschilds did not loan money to Spain to buy warships, as reported in American press Marcus Wilkerson, *Public Opinion and the Spanish-American War: A Study in War Propaganda* (New York: Russell & Russell, 1967).

43 Newspapers suppressed news reflecting poorly on rebels: Richard J. Barnet, *The Rockets' Red Glare, War Politics and the American Presidency* (New York: Simon & Schuster, 1990), pp. 128–129.

43 "You furnish the": Swanberg, p. 127.

43 "HOW DO YOU": Barnet, p. 134.

43 "Hatred and distrust": Wilkerson, p. ii.

44 "This means war": Swanberg, p. 162.

45 The Cuban rebellions: Ibid., p. 1.

45 Spain had sent: Joseph Wisan, *Cuban Crisis as Reflected in the New York Press, 1895–1898* (New York: Columbia University Press, 1934), p. 403.

45 "Spain's most important": John L. Offner, *An Unwanted War: The Diplomacy of the United States and Spain Over Cuba, 1895–1898* (Chapel Hill: University of North Carolina Press, 1992), p. 9.

46 To the Spanish, war was preferable to negotiations: Lewis L. Gould, *The Spanish-American War and President McKinley* (Lawrence, Kansas: University of Kansas Press, 1982), p. 22.

46 "The popular breeze": Offner, p. 25.

46 "Defeat ever know": Freidel, p. 6.

46 The activities of the pro-independence *junta*: Offner, p. 27.

47 "Greedy Yankees lacking": Ibid, p. 11.

47 "Passage of time": Gould, p. 22.

47 "Hand to mouth policy": Offner, p. 64.

47 The Gomez strategy: Offner, page 5.

47 The Cuban economy: Gould, p. 20.

47 "Vigorous and ruthless": Offner, p. 12.

48 The death camps: Ibid., p. 13.

PAGE

48 "Not even a dog": Ibid., p. 47.

48 "A chocolate eclair": Margaret Leech, *In the Days of McKinley* (New York: Harper & Brothers, 1959), p. 169.

48 Assigned press seats: Gould, p. 15.

49 McKinley invited reporters to New Year's receptions: Robert C. Hilderbrand, *Power and the People: Executive Management of Public Opinion in Foreign Affairs, 1897–1921* (Chapel Hill: The University of North Carolina Press, 1981), p. 11.

49 Removing Cleveland's sentry gates: Gould, p. 15.

49 Centralizing power at the White House: Hilderbrand, p. 11.

49 Shifting the focus of attention: Hilderbrand, p. 31.

50 "While others talk,": Swanberg, p. 141–153.

50 Three letters on the topic: Hilderbrand, p. 13.

50 Scrapbooks indicated public support: Hilderbrand, p. 13.

50 "The whole matter": *George B. Cortelyou Papers*, Library of Congress, Box 52.

51 Woodford agrees after big names turn McKinley down: Gould, p. 28.

51 Spanish riots in Havana: Gould, p. 32.

51 McKinley excelled at bureaucratic leadership: Hilderbrand, p. 199.

52 Four-inch high headlines for Hearst: Knightley, p. 56.

52 "The new journalism": Wilkerson, p. 83.

52 Flotilla of boats: Knightley, p. 56.

53 "Men to follow": Arthur Lubow, *The Reporter Who Would Be King: A Biography of Richard Harding Davis* (New York: Charles Scribner's Sons, 1992), p. 185.

53 Press boats rushing to shore to use the telegraph: Knightley, p. 56.

53 "His death sentence": Brown, p. viii.

54 "Fear of lese-majesty": Hilderbrand, p.12.

54 "It was a revolution": Maurice Gravier, *Luther and Public Opinion: An Essay on the Satirical and Polemical Literature in Germany During the Decision Years of the Reformation, 1520–1530* (Paris: Edition Montaigne, 1942), cited in Eisenstein, p. 310.

Chapter 4: Gutenberg's Revolution

55 Cost of Bibles: Henry Lemoine, *Typographical Antiquities: Origin and History of the Art of Printing, Foreign and Domestic* (London: S. Fisher, 1797), p. xv.

55 A goldsmith named Johann Gutenberg: Michael Olmert, *The Smithsonian Book of Books* (Washington, D.C.: Smithsonian Books, 1992), p. 113.

55 The Chinese printing history: Daniel J. Boorstin, *Discoverers* (New York: Random House, 1983), p. 501.

Endnotes

PAGE

56 "A whole year": Samuel Palmer, *The General History of Printing* (published by Samuel Palmer, 1732), p. 25.

56 Gutenberg's ink: Olmert, pp. 113–118.

56 The 1455 trial: Boorstin, p. 513–514.

57 Schoeffer claims: Encyclopedia Brittanica, *Printing, Typography and Photoengraving*, p. 71.

57 Like so much of Gutenberg's life, even this fitting ending was not to last. When the church was razed in 1742, the tablet and Gutenberg's body disappeared. For more on this, see Olmert, p. 122.

57 Some, like W. Russell Neuman, argue that "the first truly mass medium did not arise with Gutenberg's printing press, but rather with the steam-driven cylindrical press of the 1830s." The reasoning: the steam presses speeded production, and made print cheap enough to produce inexpensive material, like newspapers and magazines, in large numbers for "an increasingly literate mass populace in industrializing societies." For a fuller exposition of this view, see W. Russell Neuman, *The Future of the Mass Audience* (Cambridge: Cambridge University Press), p. 7.

57 Sorbonne as center of scholarship: Karl Schottenloher, *Books and the Western World* (Jefferson, N.C.: McFarland & Co.), p. 50.

58 "With the devil": Lemoine, p. xv.

58 Vellum: Olmert, p. 171.

58 "This will kill that": Cited in Boorstin, p. 485.

58 "Clumsy and unattractive": Olmert, p. 178.

58 François I ban on printing: See Boorstin, p. 515.

59 "Mind of Europe": Eisenstein, p. 147–150.

59 "Even in the cottage—a book": Schottenloher, p. 84.

59 The total reached 200 million: Lucien Febvre and Henri Jean Martin, *The Coming of the Book* (London: N.L.B., 1976).

59 "Obvious to all": Olmert, p. 301.

60 "Invention of typography": Lemoine, page *cix*.

61 "Let us enjoy it": Charles Mee Jr., *White Robe, Black Robe* (New York: G. P. Putnam's, 1972), p. 103.

61 Church debt: Mee, p. 288.

61 "Taxes of the church": Mee, p. 271.

62 Insipid corruption: Mee, p. 151–152.

63 "Would settle itself": Mee, p. 231.

63 600 printers in business: Mee, p. 261.

64 Ben Franklin as publisher: Thomas R. Adams, *The British Pamphlet Press and the American Controversy, 1764–1783* (American Antiquarian Society, Volume 89, Part I, April 1979), pp. 58–68.

64 Thomas Paine selling 500,000 copies of *Common Sense*: Asa Briggs, *The War of Words* (New York: Oxford University Press), p. 215.

Endnotes

64   Price of Isaiah Thomas's newspaper: Briggs, p. 213.

64   Pre-Revolutionary War public opinion: Briggs, p. 209–210.

65   "The limits of his willingness": Richard B. Morris, *The American Revolution, A Short History* (Princeton: D. Van Nostrand Company, Inc., 1955), p. 14.

65   British costs of maintaining a militia in the colonies: Ibid, p. 17.

66   "Engines of opinion": Arthur M. Schlesinger, *Prelude to Independence: The Newspaper War on Britain, 1764–1776* (New York: Alfred A. Knopf, 1957), p. 82.

66   130 new political newspapers in 1789: Hugh Gough, *The Newspaper Press in the French Revolution* (London: Routledge, 1988), p. 26.

66   "The journalist who holds the tablets": Gough, p. 36.

66   French newspaper circulation: Simon Schama, *Citizens: A Chronicle of the French Revolution* (New York: Alfred A. Knopf, 1989), pp. 177–180.

67   "The electric fire": John Thomas Gilchrist and W. J Murray, *The Press in the French Revolution: A Selection of Documents Taken from the Press of the Revolution from the Years 1789–1794* (New York: St. Martin's Press, 1971), p. 41.

67   "Torn the country apart": Jeremy Popkin, *Revolutionary News: The Press in France, 1789–1799* (Durham: Duke University Press, 1990), p. 172.

67   "Animate their patriotism": Gilchrist and Murray, p. 32.

68   *La Gazette de France* does not report storming of Bastille: Ibid., p. 7.

Chapter 5: Photography and Emotion

71   Different capture for Chinese audience: Vicki Goldberg, *The Power of Photography: How Photographs Changes Our Lives* (New York: Abbeville Press, 1991), p. 251.

71   Woodsworth, "a dumb art": Ibid, p. 10.

72   Paper money trips up Louis XVI: Schama, p. 554.

72   Politics at French Academy of Sciences: Claude Nori, *French Photography* (New York: Pantheon Books, 1979), p. 1.

73   "Starvation prices": George Hobart, *Mathew Brady* (London: Macdonald & Co., 1984), p. 1.

73   Archer's prints: William S. Frassanito, *Antietam: The Photographic Legacy of America's Bloodiest Day* (New York: Charles Scribner's Sons, 1978), p. 25.

73   Daguerre plates a thing of past: Nori, p. 2.

73   Brady may not have known how to write: James David Horan, *Mathew Brady: Historian With a Camera* (New York: Bonanza Books, 1955), pp. xiv–xv.

73   "You must never": Hobart, p. 2.

PAGE

73   Brady as media celebrity: Roy Meredith, *The World of Mathew Brady: Portraits of the Civil War Period* (Los Angeles: Brooke House Publishers, 1976), p. 5.

74   "And formidable instrument": Ibid, p. 7.

74   "The runaways mistook": Ibid, p. 7.

74   "Like Euphoria": Ibid, p. 7.

74   Brady made $12,000 a year during Civil War: Josephine Cob, "Photographs of the Civil War," *Military Affairs* (Fall 1962), p. 128.

74   Gave Gardner negatives instead of money: Jorge Lewinski, *The Camera at War: A History of War Photography from 1848 to the Present Day* (New York: Simon & Schuster, 1978), p. 44.

75   Posed pictures, for burial: Ross J. Kelbaugh, *Introduction to Civil War Photography* (Gettysburg, Pennsylvania: Thomas Publications, 1991), p. 9.

75   1,000 artists in 1901: Time-Life Books, ed., *Photojournalism* (New York: Time-Life Books, 1971), page 16.

75   "In an imaginative way": Lewinski, p. 69.

75   Few photographs of Russian Revolution: Lewinski, p.6.

76   Conditions at Andersonville: See Goldberg, pp. 20–24; also *The Congressional Globe*, January 1865.

76   Concentration camp pictures: Goldberg, p. 35.

76   "The enormity of it": Timothy McNulty, "Decisions At the Speed of Satellite," *Chicago Tribune* (Sunday, December 22, 1991).

77   *Times* review of pictures in Brady's gallery: Cited in Goldberg, p. 26; Frassanito, pp. 15–17; and in *The New York Times* (October 20, 1862), p. 5.

77   Fenton in Crimea: Lewinski, p. 37–38.

78   Heavy camera equipment: Frassanito, p. 21.

78   The first living room war: Goldberg, p. 20.

78   "It was so nearly": Ibid, p. 26.

78   Oliver Wendell Holmes background: Frassanito, p. 57.

78   "For their delineator": Goldberg, p. 26.

79   Quakers agenda: Shelby Foote, *The Civil War: A Narrative, Fort Sumter to Perryville* (New York: Vintage Books, 1974), pp. 705–706.

80   "No movies of": Betty Houchin Winfield, *FDR and the News Media* (Urbana, Illinois: University of Illinois Press, 1990), p. 16.

80   FDR at 1936 convention: Stephen Bates, *If No News, Send Rumors, Anecdotes of American Journalism* (New York: St. Martin's Press, 1989), p. 98.

80   Photographers voluntarily destroyed photo plates of FDR: William E. Leuchtenburg, *Franklin D. Roosevelt and the New Deal, 1932–1940* (New York: Harper and Brothers, 1963), p. 169.

PAGE

81   "To walk in": Winfield, p. 16.

81   Penalty for aiding the enemy: Everette E. Dennis, ed., *The Media At War: The Press and the Persian Gulf Conflict* (New York: Gannett Foundation, 1991), p. 10.

82   "Photographs seem to": Cited in Goldberg, p. 195.

82   "Was faring well": Goldberg, p. 196.

82   War Bond drive dip: Ibid., p. 198.

82   *Life* editorial: Ibid., pp. 196–199.

84   "Wartime conditions": Frank Maslowski, *Armed With Cameras: The American Military Photographers of World War II* (New York: Free Press, 1993), p. 79–81.

84   "Dying of dehydration": Maslowski, p. 82.

84   "It's a Tough War": Goldberg, p. 199.

84   CNN restraint in Mogadishu: Author's interview with CNN vice president Gail Evans.

85   Capa's photographs of D-Day: Charles Hagen, "The Essence of an Invasion in Just a Few Frames," *The New York Times* (June 3, 1994), p. C26.

85   "Realism for Breakfast": Maslowski, p. 81

86   "Record the act": Cited in Goldberg, p. 229.

86   *Life* editorial: Goldberg, p. 199; see also *Life Goes to War: A Pictorial History of World War II* (New York, Simon & Schuster, 1977), pp. 128–130.

Chapter 6: Public Opinion and World War I

89   "In that process": Paddy Scannell and David Cardiff, *A Social History of British Broadcasting, Volume One, 1922–1939* (Oxford: Basil Blackwell, 1991), p. 11.

90   "Life and death": Chas W. Freeman Jr., *The Diplomat's Dictionary* (Washington, D.C.: National Defense University Press, 1994), p. 319.

92   "Out to die": Arthur Schlesinger, "The Measure of Diplomacy: What Makes a Strategy Grand?" *Foreign Affairs* (July/August 1994), p. 147.

92   "Would be a revolution": Oron J. Hale, *The Great Illusion, 1900–1914* (New York: Harper & Row, 1971), pp. 303–304.

92   The localized war strategy: Ibid., p. 307.

93   "Cannot be improvised": Barbara Tuchman, *Guns of August* (New York: The Macmillan Company, 1962), p. 79.

93   "Not become nervous": Ibid., pp. 80–81.

93   In the new understanding of the Kaiser's use of wireless and cable, the pioneering source is Stephen Kern, *The Culture of Time and Space, 1880–1918* (Cambridge: Harvard University Press, 1983). Quote is from Bismarck, cited Tuchman.

PAGE

93 "Of their failure": Kern, p. 276.

93 "The United States": Barnet, p. 141.

94 When he learned in 1915, from a report in the *Baltimore Sun*, that military advisers were drawing up contingency plans for war, Wilson ordered the entire General Staff fired. Cited in Barnet, p. 147.

95 Editorials after Zimmermann telegram: Walter Millis, *Road to War America, 1914–1917* (Boston: Houghton Mifflin, 1935), p. 407.

96 "War with us": Millis, p. 420.

96 A buoyant Wilson sails for France: Hilderbrand, p. 165.

96 Marconi's early experiments: Gleason L. Archer, *History of Radio to 1926* (New York: The American Historical Society, Inc., 1938), pp. 56–57.

96 "Apostle of international justice": Lewis, p. 140.

97 "Mired in the minutiae": Ibid.

97 "Wireless brought home": Ibid.

97 "Just think, we": Thomas A. Bailey, *Woodrow Wilson and the Great Betrayal* (Chicago: Quadrangle Books, 1945), p. 3.

97 The 10,000-mile campaign across the country: see Hilderbrand, pp. 191–193.

97 "His missionary work": Hilderbrand, p. 195.

97 "Single whispering gallery?": Lewis, p. 139.

98 "Haggard, close to": Ibid.

100 Kaiser takes to his bed ill after newspaper interview: Tuchman, p. 9.

Chapter 7: Telephone Diplomacy

101 There are several excellent sources for the events of August, 1991, among them Michael R. Beschloss and Strobe Talbott, *At the Highest Levels: The Inside Story of the End of the Cold War* (Boston: Little Brown, 1993); Michael J. O'Neill, *The Roar of the Crowd* (New York: Times Books, 1993); coverage in *Newsweek* and *Time*, September 2, 1991, issues.

102 There was no small amount of irony in Gorbachev trying to get foreign broadcasts, since he had only stopped jamming foreign broadcasts in December of 1988. Boris Yeltsin, *The Struggle for Russia* (New York: Times Books, 1994), pp. 57–58.

103 Yeltsin wanted Bush to call him: Beschloss and Talbott, p. 433.

103 Transmitting the human voice: Catherine Mackenzie, *Alexander Graham Bell: The Man Who Contracted Space* (Boston: Houghton Mifflin, 1928), p. 8.

103 Calling him Crazy Bell: Mackenzie, p. 136.

Endnotes

PAGE

103 The best source on the sociology of the telephone is *The Social Impact of the Telephone*, edited by Ithiel de Sola Pool, (Cambridge, Massachusetts: MIT Press, 1977). The book is a collection of essays, written for the U.S. Bicentennial, about the telephone's history. Of particular note are Sidney Aronson, "Bell's Electrical Toy: What's the Use?" p. 15, and Jacques Attali and Yves Stourdze, "The Birth of the Telephone and Economic Crisis: The Slow Death of Monologue in French Society," p. 98.

103 "What use could": AT&T, *Events in Telecommunications History*, p. 5.

103 "We have plenty": Attributed to Arthur C. Clarke, quoted in *Wall Street Journal* editorial, (May 17, 1993), p. 16.

103 Carrier pigeons in Switzerland: Clare Nullis, "Swiss Fight to Keep
104 World's Last Military Carrier Pigeon Unit," *Associated Press*, Geneva (October 11, 1994).

104 "This is an": Christopher Cerf and Victor Navasky, *The Experts Speak: The Definitive Compendium of Authoritative Misinformation* (New York, Pantheon, 1984), p. 206.

105 Hoover had telephone placed on his desk within three weeks of inauguration: Richard T. Loomis, "White House Telephone and Crisis Management," *U.S. Naval Institute Proceedings* (December 1969), pp. 65–67.

105 Clinton first president to get dial tone: Author's interviews with John Carey and Harold Quan, also noted in Nick Sullivan "Joining the Online Generation Finally," *Home Office Computer* (December 1993), p. 72.

105 Bell annoyed if family answered phone at dinner: MacKenzie, p. 352.

105 "I can imagine": Walter Wriston, *The Twilight of Sovereignty* (New York: Charles Scribner's Sons, 1992), p. 40; also cited in H. M. Boettinger, *The Telephone Book: Bell, Watson, Vail and American Life, 1876–1976* (Croton-on-Hudson, New York: Riverwood Publishers, 1977).

106 "In league with it": Pool, p. 210.

106 "Inventor of the telephone": Robert V. Bruce, *Bell: Alexander Graham Bell and the Conquest of Solitude* (Boston: Little Brown, 1973), p. 285.

106 "Like a deserted infant": Pool, p. 212.

107 Buchanan's despair about how the telegraph had influenced diplomatic corps is based on a report from the Select Committee on the Diplomatic Service, 1861, cited in D. P. Heatley, *Diplomacy and the Study of International Relations* (Oxford: Oxford Press, 1919), p. 252 and Kern, p. 274.

108 "Time-consuming, diplomatic channels": Loomis, p. 67.

109 "Hang Mason and": William Bender Wilson, *From the Hudson to the Ohio: A Region of Historic, Romantic and Scenic Interest, and Other Sketches* (Philadelphia: Kensington Press, 1902), p. 47.

109 "One war at a time": Sandburg, pp. 359–369.

110 Dewey cuts cable in Manila: Loomis, p. 70.

PAGE

110 The first "scoop" by phone: AT&T, p. 6.

111 SENT BY A: Bruce, p. 218.

111 "Back in primeval darkness,": Bruce, p. 224.

111 The AP's "pony service": Robert W. Desmond, *Windows on the World: The Information Process in a Changing Society, 1900–1920* (Iowa City: University of Iowa, 1980), pp. 70–71.

111 The history of how the Lincoln assassination was reported: Donald Read, *The Power of News: The History of Reuters* (Oxford: Oxford University Press, 1992), pp. 38–39.

112 Comparative between news dissemination on Lincoln and Kennedy assassinations is from author's interview with John Carey. By the time a would-be assassin shot President Reagan in 1981, it took six minutes for taped footage of the event to reach the airwaves.

112 "The most popular": Robert Friedel, *Zipper: An Exploration in Novelty* (New York: W. W. Norton & Co., 1994), p. 1.

112 "Laborious and unsatisfactory": Carolyn Marvin, *When Old Technologies Were New: Thinking About Electrical Communication in the Late Nineteenth Century* (New York: Oxford University Press, 1988).

113 "You got it. Go.": Bob Woodward, *Commanders* (New York: Simon & Schuster, 1991), p. 273.

113 Persian Gulf deployment: General H. Norman Schwarzkopf, *It Doesn't Take a Hero* (New York: Bantam Books, 1993), p. 359.

114 Palestinians getting their own area code from Israelis: Interview with Israeli diplomat, May 1994.

115 "If, as it": Pool, p. 51.

Chapter 8: Film and the Global Village

117 "It was as if " : Peter Kenez, *Cinema & Soviet Society, 1917–1953* (Cambridge: Cambridge University Press, 1992), p. 9.

117 "Devise an instrument": Czitrom, p. 38.

118 "They didn't work": Eric Rhode, *A History of the Cinema from Its Origins to 1970* (New York: Hill and Wang, 1976), p. 15.

118 "Ceases to be absolute": Rhode, p. 18–22.

118 Hildesheim reports losing theater customers to movies: Seigried Kracauer, *From Caligari to Hitler, A Psychological History of the German Film* (Princeton: Princeton University Press, 1947), pp. 16–17.

119 Nicholas prohibited footage of labor strikes: Kenez, p. 11–17.

120 "The masses need": Paul Virilio, *War and Cinema, The Logistics of Perception* (London: Verso, 1989), p. 53.

121 "As soon as": Adolf Hitler, *Mein Kampf*, Volume 1, Chapter 6.

Endnotes

PAGE

121 "Must be true": Humphrey speech in Medford, Massachusetts, on December 6, 1965.

121 Lenin entrusted movie industry to his wife: Kenez, p. 28–31.

122 Success of *agitki*: Ibid., p. 34.

122 "Within these limitations": Ibid., pp. 39–40.

122 "The production of": Kracauer, p. 185.

123 "The primary social": Kenez, p. 5.

123 "A series of catastrophes": Raymond Fielding, *The March of Time 1935–1951* (New York: Oxford University Press, 1978), pp. 3–6.

124 "The average citizen": Goldberg, p. 34.

124 Estimates on weekly viewing of newsreels: Fielding, p. 4.

124 Theaters that only showed newsreels: Maslowski, p. 264.

124 "Of his enemies": Goldberg, p. 90.

125 FDR disliked his radio imitator: Fielding, p. 15.

125 Newsreels run from 1911 to 1967: Fielding.

125 Russian audience for film in World War I: Kenez, pp. 18–22.

126 $5 million Creel Committee budget: Knightley, p. 122.

126 "A propaganda": Clayton R. Koppes and Gregory D. Black, *Hollywood Goes to War: How Politics, Profits & Propaganda Shaped World War II Movies* (New York: The Free Press, 1987), pp. 48–49.

126 The four-minute men: Barnet, p. 160–161.

126 Creel's memoirs: Ibid., p. 158.

126 Anti-German race riots: Koppes and Black, pp. 48–49.

127 Sedition Act: Barnet, p. 159.

127 "The German authorities": Kracauer, pp. 35–37.

128 Size of Riefenstahl staff: Virilio, p. 54.

128 "To win the": Kracauer, pp. 300–301.

128 *Triumph of the Will* entered at Venice Film Festival: Roger Manvell, *Films and the Second World War* (New York: A. S. Barnes and Company, 1974), p. 57.

128 "All the more": Manvell, p. 51.

129 Goebbels's personal film habits: Curt Riess, *Joseph Goebbels* (London: Hollis and Carter, 1949), p. 185.

129 Germany's most talented cameramen: Nicholas Harman, *Dunkirk: The Patriotic Myth* (New York: Simon & Schuster, 1980), pp. 244–245.

129 *The New York Times* reports 23 German newsreel cameramen died at front: Kracauer, p. 276.

129 Diplomats abroad make use of German propaganda films: Kracauer, pp. 275–277.

130 "A first-class headache": Alvin A. Snyder, "U.S. Foreign Affairs in the New Information Age: Charting a Course for the Twenty-first Century," Annenberg Washington Program in Communications Policy Studies, Northwestern University (1994), p. 7.

PAGE

130 Steve Early campaigns against heavy propaganda: Koppes and Black, pp. 52–53.

131 "Does the picture": Koppes and Black, p. 62–67.

131 The best account of the Dunkirk: Harman.

134 "A *Mrs. Miniver* of": Koppes and Black, p. 65.

Chapter 9: Radio Goes to War

135 "Duped by misleading": Archer, p. 110.

135 Prosecutor claims: Lewis, pp. 82–85.

135 The verdict: Archer, p. 110.

136 "Collapsed" in his lawyer's arms: Lewis, p. 85.

136 "Get a common": Archer, p. 110.

136 January 2, 1914, *New York Times* page one stories: Lewis, p. 85.

136 Amateur wireless clubs: Susan J. Douglas, *Inventing American Broadcasting, 1899–1922* (Baltimore: Johns Hopkins University, 1987), p. 205.

137 "Spreading seed wide across a field": Lewis, p. 73.

137 *Broadcatching:* The term was coined by Nicholas Negroponte in *Being Digital* (New York: Knopf, 1995).

137 "The telegraph and": Lewis, pp. 1–2.

137 Sarnoff and the *Titanic*: Lewis, p. 105.

138 Marconi experiments in his father's vegetable garden: Archer, pp. 56–57.

138 "The *Titanic* disaster": Ibid., p. 107.

138 Radio boom in America: Douglas, p. 303.

138 20 million listeners: Bruce Bliven, "How Radio is Remaking Our World," *Century*, vol. 108 (June, 1924), p. 148.

138 "Nothing has approached": Douglas, p. xv.

139 "An ideal democracy": M. H. Aylesworth, "Radio's Accomplishment," *Century* (June, 1929), pp. 214–221.

139 "A gift of Providence": Morris, p. 452.

139 Reaction to radio broadcasts of 1924 Democratic National Convention: Ben Gross, *I Looked and I Listened, Informal Recollections of Radio and TV* (New Rochelle, New York: Arlington House, 1954), p. 2.

139 "Debunking of present-day oratory": "The Spellbinder and the Radio," *Saturday Evening Post* (August 23, 1924).

139 "If no man": Glenn Frank, "The Decadence of American Politics," *Century* (September 1924), p. 714.

140 "An instrument of beauty": Archer, p. 212.

140 "One of the most": Ibid., p. 323.

140 1928 speech length average fell to ten minutes: Lewis, p. 182.

140 "Why should you": Bliven, p. 147.

PAGE

140 "You cannot answer": Arthur Ransome, *Manchester Guardian*, quoted in "The Living Age," (April, May, June, 1924).

142 "From the dawn": Archer, p. 3.

142 "The human race": Douglas, p. 249.

142 "Unifying factor in national life": Mark Pegg., *Broadcasting and Society*, 1918–1939 (London: Croom Helm, 1983), p. 149.

142 "Initially, the fascination": Pegg, p. 6.

143 America's Cup coverage competition: Douglas, pp. 19–20.

143 "My fame . . . my whole future": Lewis, p. 40.

143 "We gave Marconi": Such an optimistic reading was not shared by history, or by De Forest's fellow scientists. In coming years, as the scrappy little inventor tried to take credit for pioneering work done by others, like Edwin Howard Armstrong, various engineering groups snubbed him. The courts tended always to side with De Forest, who was in court more often than most lawyers, but "what the lawyers gave, the engineers took away." In award after award, they acknowledged the work of others, leaving De Forest with his claims to the audion, and his memories of a boat race against Marconi. Lewis, p. 40.

143 Radio script about British conscription: Czitrom, p. 87.

144 Regulatory legislation against radio: Lewis J. Paper, *Empire: William S. Paley and the Making of CBS* (New York: St. Martin's Press, 1987), pp. 68–69.

144 "Reporters play poker": David Halberstam, *The Powers That Be* (New York: Alfred A. Knopf, 1979), p. 17.

145 "He knew intuitively": R. Franklin Smith, *Edward R. Murrow: The War Years* (Kalamazoo, Michigan: New Issues Press, 1978), pp. 9–11.

145 "The only way": Ibid., p. 11.

145 "I like the House": Ibid., p. 30.

146 "From English pubs": Ibid., p. 8–9.

146 "As the Germans": Media historian Erik Barnouw, cited in Smith, pp. 106–107.

146 "About an hour": Smith, p. 58.

146 "My mind went back": Smith, p. 91.

147 "There was a German": Smith, p. 89.

147 "Was of far greater": Smith, p. 107.

148 "Colorless, uninteresting and": Riess, p. 126.

148 Nazi Propaganda Ministry staff: Riess, p. 130–134.

148 "People can't stand": Halberstam, page 15–17.

148 "Speaking in simple": Nathan Miller, *FDR: An Intimate History* (New York: Doubleday & Co., 1983), p. 231.

149 FDR honed his radio skills: Ibid., p. 311.

PAGE

149 Radio sets per households: Lewis, p. 162.

149 Hooperatings: Winfield, Chicago, pp. 108–109.

149 FDR's bank holiday speech: Miller, page 311.

149 "Our president took": Lewis, p. 239.

149 A list of the Fireside Chats, and their topics, is in Winfield, pp. 119–120.

150 FDR on the lend-lease proposal: Robert E. Sherwood, *Roosevelt and Hopkins, An Intimate History* (New York: Harper & Brothers, 1948), p. 225.

150 "Gifted with a": Morris, p. 457.

150 "He changed the nature": Koppes and Black, p. 50.

150 "Preeminently": Miller, pp. 306–307.

151 "He did not want": Koppes and Black, p. 50.

151 Germans timed bombing runs: Sherwood, p. 228.

152 Editorialists had a field day: Morris, pp. 458–459.

152 "Add radio sight": Lewis, illustrations following p. 278.

Chapter 10: Cold War Politics in the TV Age

153 "A device which": Francis Wheen, *Television: A History* (London: Century Publishing Co., 1985), pp. 11–14.

153 The competition to invent television: Michael Winship, *Television* (New York: Random House, 1988), p. 4.

153 The new medium's "impact on U.S. civilization is beyond prediction," *Life* said on September 4, 1944. Cited in Loudon Wainwright, *The Great American Magazine: An Inside History of Life* (New York: Alfred A. Knopf, 1986), p. 147.

154 *One Nation Under Television*: J. Fred MacDonald, *One Nation Under Television: The Rise and Decline of Network TV* (New York: Pantheon Books, 1990) p. 6.

154 "It is the glory": David Sarnoff, *Saturday Evening Post* (August, 1926). See also, *Looking Ahead, the Papers of David Sarnoff* (New York: McGraw-Hill Book Co., 1968), pp. 87–91.

155 Cartoonists envisioned television: Sarnoff, p. 85.

155 "Existed conceptually long": Joseph H. Udelson, *The Great Television Race: A History of the American Television Industry 1925–1941* (University, Alabama: University of Alabama Press, 1982), p. 12.

155 The world television enters the language: Udelson, p. 24.

155 "Seeing by radio": Sarnoff, pp. 85–86.

155 RCA spends $50 million before television turns a profit: Ibid.

155 "Suffered as stormy a fate": MacDonald, p. 15.

155 Free long-distance calls at fair: AT&T, p. 54.

Endnotes

PAGE

155 Extra security at television pavilions: MacDonald, p. 19.

156 "The first real": *The Economist*, "Just Smile, Naturally," (December 3, 1994), p. 104.

156 Wilkie's 1940 nomination on television: *The New York Times*, June 1, 1930, cited in MacDonald, p. 9.

156 "Showmanship in presenting": Udelson, p. 140.

156 "It will be": MacDonald, p. 41.

157 "Television is going": Newton Minow, "How Vast the Wasteland Now?" Columbia University, May 9, 1991, the thirtieth anniversary of his "Vast Wasteland Speech" as chairman of the Federal Communications Commission.

157 Numbers of television sets: MacDonald, pp. 44–45.

157 "The money tree of Madison Avenue": Ibid., p. 149.

157 World audience: Wheen, p. 41.

157 "Television is not": Wheen, p. ix.

158 "Why should we": *The New York Times*, June 1, 1930, cited in MacDonald, p. 9.

158 Safe to give the gift of sound: Udelson, p. 49.

158 "Why the commission": Ibid., p. 65.

158 *New Republic* predicts television would replace newspapers: MacDonald, p. 9.

158 "Has an old soldier": Wheen, p. 57.

159 "This is the worst": Ibid.

159 "You have put": Ibid., p. 22.

159 Television's impact on diplomats: Erik Barnouw, *Tube of Plenty, The Evolution of American Television* (Oxford: Oxford University Press, 1975), p. 240–241.

160 The Kitchen Debate: Richard M. Nixon, *Six Crises* (New York: Pyramid Books, 1962), p. 273.

161 So strict was the attention that when Robert Kennedy, John Kennedy's campaign manager, came to preview the setup for the second debate, he grew upset that lighting experts had given Nixon more lights than his brother. Not understanding that John Kennedy would be better served by fewer lights, Bobby Kennedy insisted on parity. As a result, Kennedy was slightly overlit for the second debate. Source is John Carey.

161 "A seminal shift": Tom Shales, "Nixon and TV: A Strange but Fascinating Fit," *Washington Post* (April 25, 1994), p. 1.

162 "And you know": Wheen, p. 58.

162 FDR's use of Fala: Halberstam, p. 16.

163 "More an instrument": Johanna Neuman, "According to Reliable Sources," unpublished masters thesis, University of Southern California, June, 1971, p. 49.

PAGE

163   "We wouldn't have": Barnouw, p. 277.

164   "The fastest way": Michael R. Beschloss, "Presidents, Television and Foreign Crises," Washington, D.C. Annenberg Washington Program in Communications Policy Studies, Northwestern University, 1993, p. 13.

164   Kennedy speech: Barnouw, p. 316.

164   "This clandestine, reckless": Barnouw, pp. 316–317.

165   Bobby Kennedy's views: Robert F. Kennedy, *Thirteen Days, A Memoir of the Cuban Missile Crisis* (New York: W. W. Norton & Co., 1969), p. 111.

165   "He benefited from": Beschloss, *Presidents, Television and Foreign Crises,* p. 7.

165   "In the culture": Ibid., pp. 10–11.

166   CIA pictures: Donald Kegan, *On the Origins of War and the Preservation of Peace* (New York: Doubleday, 1995). Kegan notes, on page 500, that CIA Director John McCone had warned of the Soviet activity in Cuba as early as August, but that Kennedy and his advisers doubted McCone because of his reputation as a hawk and his registration as a Republican. The pictures convinced them the threat was real. Reeves, p. 368, adds an interesting footnote, that it took experts at the National Photographic Interpretation Center 18 hours, from 2 A.M. to 8 P.M., to decipher the photos, but that aides thought not to disturb Kennedy with the information until morning.

166   Washington warns delegate "to be more careful": William Rivers, *The Adversaries: Politics and the Press* (Boston: Beacon Press, 1970), p. 3.

166   FDR held 998 press conferences: Neuman, "According to Reliable Sources," pp. 43–45.

166   Questions expanded to average of fifty words: Bates, p. 100.

167   Thatcher resists calling commanders during Falklands: Margaret Thatcher, *The Downing Street Years* (New York: HarperCollins, 1993), p. 234.

168   Four in ten television sets watched Kennedy's burial: Barnouw, pp. 332–337.

Chapter 11: Television and the War in Vietnam

169   600,000 Americans in battle: Charles B. MacDonald, *Time for Trumpets: The Untold Story of the Battle of the Bulge* (New York: William Morrow & Co., 1985), jacket.

169   Casualty figures: Don Oberdorfer, *Tet: The Story of a Battle and Its Historic Aftermath* (New York: Doubleday & Co., 1971), p. 333.

169   Not doing their share: Winston S. Churchill, *The Second World War: Triumph and Tragedy* (Boston: Houghton Mifflin Company, 1953), p. 278.

PAGE

170 "So I call upon": Oberdorfer, p. 333.

170 Johnson's speech: Michael Mandelbaum, "Vietnam: The Television War," *Daedalus* (Fall 1982), Vol. 3, No. 4, p. 157.

172 "The only difference": Oberdorfer, p. 99.

172 Peoples' power in foreign policy: Anthony Lake, ed. *The Vietnam Legacy: The War, American Society, and the Future of American Foreign Policy* (New York: New York University Press, 1976).

173 Westmoreland's case: Don Kowet, *A Matter of Honor* (New York: Mac-Millan Publishing Company, 1984).

173 "We in this country": Kathleen J. Turner, *Lyndon Johnson's Dual War: Vietnam and the Press* (Chicago: University of Chicago Press, 1985), p. 6.

174 "History provided": Harry G. Summers Jr., *On Strategy: A Critical Analysis of the Vietnam War* (Novato, California: Presidio Press, 1982), p. 35.

175 "Who would you say": Knightley, p. 402.

175 Greenfield urges LBJ to appeal to public: Turner, p. 113.

175 "One television fireside": Hammond, p. 261.

176 "I wanted to see": Wheen, p. 63.

176 Johnson's popularity ratings: Altschuler, figure 1.

177 "Tet demonstrated that": Mandelbaum, p. 159.

177 "The best of a generation": Oberdorfer, p. 329.

177 "And inconclusive war": Oberdorfer, p. x.

178 "Piddling platoon action": Ibid., p. 5.

178 "Standing in the ruins": Oberdorfer is quoted by Peter Braestrup, *Big Story: How the American Press and Television Reported and Interpreted the Crisis of Tet 1968 in Vietnam and Washington* (New Haven: Yale University Press, 1978), pp. 120–121.

179 "The only rational": Steven Cohen, ed., *Vietnam, Anthology and Guide to a Television History* (New York: Alfred A. Knopf, 1983), p. 214.

180 Westmoreland to his troops: Oberdorfer, p. 333.

181 Television at Khe Sanh: Braestrup, p. 292.

182 Laurence-Cronkite exchange: Ibid., p. 295.

182 Actual loses at Khe Sanh: Ibid., p. 256.

182 Length of network news shows grows from 15 minutes to 30 minutes: Mandelbaum, p. 158.

183 For the best explanation of journalism's trend away from factual reporting toward analysis, see Tom Patterson, *Out of Order* (New York: A. Knopf, 1993).

Chapter 12: The Media and Revolution

185 "It's become technically": Philip Revzin, Peter Waldman and Peter Gumbel, "Scoop or Goof?" *Wall Street Journal* (February 1, 1990), p. A1.

186 "Because the satellite": Minow, p. 17.

PAGE

187 "I'm ready": ABC News, "This Week With David Brinkley," transcript, November 3, 1985, pp. 10–11.

188 Marcos's $160 million war chest: George Russell, "Standoff in Manila," *Time* (February 17, 1986), p. 35.

188 "Marcos had the": Corazon Aquino, "Freedom and the Media," *Time* (September 29, 1986), p. 45.

188 "It is easier to": Ferdinand E. Marcos, *Time* (June 6, 1977).

189 Emergency crews at Chernobyl: Among the sources: Robert G. Kaiser, *Why Gorbachev Happened: His Triumphs and His Failure* (New York: Simon & Schuster, 1991), pp. 125–129; David Remnick, *Lenin's Tomb, the Last Days of the Soviet Empire* (New York, Random House, 1993), pp. 244–247.

190 Kremlin in denial: Kaiser, pp. 125–129; Remnick, pp. 244–247.

192 Faxes to China: Larry Martz, "Revolution by Information," *Newsweek* (June 19, 1989), pp. 28–29.

192 Chinese exhibit photograph to show restraint: Goldberg, pp. 250–251.

193 Later Bush sent national security adviser Brent Scowcroft on just such a private mission. Reporters accused the administration, in approving the mission, of violating its own ban on high-level meetings.

193 "They didn't give a damn": Author's interview with Bob Gates.

194 "Today's Electronic Bastille": Minow, (May 9, 1991), Columbia University.

194 "It was a heady fall": Author's interview with William Hill.

195 "Would there be land": Johanna Neuman, "Media: Partners in the Revolution of 1989," (Washington, D.C.: The Atlantic Council of the United States, 1991), p. 10.

195 Numbers of East Germans who watched American television: Ibid., p. 24.

196 "When we saw": Ibid., p. 20.

196 "This piece of": Ibid., p. 13.

198 "It came from": William Echikson, *Lighting the Night, Revolution in Eastern Europe* (New York: William Morrow & Co., 1990), p. 3.

199 180 East Germans died trying to cross Wall: Neuman, "Media: Partners in the Revolution of 1989," p. 19.

201 "It is too soon to tell": Schama, p. xiii.

Chapter 13: Persian Gulf War

203 British claims on Falklands: Thatcher, p. 174.

204 Navy's attempt to limit number of reporters on board: Robert Harris, *Gotcha! The Media, the Government and the Falklands Crisis* (London: Faber & Faber 1983), p. 17.

Endnotes

PAGE

203 "The most violent": Valerie Adams, *The Media and the Falklands Campaign* (London: The Macmillan Press, 1986), p. 6.

203 "Pens or bayonets?": Harris, p. 17.

203 Television tapes sent by ship: Adams, p. 6.

204 Early radio reports from Bluff Cove: Jacqueline Sharkey, *Under Fire: U.S. Military Restrictions on the Media from Grenada to the Persian Gulf* (Washington, D.C.: The Center for Public Integrity, 1991), pp. 63–64.

204 "Reporting live propaganda": Harris, p. 75.

204 "Totally offensive and": Sharkey, p. 64.

204 "I became very": Thatcher, p. 181.

205 "What I am trying": Ibid.

205 Pentagon's review of Falklands: Sharkey, pp. 65–66.

206 In the North, the government prosecuted newspapers that published information helpful to the enemy, denying them access to the mails and supervising the content of telegraphic messages sent over government lines. Three newspapers were ordered to cease publication, at least temporarily—two, the *New York Journal of Commerce* and the *New York World*, because they had printed false rumors thought harmful to the North and one, the *Chicago Times*, because it continuously attacked the Lincoln administration. Cited in Everette E. Dennis, "The Media at War: The Press and the Persian Gulf Conflict," (New York: Gannett Foundation, 1991), p. 8–9.

206 Importance of controlling transportation: Ibid., p. 14.

206 Early U.S. mistakes in Grenada: Philip L. Hilts, "565,000 Jam ABC's Phone Lines, Call-In Poll Endorses Invasion of Grenada, 8 to 1," *Washington Post* (October 30, 1983).

207 "The most astounding": William A. Henry III, "Journalism Under Fire: A Growing Perception of Arrogance Threatens the American Press," *Time* (December 12, 1984), p. 76. Cited in Sharkey, p. 87.

207 Pool arrives four hours after fighting begins: Sharkey, p. 93.

208 "We were right there": "Panama, One Year Later," C-SPAN, December 20, 1990, transcript, p. 1, cited in Sharkey, p. 94.

208 Noriega's headquarters: William Boot, "Wading Around in the Panama Pool," *Columbia Journalism Review* (March 1990), pp. 18–20.

208 Pool numbers in Persian Gulf: Dennis, "The Media at War," p. 27.

209 Film took 36 days to reach its destination: Fialka, p. 5.

209 Pentagon uses media to spread disinformation to Iraqis: Dennis, "The Media at War," p. 20.

210 "A media event" instead of a surrender: HRH General Khaled bin Sultan, with Patrick Seale, *Desert Warrior: A Personal View of the Gulf War by the Joint Forces Commander* (New York: HarperCollins, 1995), p. 425.

Endnotes

PAGE

210 "The first casualty": Knightley, frontispiece.

210 Israelis private intelligence: Author's interview with Israeli source.

210 No intent to deceive: Author's interview with Thomas Kelly.

211 "War is messy at first": W. Lance Bennett and David L. Paletz, eds., *Taken by Storm* (Chicago: University of Chicago Press, 1994), p. 284.

211 "Tie the world together": Revzin, Waldman and Gumbel, p. A1.

213 "A war, any": Cited in Goldberg, p. 24.

214 "Junk food journalism": Michael Crichton, "The Mediasaurus," *WIRED* (September/October, 1993).

214 "Media circus": Howard Kurtz, *Media Circus: The Trouble with America's Newspapers* (New York: Times Books, 1993).

214 "Feeding frenzy": Larry Sabato, *Feeding Frenzy: How Attack Journalism Has Transformed American Politics* (New York: Free Press, 1991).

215 Gulf War was a wake-up call for the networks: Jon Katz, "Say Goodnight Dan," *Rolling Stone* (June 27, 1991), p. 81.

216 "A small electric current": Arthur Ransome, *Manchester Guardian*, quoted in "The Living Age," (April, May, June, 1924).

216 "We turned on the lights": Author's interview with CNN producer John Towriss.

217 Angry calls to CNN about Peter Arnett: Peter Arnett. *Live from the Battlefield, From Vietnam to Baghdad: 35 Years in the World's War Zones* (New York: Simon & Schuster, 1994), p. 409.

217 "A sympathizer": Ibid., pp. 409–410.

217 "A conduit for": Ibid., pp. 388–389.

218 Ho Chi Salisbury: Knightley, p. 416.

218 "War will never be the same": Johanna Neuman, "Ambassadors: Relics of the Sailing Ships? A Gentle Inquiry into the Diplomatic Trade in the Age of Cyberspace," The Annenberg Washington Program in Communications Policy Studies, Northwestern University, (1995), p. 7.

218 "By God, we've": Harry G. Summers Jr., *On Strategy II: A Critical Analysis of the Gulf War* (New York: Dell Publishing, 1992), p. 7.

219 The next Saddam: See Jeffrey Record, *Hollow Victory: A Contrary View of the Gulf War* (Washington, D.C.: Brasseys, 1993), for a fuller explanation of the differences that make a repeat of the Gulf War unlikely.

219 Army needs a winning story: Author's interview with Thomas Kelly.

219 "When it comes to war": Neuman, "Ambassadors: Relics of the Sailing Ships?" p. 7.

222 "Iraq's invasion of": Thatcher, p. 819.

222 "This will not stand.": *Commanders*, p. 260.

223 "They die for God and country.": Author's interview with Marlin Fitzwater.

PAGE

223 Bush had to reassure Mideast leaders about congressional debate: Author's interview with Frank Sesno.

223 Bush planned to defy Congress: Author's interview with Marlin Fitzwater.

224 Debate proved a valuable tool: Author's interview with Marlin Fitzwater.

224 "Did Stuart have": Lawrence Freedman and Efraim Karsh, *The Gulf Conflict, 1990–1991: Diplomacy and War in the New World Order* (Princeton, New Jersey: Princeton University Press, 1993), p. 155.

224 "Slumped in their chairs,": Paul Hofmann, *The Viennese* (New York: Anchor Books, 1988), p. 70.

Chapter 14: The Satellite Spotlight

227 "My immediate reaction": Quoted in Johanna Neuman, "Military's Photo Op 'Got Out of Control,'" *USA TODAY*, (December 10, 1992).

227 "You are defiling": Debby Webber, quoted in "Controversial Photo," *Editor & Publisher* (October 23, 1993), pp. 14–15.

228 "Once again, television": "Foreign Policy: In, or Out, or What?" *The Economist* (October 9, 1993).

229 CNN Library research shows the network ran stories about the drought or refugee situation in the Sudan on March 5, 1991; April 29, 1991; June 6, 1991; June 12, 1991; June 17, 1991; June 18, 1991; June 19, 1991; June 20, 1991; June 21, 1991; January 7, 1992; April 23, 1992; May 26, 1992; October 27, 1992; January 28, 1993; April 7, 1993; April 8, 1993; May 13, 1993; May 17, 1993; May 20, 1993; July 9, 1993; July 13, 1993; August 17, 1993; September 9, 1993. By this time, world attention had switched to Somalia, where U.S. troops came ashore on December 9, 1992.

230 "The reaction is" : George F. Kennan, "Somalia: Through a Glass Darkly," *The New York Times* (September 30, 1993), p. A25.

231 "But it's wrong": Dan Rather, "Don't Blame TV for Getting Us Into Somalia," *The New York Times* Letters to the Editor (October 14, 1993).

231 Red Cross investigates reports of concentration camps: Samantha Power, *Breakdown in the Balkans: A Chronicle of Events, January 1989 to May 1993* (Washington, D.C.: Carnegie Endowment for International Peace, 1993), pp. 47–50.

233 "The images came,": Peter Jennings Reporting: *While America Watched: The Bosnia Tragedy*, ABC News, aired March 17, 1994.

234 "France was pressing": Nik Gowing, "Real-Time Television Coverage of Armed Conflicts and Diplomatic Crises: Does It Pressure or Distort Foreign Policy Decisions?" Cambridge, Massachusetts: Joan Shorenstein Barone Center on the Press, Politics, and Public Policy, John F. Kennedy School of Government, Harvard University, (1994), p. 72.

PAGE

235 "We had to keep": Author's interview with Marlin Fitzwater.

236 "I don't care": Bush quoted on *While America Watched.*

236 Propelling Bosnia to the top of international agenda: Author's interviews with Margaret Tutwiler.

238 "Until those folks": Clinton quoted on *While America Watched.*

238 "Mass murders, systematic beatings": Warren Christopher, remarks, February 10, 1993.

238 "Problem from hell": *Face the Nation*, Sunday, March 28, 1993.

240 "The most promising": Elaine Sciolino "What Price Peace?: Balkan Agreement Offers All Parties a Practical, but Not Ennobling, End," *The New York Times* (September 9, 1995) p. A4.

241 "Bosnia was a subject": Elizabeth Drew, *On the Edge: The Clinton Presidency* (New York: Simon & Schuster, 1994) p. 150.

242 "Often give a": Roger Rosenblatt's essay, *MacNeil-Lehrer News Hour*, November 9, 1993.

243 Ethiopian aid budget: Hess, p. 48.

244 Clinton played golf to disguise emotional reaction: Gowing, p. 71.

245 "That amounted to": Author's interview with Marlin Fitzwater.

246 "Now we don't": Author's interview with Rozanne Ridgway.

246 "He was on the phone": Author's interview with Richard Perle.

247 "Still damp from the printer": Frederic Morton. *The Rothschilds: A Family Portrait* (New York: Atheneum, 1962), p. 49.

Chapter 15: Cyberspace and War

249 "Thank you for": Digital Flubs, *Washington Post*, Washington Business, (October 24, 1994), p. 21.

250 "An hour's worth": *The Economist* (February 12), 1994, p. 6.

250 "Defies the laws": "From Idiot Box to Information Appliance," *The Economist*, Television Survey, (February 12), 1994, p. 5.

251 "I'm on the lunatic fringe of believers": *Television: What If They're Right?* in *The Economist* (February 12, 1994).

251 "An all-seeing discriminatory technology": Oscar Gandy Jr., "The Yellow Brick Road," *Phi Kappa Phi Journal* (Spring 1994), p. 26.

252 "This is a time": Quoted in John Markoff, "The Rise and Swift Fall of Cyber Literacy," *The New York Times* (March 13, 1994), Section 4, p.1.

252 Term *cyberspace* is coined: Raymond Gozzi Jr., "The Cyberspace Metaphor," *Et cetera* (Summer, 1994), p. 220.

253 "Millions of new users": Ross Stapleton-Gray, "Ambassador to Cyberspace," *HotWired* (October-November 1994).

253 "Information has now": Quoted in "We are the Wired: Some Views on the Fiberoptic Ties that Bind," *The New York Times* (October 24, 1993), p. E16.

254 "This distorted top-to-bottom": Kevin Phillips, "Virtual Washington," *Time* (Spring 1995), p. 65.

254 See James J. Cramer, "We're All 'Journalists' Now," *Washington Post* (April 7, 1995), p. A27.

257 I am indebted for this insight to a symposium on the future of newspapers conducted by Ellen Hume for the Annenberg Washington Program in 1995.

258 "It is not technology": Max Frankel, "The Daily Digital," *New York Times Magazine* (April 9, 1995), p. 38.

258 The trend toward newspaper analysis: See Patterson.

259 25-year drop in news consumption: "Did O. J. Do It? Network News Viewing and Newspaper Reading Off," (Washington, D.C.: Times Mirror Center for the People & the Press, April 6, 1995).

259 Trend of consumer buying of media products: U.S. Department of Commerce, *Historical Statistics of the United States*.

261 "And it doesn't need": Associated Press, dateline Jerusalem, 11:15 A.M. EDT, April 22, 1995, V0767.

264 Subcomandante Marcos's use of laptop computers: Tod Robberson, "Mexicans Using a High-Tech Weapon: Internet Helps Rally Support," *Washington Post* (February 20, 1995), p. 1.

Chapter 16: Leadership in the Information Age

267 "Pernicious influence": John B. Anderson, "The House on TV: Who Should Control the Cameras?" *Washington Post* (January 19, 1978).

270 "Now they ask me": Henry Kissinger remarks to Everette Dennis.

270 "The aggressiveness of": Author's interview with Bob Gates.

270 "Embassies are relics": ABC News, *20/20*, aired May 29, 1992.

271 "Telegraph, steam [engine],": S. S. Cox, *The Folly and Cost of Diplomacy* (Washington, D.C., 1874), cited in Vary T. Coates and Bernard Finn, *A Retrospective Technology Assessment: Submarine Telegraphy, The Transatlantic Cable of 1866* (San Francisco: The San Francisco Press, 1979).

272 "The journalism of anarchy": Quoted in Stephen Bates, *If No News, Send Rumors: Anecdotes of American Journalism* (New York: St. Martin's Press, 1985), pp. 243–244.

273 "I knew nothing": Knightley, p. 8.

273 World War I supply scandal: Ibid., p. 129.

273 "The Bolsheviks must fall": Ibid., pp. 148–149.

273 *The New York Times* loses in 1896: Harrison E. Salisbury, *Without Fear or Favor, An Uncompromising Look at The New York Times* (New York: Ballantine Books, 1980), p. 15.

PAGE

273 Ochs's road back to respectability, and profitability: Ibid., p. 26.

274 Delayed victory in the Philippines: Loomis, p. 70.

277 "Was the beginning": Stephen B. Oates, *With Malice Toward None, The Life of Abraham Lincoln* (New York: Harper & Row, 1977), p. 231.

Index

Index

Index